M000222551

This study presents the evidence, derived from letters and theological works, for theories of Christian friendship as they were developed by the leading fourth-century Church Fathers, in both the East and the West – men such as Augustine, Jerome, Basil the Great and John Chrysostom. The author attempts to find out how consistent and positive is the picture of friendship between Christians at this time, and considers friendship in the context of the relation between pagan theory and Christian ideas. All of the writers considered had a profound influence on later ages as well as on their own period, which means that the survey provided will be of wide interest both to ancient historians and to theologians.

CHRISTIAN FRIENDSHIP IN THE FOURTH CENTURY

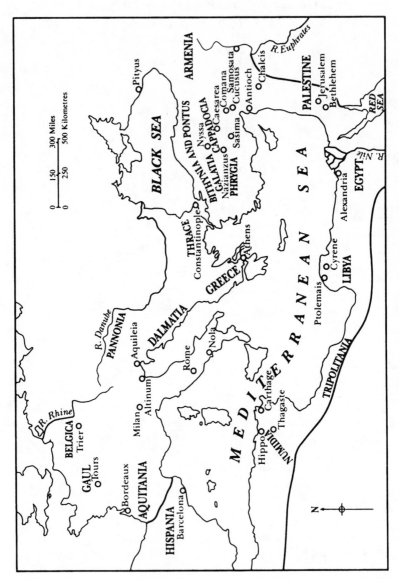

The world of the Church Fathers (around A.D. 400)

CHRISTIAN FRIENDSHIP IN THE FOURTH CENTURY

CAROLINNE WHITE

CAMBRIDGE
UNIVERSITY PRESS

PUBLISHED BY THE PRESS SYNDICATE OF THE UNIVERSITY OF CAMBRIDGE
The Pitt Building, Trumpington Street, Cambridge, United Kingdom

CAMBRIDGE UNIVERSITY PRESS
The Edinburgh Building, Cambridge CB2 2RU, UK
40 West 20th Street, New York NY 10011–4211, USA
477 Williamstown Road, Port Melbourne, VIC 3207, Australia
Ruiz de Alarcón 13, 28014 Madrid, Spain
Dock House, The Waterfront, Cape Town 8001, South Africa

http://www.cambridge.org

© Cambridge University Press 1992

First published 1992
First paperback edition 2002

A catalogue record for this book is available from the British Library

Library of Congress Cataloguing in Publication data
White, Carolinne.
Christian friendship in the fourth century / Carolinne White.
p.   cm.
Includes bibliographical references and index.
ISBN 0 521 41907 7 (hardback)
1. Friendship – Religious aspects – Christianity – History of
doctrines – Early church, ca. 30–600.
BR195.F75W45   1992
241′676′09015–dc20   92-330   CIP

ISBN 0 521 41907 7 hardback
ISBN 0 521 89249 X paperback

For Hugh
'Cor unum et anima una'

Contents

ix

Preface

When I first read Augustine's *Confessions* I was intrigued by the prominence of the theme of friendship. As I explored the literature of the fourth and early fifth centuries it became clear to me that this was not unusual in the writings of the time. Thus I was led to the present investigation in which I aim to see how consistent is the picture of the nature and duties of friendship in a Christian context emerging from the letters, theological and ascetic writings of some of the leading patristic writers. This investigation also necessarily related the Christian ideas closely to the main Classical – Greek and Roman – theories on friendship developed in antiquity which generally formed the basis for the Christian theories and therefore offers further evidence for the relations of pagan and Christian at an important stage in the development of the early Church as it negotiated the move from pagan antiquity to Christian Middle Ages.

I am grateful to Andrew Louth not only for introducing me to the world of the Church Fathers, but for all his advice and guidance along the road which led to this book. I was also assisted by Steven Collins who read it through at an early stage, and by the comments of O. M. T. O'Donovan and P. G. Walsh. I am greatly indebted for practical support to my parents and parents-in-law, and to my friends Richard Rutherford, Emily Kearns and Nicholas Purcell for discussion and learned advice on so many occasions. My greatest debt is to my husband, to whom this book is dedicated.

Abbreviations

ACW	Ancient Christian writers. The works of the Fathers in translation, J. Quasten *et al.*
CCL	Corpus Christianorum, series Latina
CPh	*Classical Philology*
CQ	*Classical Quarterly*
CSCO	Corpus Scriptorum Christianorum Orientalium
CSEL	Corpus Scriptorum Ecclesiasticorum Latinorum
FotC	Fathers of the Church
GCS	Die Griechischen Christlichen Schriftsteller der ersten Jahrhunderte
HSPh	*Harvard Studies in Classical Philology*
JbAC	*Jahrbuch für Antike und Christentum*
JEH	*Journal of Ecclesiastical History*
JRS	*Journal of Roman Studies*
Paroem.Gr.	Corpus paroemiographorum Graecorum, E. Leutsch, F. Schneidewin
PCPhS	*Proceedings of the Cambridge Philological Society*
PL	Patrologiae cursus completus, series Latina, J. P. Migne
PG	Patrologiae cursus completus, series Graeca, J. P. Migne
RecAug	*Recherches Augustiniennes*
Rec.Theol.	*Recherches de Théologie ancienne et médiévale*
RLAC	*Reallexicon für Antike und Christentum*
Sir.	Sirach (= Ecclesiasticus)
StudClas	*Studii Clasice*
SVF	Stoicorum Veterum Fragmenta, J. von Arnim
TGF	Tragicorum Graecorum Fragmenta, A. Nauck

ThZ	*Theologische Zeitschrift*
ZKG	*Zeitschrift für Kirchengeschichte*
ZRGG	*Zeitschrift für Religions-und Geistesgeschichte*

CHAPTER I

Introduction

The theme of this book is friendship, an area of ethics which is not of central concern nowadays, especially when regarded as a relationship of affection between members of the same sex.[1] And although it may in some form still have a part in our everyday lives, possibly offering a pleasant means of passing our spare time, we do not tend to regard it as something to which definite rules of conduct apply. Family relations have taken centre stage in our society and friendship has consequently moved into the wings. The modern view of friendship has little in common with that held in antiquity, even if occasionally, in literary writings, we may find sentiments expressed about friendship which seem to conform to generally accepted ideas on the subject, handed on through the ages and discovered anew to be accurate by each generation of articulate people, as when Charlotte Brontë writes in a letter of 1 March 1847, 'To keep friendship in proper order, the balance of good offices must be preserved, otherwise a disquieting and anxious feeling creeps in, and destroys mutual comfort.' But in general it is not a topic about which we theorise or which is regarded as demanding or problematic.[2]

It may then seem surprising that it should have been such a popular topic and so highly valued in Greece and Rome and even more surprising that it should have been regarded as important within Christianity. In showing in what ways this was true, I aim to consider friendship primarily from a theoretical point of view rather than from the perspective of biography, social history or politics, though the book will inevitably touch on these areas as well as on early Christian theology: its aim is to describe and compare the ideas about friendship developed in antiquity, first by writers and thinkers of pagan culture and then by the Christians whose culture was in many ways dependent on its pagan background,[3] while differing radically from it in other respects. In outlining the Classical theories my concern will be not primarily with political friendships, with the question of alliances and patronage, but rather with philosophical discussions and pronouncements and popular expressions of the nature and value of friendship.

With regard to the Christian writers of the fourth century, their theories will be considered in the context of their personal lives, where relevant, and also in the context of their relations with one another, for there is usually a correlation between the theory held by an individual and his personality and experience. All the writers considered here were men of great stature and influence on later ages as well as on their own period, deeply involved as they often were in current political and ecclesiastical affairs from the vantage point of high office, at least at some stage in their lives: such involvement meant that they were people of 'high profile' who were looked to for advice by many others from all parts of the Roman Empire. Furthermore, the fact that at this stage the Christian Church still felt itself under some threat from pagans and heretics and was spending much effort on consolidation and extension meant that orthodox Christians in positions of responsibility felt the need to communicate with one another to discuss various problems, to chastise[4] and encourage, and to canvas support for their cause. These circumstances provided a fertile field for the growth of alliances which were often regarded as sufficiently intimate and personal to merit the name of friendship.

But why should one consider the theories of Christians in the late fourth century and early fifth century in preference to other periods? To be sure, these are years of enormous interest that witness the development of the Church from a persecuted sect before the accession of Constantine to a tolerated, even favoured, creed under Constantine in the first half of the century, to the official religion under Theodosius at the end of the century, a religion in power which was to dominate Western civilisation at least for the next millennium. The voices of more and more Christians are to be heard as Christianity takes its place at the centre of the contemporary culture, and yet the influence of Classical civilisation is still very strong, a source of pride as well as a cause of conflict. Each Christian, and the Church as an instrument of power, must come to terms with this heritage which had much to offer that was admirable as well as much that had to be condemned. This was also the crucial period when the members of the intelligentsia were being converted to Christianity in greater numbers than ever before, a fact which would inevitably influence the way the Christian religion presented itself to the world, as well as affecting the concerns and outlook of many Church leaders.[5]

But more specifically, it seems that in the fourth century, despite the problems of compatibility between Christianity and the traditional theories of friendship (which will be considered in chapter 3), Christians began to consider the subject in more serious and positive terms than heretofore. It is true that the traditional views peer forth occasionally in the writings of some earlier Christians who had been educated to a high standard in pagan literature and thought: in the second century Clement of Alexandria referred to the proverb 'Friends hold all things in common' and to the theory of three kinds of friendship in his *Stromateis* (2.19), as well as mentioning pagan usages of the concept of friendship (4.3). In the work *Quis dives salvetur* he observed that friendships need a long time to develop, an idea frequently found in pagan writings. In about 200 A.D. the Christian apologist Minucius Felix wrote of his friendship with Octavius in the eponymous dialogue, 'In our moments of relaxation as well as in times of seriousness, we had been in complete harmony together with but a single will; you might have said of us that we had one mind shared between us' (1.3), while he later refers to a Classical proverb when he writes (4.6), 'Friendship always either finds or makes equals'.[6] However, these ideas are not developed and at this early Christian period the terminology of friendship is usually used of the relations between God and man rather than of the purely human relationship.

It is not until the fourth century that friendship began to play an important part in the lives and thought of Christians.[7] It is indeed striking to see how often friendship is praised in the writings of those Christians who had an important part to play in the development of orthodox Christian theology at this crucial time in the Church's history, the golden age of patristic thought. In facing the challenge of bringing the Church to maturity, these men, the majority of whom had been highly educated in the academic capitals of the Roman Empire – Athens, Alexandria, Antioch and Rome – were often able to put their knowledge of Classical philosophy and literature to good use,[8] for although they were critical of their cultural heritage, they saw, in varying degrees, that it could not be wholly rejected. As part of this, they recognised that certain characteristics of the ideal pagan friendship, such as spiritual unity and harmony of interest, reciprocity and sharing, could accord with Christian ideals and even be developed further within a Christian context. This book aims to show the variety of ways in which some of the Christians of late antiquity assimilated the ideas worked out by their Greek and Roman forbears.

Another factor which could be said to have favoured a rekindling of interest in the concept of friendship at this period was the new social status of Christianity which had spread to all parts of the Empire. People could thus feel that wherever they lived, whether in what is now the Middle East or in Germany, whether in North Africa or in Turkey, they were bound together by a common faith. Christians were no longer merely members of individual, isolated churches but of one Church under the emperor's patronage, ideally forming a harmonious unity, were it not for the difficulty of establishing what was heterodox and suppressing it. Moreover, the cosmopolitan atmosphere of the time was also conducive to the formation of friendships all over the Empire, with people often making friends during their student days when they came together from different countries, friendships which they managed to maintain for many years after, even when separated by great distances on return to their homeland or on appointment to some administrative post in whatever corner of the Empire.

These particular circumstances meant that letters were of enormous value in communication and in maintaining links between fellow Christians. As the Church was now a vast network of interrelating communities, each represented by a bishop who had a very important part to play in ecclesiastical politics and in theological matters, letters as well as prayer were essential for maintaining the unity of the Church in these difficult times.[9] The problems of meeting one's friend and the advantages of epistolary communication are well expressed by Paulinus of Nola in a letter to Pammachius (Ep.13.2) when he writes:

Writing was the only way by which I could make the journey to your holy and loving person. I could not put the same limits on my mind as on my body; for the flesh is always weak and refused to be transported too far in winter, whereas the spirit, always more willing, flew to you in fervent longing so that though I did not embrace you in person, I was able to do so in mind.[10]

Of course, these letters, concerned most often with theological controversies or with details of the Church's organisation as an institution, did not have to include a personal element, and sometimes such an element is indeed lacking. But the majority of the vast output of letters at this period, especially when addressed to individuals, did contain some form of appeal to friendship and human affection, based on common faith in Christ and the bond of Christ's love which characterised Christian friendships. Another characteristic of these letters is that they are of a literary nature, usually elegantly expressed and studded with Classical and Biblical quotations, as we might expect from men educated according to the traditional values and probably conversant with the theories of literary letter-writing.[11] Although some of these writers were unable ever to meet, they managed to maintain a correspondence over many years and developed an intimate spiritual and intellectual relationship by this prolonged association, as in the case of

Augustine and Jerome – though this relationship was not without its vicissitudes!

Correspondence by letter undoubtedly presented many problems at this time and it is clear that it was not easy to keep up a friendship in this way: letters often went astray *en route* or the difficulty of procuring trusty messengers, especially during the winter months when travel was dangerous and restricted, caused letters to be long delayed in reaching their destination.[12] In the spring of 371, from Caesarea in what is now central Turkey, Basil writes to his friend Eusebius, bishop of Samosata (Samsat), an important city on the Euphrates some 150 miles to the south-east, excusing himself for his delay in writing:

> We have had great difficulty in obtaining a carrier for our letter to you, because in our land people so shudder at the winter that they cannot bring themselves even to put their heads out of their houses for a moment. Indeed, we have been overwhelmed with such a mass of snow that for two months now we have been lurking in our burrows, buried with our very houses.[13]

Sometimes the letters would be entrusted to a friend to be delivered to another friend, in which cases the actual letter was often no more than a brief note, for it was expected that the messenger, as a trusted friend, would be able to give all the news by word of mouth.[14] In Ep.27 Paulinus writes of his joy at the personal message and the news of his friend conveyed to him at Nola by the messengers by word of mouth. He tells Severus, 'I cannot express the pleasure with which they filled me as they recounted your activities and words and told me of your heart made perfect by knowledge of the divine love.' Paulinus also clearly regards the messenger as important in forming a link between the two friends, as Victor does between Paulinus and Severus: 'Victor is our joint pledge of affection', writes Paulinus in Ep.28, 'our faithful attendant, our regular consolation. Victor is mine in you and yours in me.'

Such facts provide a salutary reminder of the problems involved in drawing conclusions about friendship from the available evidence: the many letters which survive presumably represent only a small fraction of the complete picture of Christian friendship at this period. Not only are many lost, but

we have little record of the friendships between men living in
the same place who would not be so dependent on letters for the
maintenance of their relationship of which there may consequently be no written record. But although our knowledge of
both theory and practice of friendship is limited to the evidence
provided by the letters and theological works of a few eminent
Christians, these do nevertheless offer a fascinating insight into
the network of friendly relations formed by a number of the
leading figures in the Christian Church, whether within the
Church hierarchy or in the ascetic movement, and covering the
whole Mediterranean area, from Ambrose in Milan to Basil in
Cappadocia, from Paulinus in Campania to Jerome at Bethlehem. And did not Cassian meet John Chrysostom in
Constantinople before moving to the West, Augustine meet
Ambrose in Milan before returning to North Africa and Jerome
meet Pammachius in Rome before retiring to Bethlehem?

Despite the problems involved in letter-writing it is evident
that all these men regarded letters as invaluable both for
providing information about important events in different
parts of the Empire and for maintaining affectionate spiritual
relationships: a letter could treat both of theological questions
or Church business and more personal matters such as spiritual
development and affectionate feelings. On the personal level
letters and other writings were considered to enable friends to
know one another without meeting. In Ep.40 to Jerome,
Augustine argues wittily:

For if the reason I do not know you is that I have not seen your actual
face, then by the same argument you do not know yourself, for you do
not see it either. But if you are only known to yourself because you
know your own mind, then I too know it quite well through your
writings and I bless the Lord for giving a man of your calibre to
yourself, to me and to all the brothers who read your works.

Basil often[15] praises the ability of letters to reveal the writer's
soul and Paulinus writes to his dear friend Pammachius in
Ep.13 that a man's words are the mirror of his mind,[16] applying
the idea of the Classical proverb that the face is the mirror of
the soul to a situation which could be relevant also for the many
times when you were unable to see your friend's face. For letters

could, it was felt, make the absent one present to his friend –
and here the Fathers were keeping alive a belief which had
been formulated by many Classical writers on epistolary theory
and had appeared in personal letters, too, as in those of
Cicero.[17] Jerome writes that letters allow friends to be present
to each other 'in love and in spirit' while Ambrose expresses this
popular idea in writing to his friend Sabinus: his Ep.49 (26)
opens on this deeply personal note:

Since our practice of writing letters gives you pleasure, too, so that
those who are far apart indulge in conversation as though they were
near, I shall continue often to address my writings to you, even when
I am alone. For I am never less alone than when I seem to be so, nor
less at leisure than when I am at leisure. Then, at least, I can summon
at will whomever I wish to and I can bring to my side those whom I
love more dearly or whom I consider more suited to me. No one
speaks, no one interrupts our talk. Then do I have you closer to me
and then I can talk about the Scriptures and we can chat together at
great length.

More generally, letters were useful as proofs of affection and as
providing evidence of spiritual development. Paulinus writes to
Aper in Ep.38, begging him to write again, 'so I may simul-
taneously obtain the consolation of love and joy, when by
reading your letter I shall see that you are mindful of me in
your holy dealings with God and attentive to yourself in the
progress of your spiritual knowledge and in the understanding
of your heart which yearns for God'. Letters were not regarded
as merely a means of transmitting news – and this was the view
of pagans such as Symmachus as well as of Christians.[18]

And yet in more despondent moments it was felt that letters
were only a second best, unable to provide an adequate
substitute for a friend's physical presence and conversation.
Often the writers of these letters express their intense longing to
see their friends[19] which is not surprising considering the
frustrations of correspondence and the fact that many of them
lived in isolated regions, far from like-minded people. Such
expressions may be common but they are not therefore mere
clichés: at such points personal human feelings are very much
to the fore, pushing theory into the background.

The growth of interest in the possibilities of friendship on a personal, ecclesiastical and theological level may also be connected with the growth of the ascetic movement which was regarded by some as offering the ideal Christian life, by others as a threat to the Church and by many pagans as worthy of scorn and disgust.[20] It is certainly the case that it encouraged a radical break with secular society and with ties of kinship, thus liberating men and women from, amongst other things, the concerns and responsibilities of marriage and the education of children and allowing them to form other human relationships according to different values. Did not Augustine feel that in order to devote himself whole-heartedly to Christianity, he must renounce his career as an orator as well as his desire to marry? For him and most of his friends, as for many at this period, a genuine Christian could not continue to live in the world once the decision to dedicate himself to Christ had been made. But their natural affections could then be channelled into relationships based primarily on a shared devotion to Christ rather than on any kind of secular or sexual concerns. It is significant that such intimate Christian friendships were to thrive throughout the Middle Ages primarily within monasticism which offers us plentiful documentary evidence of affectionate relationships, mostly in the form of letters but also in more theoretical works such as the dialogue on spiritual friendship by the twelfth-century Cistercian, Aelred of Rievaulx. Indeed, the Middle Ages are generally considered to be the time of the flowering of Christian friendship, with much play made of the extravagant language used by the monks in their expressions of devotion to one another.[21] And yet medieval monasticism is greatly indebted to the exciting and far-reaching ideas developed by the Church Fathers of the fourth century in this respect as in so many, for it was among these earlier Christians, educated within the traditional pagan system but often opting for an ascetic life on rigorously Christian tenets, that coherent theories of Christian friendship were first worked out.

The formation of groups of ascetically minded men and women, strictly separated from each other, obviously encour-

aged friendships between members of the same sex, but friendships between men and women were also possible though there
is unfortunately far less evidence for them. The question of
exactly how far they were possible is part of the much wider
question of the relations between the sexes within the Church in
late antiquity, some aspects of which have been expansively
treated by Peter Brown in his book *The Body and Society*.
Particular aspects will be considered in association with the
friendships between Jerome and the circle of ascetic aristocratic
women at Rome and between John Chrysostom and Olympias
in the Eastern capital, Constantinople, as well as between
Paulinus and his wife Therasia. Although there are instances of
close spiritual relationships between members of the opposite
sex, it remains true that the men of this period were very severe
on women, not only in their theoretical writings but also in
practice. In most of his writings Augustine, for example,
refused to allow women anything but a procreative role in
relation to men and in the *De Genesi ad litteram* (9.5.9) he
admits that he does not believe that Eve could have been
created primarily to be Adam's companion for 'how much
better would two male friends live together, alike for company
and conversation, than a man and a woman'.[22] Jerome's harsh
ideal of women recurs with greater regularity in his writings
than almost any other theme – most frequently expressed in
letters addressed to women – and it was only by dint of living
up to this ideal to an amazing degree that his own close female
friends were able to maintain a relationship with him. In the
case of Augustine, after his conversion he was very strict with
himself and with those around him when it came to personal
meetings with women – these men would not allow themselves
to indulge in relaxed *tête-à-têtes* alone with women of any kind,
especially outside their immediate family.[23] They were very
wary of the temptations of sexual desire which they felt they
might fall victim to at any moment. This prevented them being
more open to the possibilities of friendships between men and
women even within marriage, although such relationships were
regarded as possible, and admirable, if both husband and wife
agreed to live in continence. Such caution meant that the

closest relationships between ascetic Christians of the opposite sex were predominantly between members of the same family: Monica's extraordinary closeness to her son Augustine is well-known, but other instances of female influence on the men to be considered in this book are Therasia's on her husband Paulinus and that of Macrina (another saint in her own right) on her brother Basil – all women who encouraged the men close to them to dedicate themselves to Christ and adopt a more or less ascetic life.

In the light of the fact that it was regarded as possible, if difficult, for a married couple to renounce their sexual desires and obligations and to continue to live together in a close spiritual relationship, it is perhaps surprising to find such unequivocal condemnation among these Christian writers of those relationships which, it seems, had been quite common within the Church for a couple of centuries[24] and which, one might think, would qualify as Christian friendships between the sexes. This was the practice which appears to have developed at a time when the Church was less highly organised and there were not monastic communities for men or women to join members of their own sex in an ascetic life, whereby a man and woman (always portrayed as a young and attractive virgin in the polemical literature) decided to live together in perfect chastity and devotion to Christ. Although the polemicists such as Jerome (who was himself accused of having a not wholly innocent friendship with Paula at Rome, though he protests that he never even saw her eating[25]) and John Chrysostom admit that such couples may have been able to maintain their vow of chastity despite the temptations occasioned by such intimacy,[26] the main objection seems to have been that they would bring scandal on the Church. It was hard to believe that their motive for such an intimate relationship was anything but lust, whether conscious or unconscious, at least on the part of the man, and ostentation on the part of the woman. Although the defence is countenanced that the man needs the woman's practical domestic help and the woman, in her weakness, needs a man's support, it is never suggested that companionship and shared ideals might be the motives. John Chrysostom, in addressing such women, pours scorn on the idea that they need a man's protection. Surely if they can help the men, they can also help themselves or one another – why not live chastely with other women? And in his work written to persuade men not to enter into such relationships, Chrysostom gives the reason why he will not allow them but will admit that a chaste Christian friendship can exist between husband and wife: the difference is that a virgin will remain a sexual temptation for much longer while a chaste friendship can only develop once the strains of child-bearing and child-rearing have rendered the wife physically exhausted and unattractive!

In conclusion: it may be true that many similarities will be seen, both between the pagan and Christian and between Christian and Christian at this period in their attitude to friendship; and yet it is certainly not the case, as I hope this book will show, that the experiences of friendship of those considered here, and their views and theories on the subject were uniform or lacking in individuality and personal feeling. Without disregarding individual variations, we can only say that, both as committed Christians and as Christians with a strong sympathy for the philosophy and literature of the past, each of them would have recognised to some degree the experience of friendship in God described thus by the product of a very different Christian world, the American Quaker Thomas Kelly who, like them, sees it as an attempt to reproduce the life of the early Christians and to prefigure the heavenly life to come:

When we are drowned in the overwhelming seas of the love of God, we find ourselves in a new and particular relation to a few of our fellows. The relation is so surprising and so rich that we despair of finding a word glorious enough and weighty enough to name it. The word 'fellowship' is discovered, but the word is pale and thin in comparison with the rich volume and luminous bulk and warmth of the experience which it would designate. For a new kind of life-sharing and of love has arisen of which we had only dim hints before. Are these the bonds which knit together the early Christians, the very warp and woof of the Kingdom of God?[27]

Classical theories of friendship

Although the focal point of this book is to be the writings concerning friendship of certain prominent Christian writers of the fourth century, their thoughts must be considered against the background of the ideas on the subject formulated and discussed by Greek and Roman writers over a period of more than one thousand years.[1] The outline of this background material must necessarily be brief, concentrating on those theories and expressions concerning friendship which will be referred to and developed later in a Christian context; for more detailed discussions of particular topics the reader must consult those books which provide more elaborate treatments of various aspects of the Classical concept of friendship. But however brief this survey, which aims at pointing out the main developments and continuities in the cultural heritage, must cover not only some of the philosophical theories and the changes in meaning or application of the terms involved (as far as this can be deduced from the available sources),[2] but also the more popular views of the subject as they were handed down, often in the form of proverbs of unknown origin: both these strands are evident in later thought.

To begin with the evidence from Greek literature it must be remembered that in Greek thought the term *philia* (or *philotes* in early Greek writings) which is usually translated as friendship, had a far wider extension of meaning and application than our term friendship.[3] It could be applied not only to one-to-one relationships of affection and loyalty but also to the network of family relations, to the political sphere and society as a whole or even, as in the case of the Presocratic philosophers Empedocles and Pythagoras, to the cosmic sphere; each writer might be concerned with one or more of these aspects.

In this study our main concern will be with the *philia* of personal relationships, the so-called *philia hetairike*, which is already represented, with a certain moral code of its own, in the Homeric poems.[4] In fact, the noun *philia* does not occur in the *Iliad* or *Odyssey* and even the frequently used adjective or noun *philos* is not easy to define in these, the earliest representations in Greek literature of a reciprocal bond of obligation and affection offering security to those involved and demanding actions as proofs of affection and trust.[5] There has been much discussion of the origins and meanings of the words *philos* and *hetairos*;[6] it is clear that the former most frequently occurs as an adjective meaning either 'one's own' (i.e. used as a possessive) or 'dear' and can be applied to parts of the body, family relationships or to one's comrades on the field of battle, i.e. anything which belongs to one, while *hetairos* is usually used to express the relationship between a hero and his followers, as for example at *Il.*17.117, when Menelaus in the midst of battle notices Ajax encouraging his comrades and urging them to fight. The relationship between those people who are *philoi* may be based on the family or on the important obligations of hospitality, as in the case of the Trojan Glaucus and the Greek Diomedes who, on the battlefield, realise that their families are linked by such ties and that their grandfathers' friendship means that they are *philoi*, too – despite being on opposite sides and never having previously met! – and must treat each other accordingly (*Il.*6.119–236). And so even when *philos* is used substantivally it does not necessarily bear the connotations which we associate with the word 'friend'; the closest the Homeric poems come to the expression of such a concept seems to be by the combination of *philos* and *hetairos* as at *Il.*17.655 when Menelaus is told to send Antilochus to break the news to Achilles that his best friend Patroclus has been killed or at 18.80–2 when Achilles, after the news has been broken, addresses Thetis with the words, 'What pleasure is this to me since my dear companion is dead, Patroclus, whom I loved beyond all other companions, as well as I love my own life.'

This relationship, of course, not only forms the focus and motivates the climax of the *Iliad* but also provided the most famous example of a close friendship in antiquity.[7] Achilles' reference to the strength of his love for Patroclus is noteworthy as it reveals the intensity and special nature of the relationship, and the comparison between his love for his friend and for his own life is interesting, for in the same speech to his mother, Achilles reveals his awareness that he will indeed lose his life if he returns to battle to avenge the friend he has lost (*Il.* 18.95–6). But on what was their special relationship based? Later the answer would probably have been 'sexual attraction'[8] but in Homer the only indications are that their affection, of whatever kind, developed because they were brought up together from childhood (Patroclus apparently being the elder, by a few years) in the home of Achilles' father and because Patroclus was appointed Achilles' squire (*therapon*), which provided a further reason for continued intimacy.[9] Here the bonds of hospitality and family seem to have combined to produce a strong relationship (as between brothers) between two who were not blood relations.

A more theoretic example of the positive value attached to friendship in the Homeric world is provided by Alcinous' words at the end of *Odyssey* 8 (585–6), 'A wise friend is just as good as a brother', but the line of Homer which was to figure most prominently in later writers on friendship was undoubtedly *Od.* 17.218, 'God always brings like and like together', which was regarded as offering a general truth.[10] It is from this line, for example, that Socrates in Plato's *Lysis* deduces that it is God himself who is the author of human friendships, for Socrates feels that the Homeric statement is supported by what the 'learned men' i.e. the natural philosophers say, namely that like must of necessity ever be attractive to like.

But if Homer saw *philotes* primarily in terms of family relationships, his successors among the early Greek poets, Hesiod and Theognis, applied the term rather to a special relationship between two *hetairoi*, distinct from family ties. Both poets expressed their views on friendship in the form of maxims which gave them a popular appeal, reflecting as they did common-sense views in Greek society. Hesiod, for example, warns against deceiving a friend and counsels openness and honesty, while Theognis, in writing to his patron Kyrnos, curses hypocritical friends. However, if your friend initiates the wrong-doing, Hesiod advises that you should repay the wrong twofold to punish him, with which we may compare Theognis' prayer to Castor and Pollux (1089–90),'If I plan anything bad for my friend, may I suffer it myself; if he wishes me ill, may he suffer it himself twice over': this attitude was in accordance with a general law of revenge[11] which represented the other side of the coin in the Greek idea of friendship.

At lines 713–14 of the *Works and Days* Hesiod condemns the man who changes friends too frequently and then advises against being either too hospitable or not sufficiently so. Both these pieces of advice were taken up by later writers on friendship: we may compare Theognis 1151–2,'Never succumb to the suggestions of wicked men and desert the friend that you have, to search for another', and Cicero in the *Laelius* (19.67–8), where we find criticism of those who keep making new friends while neglecting the old. Aristotle, too, in the *Nicomachean Ethics* warns against *polyphilia* or the over-accumulation of friends, as does Plutarch in his short moral essay on the subject – indeed, Aristotle quotes a line from Hesiod in support of his view, applying it to those who become friends with a view to their mutual usefulness. Another of Hesiod's statements touching on friendship which proved influential was the idea that friendship is best established between people of different characters and interest – 'For potter is the rival of his fellow potter and the builder of his fellow, one beggar is jealous of another as is one singer of another' is how he puts it – an idea which contrasts with the view expressed in *Od.*17.218 but which found philosophical support in the views of Heraclitus and was often cited in later literature.[12]

In fact Theognis offers a fuller picture of the advantages and dangers of friendship than Hesiod, mainly in lines 31–128 of his poem in the form of gnomic statements. He advises Kyrnos to mix only with good men from whom he can learn goodness, an exhortation referred to by Aristotle in his discussion of friendship and happiness[13] and one which was to be taken seriously

by many later writers in various forms. Another idea popular-
ised by Theognis is that a good friend will stand by you in
adversity as well as in prosperity, but Theognis was also aware
of the difficulties involved in recognising whether you could
trust someone and indeed of the difficulty of finding anyone
trustworthy:[14] 'One cannot know the mind of a man or woman
until they have been tested like a beast beneath the yoke.'

Such practical and moral advice on friendship, evidence of a
rather pessimistic view of life, was to influence the thoughts of
tragedians and rhetoricians alike and pass into the mainstream
of popular philosophy in the course of the fifth and fourth
centuries B.C. In later writers, however, the harsh advice was
tempered by a more positive view of friendship as a harmon-
ising force. This was perhaps due to the influence of Presocratic
and Pythagorean thought which added a cosmic element[15] to
philia, as well as to the more settled, civilised society of fifth-
century Greece, when friends were not regarded primarily as a
defence against a generally hostile environment but were
appreciated in their own right as companions with similar
interests. The particular interest of Hesiod and Theognis'
attitude to friendship is that it reveals that the link between
virtue (*arete*) and *philotes*, evident in Homer, continued to be
regarded as the basis for stable friendships and also that
particular rules for behaviour in friendship were already
developing.

It was in fact Pythagoras, in the sixth century B.C., who
appears to have been the most influential of the Presocratic
philosophers on the subject of *philia*, for his exciting ideas were
seen to have wide-ranging implications for theories about
human relationships. There are of course problems in establishing how much of the thought attributed to Pythagoras actually
originated with him and was not merely the invention of later
biographers,[16] but it seems that friendship was an important
element in his personal life as well as in his thought, where *philia*
was discussed in a number of different contexts,[17] whether in
connection with the relations between gods and men, between
man's soul and body, between man and his fellow men or
between different forces within the human body. This wide

application was in accordance with Pythagoras' belief in universal harmony as a cosmic principle, a principle which influenced his view of human relations. Harmonious personal relations were supposed to extend, at least in theory, throughout the world, although in practice it was believed that friendship with those unworthy of it or with those who did not share the Pythagorean world-view, ought to be avoided. Pythagoreans, however, would be friends even if they did not know one another.[18] In one's relations with others, reprimands and advice were welcome but must be administered gently. One of the salient characteristics of Pythagorean friendship was its insistence on loyalty in all circumstances:[19] such loyalty was exemplified in two stories about Pythagorean friends, that about Lysis and Euryphamos and that about Damon and Phintias recorded both by Iamblichus and Porphyry.[20] Lysis and Euryphamos were two Pythagorean friends who happened to meet when Euryphamos came to worship at the temple of Juno and Lysis was just coming out of the temple; Lysis promised to wait outside until his friend had also worshipped the goddess. But when Euryphamos had finished in the temple he was so absorbed in his own thoughts that he forgot that Lysis was waiting for him and he left the temple by a different gate. Lysis, however, a paragon of fidelity, remained waiting for his friend for the rest of the day, that night and most of the following day until Euryphamos was reminded of Lysis and his promise and went back to the temple to release him.

The more dramatic account of the loyal friendship between Damon and Phintias involved an incident when Phintias, as a result of a plot by non-Pythagoreans, was accused of conspiring against the Sicilian tyrant Dionysius. Phintias, though innocent, calmly accepted the charge on condition that he might have the rest of the day to arrange the affairs of Damon and himself (being friends, their property was held in common). Dionysius agreed but demanded that Phintias produce someone as surety for his death; to everyone's surprise Phintias offered Damon who willingly agreed to stand surety. But Phintias returned at sunset as he had promised and so impressed was Dionysius by the honourable and loyal conduct of these men that he released them both, asking only that he might become their friend too – but this request was refused. The latter story was clearly popular in antiquity – we find it referred to by Cicero, Diodorus, Valerius Maximus, Plutarch, Hyginus, Ambrose and Jerome![21]

Another principle fundamental to Pythagorean friendship was that of *koinonia*, a concept which was to recur numerous times in various contexts in later Greek and early Christian thought.[22] This broad concept of a community of members holding all things in common may have grown out of the practice of the Pythagorean community in which everything was apparently shared and indeed, to Pythagoras was attributed the enormously popular proverb, 'Friends have all things in common' (*koina ta ton philon*). According to Diogenes Laertius (8.10), Pythagoras was also the first to formulate the saying 'Friendship is equality' (*philotes isotes*)[23] which was perhaps also a prescription for the equal sharing of property but which was later interpreted as meaning that friendship involved equality of status and interests. Pythagoras too, may have been the author of the idea that a friend is a second self, an idea which occurs very often in both Greek and Latin writings on friendship and in personal letters, as does the idea, attributed to Pythagoras by Cicero,[24] that in friendship many become one. In conclusion one may claim that Pythagoras' ideas on friendship were to be influential for the development of the ideal of *philanthropia* and a more humanitarian philosophy than was hitherto evident in Greek thought, for political theory as well as for the concept of friendship as an intimate and mutual relationship of affection between those of like minds, based on a natural and universal harmony.[25]

During the next century or so, down to the end of the fifth century, many of these ideas were developed, appearing in different forms and contexts in the writings of dramatists and philosophers. Professor Blundell has shown, for example, how prominent the idea of helping one's friends was in the tragedies of Sophocles, particularly in the *Philoctetes*, but it is Euripides who appears to have made the most significant contribution to the picture of valuable friendships,[26] offering instances of exemplary relationships between those who were brought together not by blood ties but by mutual sympathy, affection and benevolence. In the case of some thoughts he accepts what was becoming part of a traditional view of friendship: like Sophocles, he accepted that it is right to help one's friends and harm one's enemies, a moral imperative which remained more or less undisputed until challenged by Socrates;[27] he also expresses the belief that men should be useful to their friends and that friends are a valuable possession,[28] but that it is hard to find a trustworthy friend who does not desert in time of trouble. A further sign of his continuity with the past is the fact that Euripides refers to the Pythagorean maxim *koina ta ton philon* at *Orestes* 735 and *The Phoenician Women* 243.

But Euripides differs from his predecessors in cutting friendship loose from any ties with cosmic laws;[29] it is up to men to create firm friendships in the face of all life's difficulties and to share one another's sufferings. One of the most important criteria of true friendship is that it perseveres in adversity. But it is no all-embracing *philanthropia*, rather an intimate relationship between two people developing out of a long acquaintance and being a result of deliberate choice on the part of each friend. About such friends it can be said that they have one soul, as at *Orestes* 1045–6. It is a friendship of such an ideal kind which is depicted by Euripides as exisiting between Orestes and Pylades in the *Orestes* and the *Iphigeneia at Tauris* and between Theseus and Heracles in the *Heracles*. These friends greatly appreciated each other's loyalty and it was for this virtue above all that Orestes and Pylades were celebrated in antiquity and the Middle Ages and allowed to take their place beside Achilles and Patroclus, Theseus and Peirithous as a perfect example of true friendship.[30]

The idea expressed by the eponymous hero in *Orestes* 665–6 is indeed fundamental to Euripides' view of friendship and to that of many of his contemporaries,[31] for the utilitarian element, though always present in Greek thought about friendship, is particularly evident at this period. This did not mean that one should or could enter into a friendship merely for selfish reasons: the fact that the relationship, in order to be good and stable, must be completely reciprocal meant that one had to offer much for one's friend, even perhaps life itself, as Orestes and Pylades were willing to do.

The emphasis on the purely human aspect of *philia* is found also in the thought of the contemporary Sophists, but their main interest seems to have lain in the political and social sphere rather than in the nature of personal relationships among a few people. A friendly relationship of mutual interest was, they believed, natural to all men in virtue of their common humanity. However, their ideas clearly did have some impact on popular opinion and confirmed certain theories found in earlier thought; for example, the idea that friends are a useful possession is found in many different writings surviving from the years following the heyday of the Sophists, as is the idea of the importance of justice and equality in human relations[32] and of the sharing by friends of all their emotions and interests.[33] It is not surprising that their ideas should have passed so quickly into the mainstream since the Sophists' teaching methods helped to spread them to a large audience in democratic Athens,[34] as did the fact that they were presented to the public in the popular form of Euripidean – and maybe other – drama.

Perhaps the fullest discussion of the nature of friendship in the light of Sophistic ideas is the one put into the mouth of Socrates by Xenophon at *Memorabilia* II.4–6. Xenophon's Socrates says that he has often heard it said that of all possessions the most precious is a good and sincere friend (II.4.1), while the idea that a friend is the most useful possession is expressed at II.4.5–6. In the following passage Socrates praises the sympathy and helpfulness offered by good friends, although he also stresses that such benefits must be reciprocal (II.6.4). This emphasis on usefulness, which is evident also in the summary Socrates gives of the desirable characteristics to be looked for in a friend, is likely to be due to Sophistic influence, as is the idea that friendship is natural to man which lies behind the statement at II.6.21,'Some elements in man's nature make for friendship: men need one another, feel pity, work together for their common good and conscious of this they are grateful to one another', and which was later taken up by Aristotle.[35] But these statements about the nature of friendships and the moral code which it implied did not result from any profound investigation into the subject and although they provide evidence of the popular view of the times and the importance of the subject at an early stage in Greek thought, it is only with Plato and Aristotle that we find developed discussions on the nature of friendship which, while referring frequently to the popular ideas, do break new ground and contribute enormously to the later conceptions of *philia* and *amicitia* in Greek and Roman thought, not only in philosophical circles.

The main work of Plato in which *philia* has a place is the *Lysis*[36] where it bears the kind of importance we find attached to *eros* in later works such as the *Phaedrus* and *Symposium*.[37] In this early dialogue Plato's Socrates, unlike the one portrayed by Xenophon, seems to be concerned with something more than merely human *philia*, whether in its political or personal aspect, at least in the second half of this dialogue. Despite the difficulty of the dialogue and the inconclusiveness of the argument, the *Lysis* does offer certain signposts which enable the attentive reader to understand more of what Socrates is saying than his interlocutors Lysis and Menexenus do at the end. It seems that Socrates moves during the course of the dialogue from an examination of certain implications of the traditional ideas about friendship (such as that a friend, if sincere, is more valuable than anything else, that like is attracted to like or the opposite view, that a friend should be virtuous and useful and that friendship must be a reciprocal relationship to warrant the name) to a tentative discussion as to the possibility of finding a more stable cause of friendship, something external to the two friends. Moreover, the rather banal ideas introduced in the first half of the dialogue, which prove to have been red herrings according to the way Socrates steers the argument, are later transposed into a more profound context and are therefore not wholly rejected in the move to the more characteristically Platonic philosophical discussion: the question of whether the statement made in *Od.*17.218, that God always leads like to like, is accurate occurs later in the guise of the important concept of *oikeiotes*, while the question of whether only good men can be friends passes into a discussion of the Good as an impersonal object of our desire.

Having concluded that neither people who are completely good nor those who are utterly bad can be friends, Socrates introduces the idea that it is that which is neither good nor bad which is attractive to the good[38] on the grounds that it is not so completely bad as to have no knowledge of the good but it does lack the good to such a degree as to make it desire the good in order to make itself whole. And it is in the context of the main discussion that we must view Socrates' earlier desire to advise Lysis' lover Hippothales not to praise his beloved too highly but rather to arouse him to an awareness of his faults and a desire for the good: this is the best way to show one's love.[39] For *philia* implies imperfection and loss and has an essential role to play in the search for the Good. But it is not sufficient to love a good man as our friend, for according to Plato there is something beyond that friend which causes us to love him. This conclusion is reached from the premise that everything is loved for the sake of something else and therefore, to prevent a *regressus ad infinitum* Plato posits a being for the sake of which everything else is ultimately loved. This is the *proton philon* or 'thing to which we are in the first instance friends' which is to be loved for its own sake and for the sake of which we will love our friends.[40]

The search for a definition of *philia* is confused by the fact that Socrates uses three different meanings of the word *philos* ('friend', 'dear' and 'fond') without specifying the variations in meaning at any point. It is therefore impossible for Menexenus, Socrates' interlocutor in the second half of the dialogue, to follow the argument and this leads to an unsatisfactory conclusion of the question of how one person becomes another's friend.[41] A further source of confusion is the introduction of the concept of *epithumia* ('desire') at 221d 3 as the basis for friendship, as more or less synonymous with *philia*. It is agreed that this, like the related concepts of *philia* and *eros*, naturally strives for what is *oikeion* (closely related to the self).[42] In some way, therefore, a man must belong to the object of his love 'either in his soul or in some quality of his soul or in disposition or in form', and this is true not only of a friend but also as regards the *proton philon*. But how does this conclusion differ from the original definition at 214a–b that like must be the friend of like? And so the dialogue ends with the admission that the argument has apparently been circular and that no conclusion as to the nature of friendship has been reached.

However, certain suggestions have been made which will be developed in other dialogues where Plato's concern with the metaphysical and transcendental, and with the end rather than the means, will be more to the fore. Such is the idea adumbrated here that the object of proper desire, the *proton philon*, unites those who seek for it and makes them truly belong both to it and to their fellow seekers.[43] In the new concept of the nature and role of friendship based on this idea the familiar utilitarian basis has not been wholly rejected but rather refined and transformed: friends are no longer useful only because they stand by us in danger or provide us with various external benefits but because they are the means whereby we may be led to wisdom and truth. It is in this search for truth that friends can be united in a true *Wesensverwandtschaft* which goes much deeper than the external similarities discussed earlier in connection with the problem of 'like to like'. Yet it would seem that from such a view followed the conclusion that once the good man attained the object of his desire, viz. wisdom, he would no longer need the friends who were only a means to a higher end. In other words, friendship was regarded as propaedeutic rather than as part of the genuinely wise man's life. It is possible that there are traces in the *Lysis* of different, potentially contradictory strands in Plato's thought. On the one hand is the mystical, contemplative side with its ascent to pure Beauty and the form of the Good while on the other hand is the concern with the life of the community and dialectic with friends.[44]

It is this latter aspect of *philia* on which Aristotle was to concentrate in his ethical discussions on the subject. It is fortunate that we have Aristotle's discussions for they develop and help to clarify some of the obscurer points adumbrated by Plato in the *Lysis*, as well as providing a systematic and widely

influential account of this far-ranging topic.[45] Aristotle sets his
main analysis of *philia*, in the *Nicomachean Ethics*, in the context of
a definition of happiness as man's *summum bonum*, of which *philia*
is regarded as an essential element: although Aristotle restricts
friendship to a human secular relationship (albeit one which can
obtain between members of a family as well as people more
generally), he does seem to accord it greater value than does the
modern view of friendship which restricts it even further.

Aristotle's discussion begins with the following description of
his subject: 'It is some sort of excellence or virtue, or involves
virtue, and it is, moreover, most indispensable for life'.[46] He
does not explain in what way *philia* is a virtue but this statement
can presumably be interpreted in the light of his later declara-
tion that the perfect form of friendship is that between good
men who are alike in excellence or virtue, for these friends wish
alike for one another's good because they are good men and
they are good *per se* (1156b 7–8), which is then developed into
the idea that friendship allows good men to put their virtue into
practice; moreover, friendship based on virtue is stable and
long-lasting because such is also the nature of virtue. At
*Rhet.*1381a a rather different definition is given, whereby a
friend is someone who is loved by us and loves us in return,
someone who shares our happiness and sorrow and who has the
same view of what is good and bad as we do, and this may be
compared with the statement made about friends later in the
discussion in the *Nicomachean Ethics*, showing that friendship
ought to be mutual, benevolent and disinterested. Another
important element in the Aristotelian view of friendship, and
one in which we can detect Sophistic influence, is that it is a
relationship which is not only natural to man but must also be
based on rational choice between equals. Aristotle, however,
lays more emphasis than his predecessors on its significance for
the truly moral life, refining his definition of *philia* to produce a
clear and psychologically realistic account of the subject.

Such an idealistic view of friendship was made realistic
because it formed only part of Aristotle's whole scheme; true
friendship, the best kind, existed side by side with the far
more common types of friendship motivated by enjoyment and

usefulness rather than by the good. This threefold categoris-
ation was to be enormously influential on later thought about
friendship and was indeed what was needed at this stage of
philosophical progress to tidy up the various ideas on virtue
and utility in connection with friendship. The differences and
relations between the three kinds of *philia* are discussed by
Aristotle in Book 8 of the *Nicomachean Ethics*. While what is good
is loved for its own sake, the useful and enjoyable are loved for
the sake of the benefit or pleasure they produce and because
people do not often consider the same thing to be useful or
enjoyable for long, friendships based on such grounds are
unlikely to be either stable or long-lasting. Friendship based on
virtue, however, will last and will also bring with it pleasure
and usefulness; such relationships are however rare, both
because good men are few and far between and because these
friendships need time to mature.[47]

As in earlier views of friendship, so in the Aristotelian version
we find the idea that actions are necessary in friendship;
benevolent feelings are not sufficient and faith must, as it were,
be accompanied by works. A friend must continually prove his
affection by his actions and that is why living together is such
an important element in Aristotle's highest kind of friendship,
for communal life allows one greater opportunity to behave
actively as a friend. Aristotle even believes that if friends are
absent from one another for a long time, their friendship is
likely to dissolve. This is the reason why his Peripatetic
followers insisted so strongly on the importance of maintaining
the relationship by means of letters, for if an effort is not made
to continue the friendship during periods of absence, the friends
may be said to have affection towards one another but without
fulfilling all the essential duties of true *philia*.

Although such a relationship, based on rational choice,
motivated by virtue and implying complete equality, is to be
admired and encouraged, Aristotle rejected the idea that one
should cultivate as many friends as possible (*polyphilia*). This is
a question to which he returns in Book 9 of the *Nicomachean
Ethics* where he quotes the Hesiodic line, 'Do not be known as a
man of many guests nor of none';[48] he concludes that it is not

practicable for a man to live with a large number of friends or to share all their joys and sorrows as he ought. Such an attitude is indicative of how intense a relationship his ideal friendship was considered to be, while a friendship which embraces a large number of friends resembles rather a general social or political relationship, i.e. *homonoia*, not *philia*, though the two do have a number of characteristics in common.[49]

Aristotle's effective categorising of different kinds of friendship did not disregard certain potential problems such as the extent of mutual obligations in each kind and the problem of self-love, which he considers in the final chapters of Book 8 and in Book 9. To the modern reader both questions often seem to be a source of embarrassment for they appear to imply an unattractive calculating materialism and a lack of altruism in the Aristotelian concept of friendship. But the problems lie not with the perfect form of friendship but with the inferior kinds: in true friendship neither friend will mind if he gives more than is strictly necessary or just, because his aim is to do as much good as possible to his friend, but in the case of friendship based on usefulness or where one friend is superior to another problems often arise for, as Aristotle remarks perceptively, 'Where material advantage is the purpose of the relationship, people always want more and think they have less than they should have.'[50] Such problems he attempts to resolve by saying that in friendships based on usefulness the conditions of the friendship must be made clear to both parties at the outset, while in the case of unequal friends the superior partner should expect to gain more honour and the needy partner a larger share of the profit.

With regard to the problem of self-love, can Aristotle be accused of advocating selfishness by referring all our affection towards our friends to our love of ourselves? But he does not seem to regard a man as selfish if he behaves in accordance with the highest part of himself, namely his reason, even though, by so behaving, he also happens to do what is best for himself. This is considered to provide a stable basis for friendship rather than a source of conflict. It is against the background of a positive view of self-love that he interprets the proverbial phrases to which he refers at 1168b 6–8 where he explains that 'all friendly feelings towards others are an extension of the friendly feelings a person has for himself. Furthermore, all the proverbs express a similar opinion, e.g. (friends have) "one soul", "friends hold in common what they have", "friendship is equality" and "the knee is closer than the shin"'.[51] In conclusion: if true friendship is based on a form of self-love, it is a self-love which does not prevent a man giving his life for his friend.[52] It is the distinction between a proper self-love and an improper one which is crucial.

A further question discussed by Aristotle which will recur in later writings about friendship, notably in those of the Stoics, is whether the supremely happy man is so self-sufficient that he will have no need of friends. While Plato appears to have concluded that the man who had attained wisdom would not need friends,[53] Aristotle's answer is that the happy man will need friends that he might exercise his virtue on them; furthermore, how can one deny friendship, which is the greatest external source of happiness, to the happy man? However, he will have no need of friends of the inferior, merely useful sort for he already possesses all the good things of life which such friends might provide.

Even after Aristotle's wide-ranging treatment of the subject of *philia*, friendship remained a topical subject among philosophers of various schools.[54] There is, for example, evidence that treatises on friendship (*peri philias*) were written by many Platonic and Peripatetic philosophers. Theophrastus, Aristotle's successor as head of the Lyceum in the fourth century B.C., is known to have written such a work in three books. Although no longer extant, it was apparently familiar to Cicero when he came to write the *Laelius*, while Plutarch mentions Theophrastus' work twice and Gellius provided a summary of the work which may have been the source of Jerome's knowledge of it. From later references to it and quotations from this treatise, it has been deduced that Theophrastus' ideas on friendship were less harsh than those of Aristotle, though he also reproduced much of his predecessor's discussion, such as the threefold division of the subject. Theophrastus does however seem to have been the originator of one of the most famous dicta connected with friendship and referred to by Cicero, Plutarch, Ammianus Marcellinus and others, namely that it is better to make judgements before one makes friends rather than be critical once the friendship is formed;[55] he also appears to have discussed in some depth the popular problem of what to do in the case of a conflict between one's duty to a friend and other duties.

In contrast to the central position accorded to friendship in Peripatetic philosophy, in Stoic ethics it seems to have played only a secondary role. It is true that Cleanthes and Chrysippus are said to have written works on friendship and that we have discussions of the subject by Epictetus and Seneca and a warm recommendation by Dio Chrysostom, as well as Cicero's treatment of the subject largely inspired by the moderate Stoic Panaetius. Yet the Stoics on the whole seem to be more concerned with the nature of virtue and the behaviour of the sage, or with the nature of society on a wider scale, with concepts such as *homonoia* (unity in agreement) and *symphonia* (harmony) rather than with the relationship between a few individuals. It is only among the later Stoics that friendship came to be accorded a higher value. While Zeno, the founder of Stoicism, regarded the cultivation of friendships as one of the duties (*kathekonta, officia*) which a man ought to perform because it is in accordance with nature and reason,[56] he also taught that a friend and the advantages derived from him are but means to the good.[57] On the other hand, later Stoics under the influence of such men as Posidonius and Panaetius, seem to have proposed that friends were a good that was to be chosen *per se* rather than for any benefit we may gain from them.[58] Both early and later Stoics agreed that friendship was natural to man, this belief being founded on their idea of *oikeiosis*, whereby men naturally appropriate to themselves what is around them or what they regard as similar to themselves.[59] This natural instinct for self-preservation brings man into friendly and harmonious relations with others and these relations gradually spread out from his immediate family circle to embrace more and more people. The likeness between all men by virtue of their common reason is an essential element in the Stoic view of friendship, although Epictetus points out that men are only truly friends if they agree that the highest good lies in moral purpose.

Another belief which seems to have been held by most Stoics from Zeno to Seneca, with only minor divergences, was the idea that only the wise are friends. Zeno, in the *Politeia*, said that only the truly good can be proper citizens, friends and free men. Posidonius, in the first book of his *De officiis* (*On Moral Duties*) and Hecato in the third book of his work *On Paradoxes* apparently claimed that friendship only exists between wise men because of their likeness. Cicero perhaps found this idea in Panaetius, too, in a moderate form, for although they both rejected the very strict definition of the wise man put forward by earlier Stoics, Cicero does still agree that friendship can exist only between good men, while Seneca quotes the Stoic saying, 'Only the wise man is a friend'.[60] Conversely the Stoics also believed that all wise men are friends[61] even if they are unacquainted with one another. Concord and friendship on a large scale seem to have been regarded as natural concomitants of virtue and Chrysippus went so far as to deduce that, since all wise men are friends to one another and friends have everything in common, the wise man's actions will consequently be beneficial to all the wise. This aspect of universality in the Stoic view of friendship is also evident in their approval of the impulse to have many friends (*polyphilia*), which, as we have seen, was rejected by most writers on friendship.

On the other hand, the idea that friends have all in common is one that runs right through the history of this concept in antiquity, though it seems to be particularly prominent in the writings of Seneca who discusses its implications within the context of Stoic philosophy.[62] In the *De beneficiis* (7.12.1) he considers the difference between the sharing of property by business partners and friends; after referring to the proverbial 'Friends share everything', he goes on to explain that one does not share everything with a friend in the same way as one does in a business relationship where one partner owns a part and the other another part; friends share things in the way parents share their children, where all the children belong to both parents equally. In the next paragraph Seneca connects the belief that only wise men can be friends with the idea that complete community of goods is only possible amongst the wise, while in Ep.48.2 he shows that the idea of having all in common was not restricted to property but applied to interests and to good and bad fortune alike which were to be shared by friends. This letter also shows how a Stoic viewed the fellowship which bound him to his fellow men as the basis for the more intimate fellowship between friends, when Seneca writes that, since a man has many things in common with his fellow man, he will *a fortiori* have everything in common with his friend.[63]

The main problem facing the Stoics was that a conflict appeared inevitable between their belief that only the wise could form true friendships and the belief that the wise man was self-sufficient. It was a problem which had already been raised by Plato and Aristotle but it recurred in Stoic philosophy in a more acute form because of the Stoic emphasis on self-sufficiency (*autarkeia*). The early Stoics apparently took a rigorous line, conceding only that friendship is one of the things by nature (*kata physin*) providing the material on which virtuous action is based and therefore in some sense to be desired even by the truly good man who nevertheless does not compromise his self-sufficiency. Later Stoics such as Antipater, Panaetius and Posidonius were forced to admit that external benefits were indeed necessary to the life of the good and wise man and that virtue was not the sole object in life. When Seneca expounds this problem in Ep.9 he reaches a positive conclusion by explaining that the wise man does not have friends for the benefit he can derive from them but for the help and support he can give them. Indeed he turns the problem on its head by concluding that only the man who is self-sufficient can be helpful in a completely selfless way and therefore the wise man, who is by definition self-sufficient, is the person best suited to true friendship.[64]

Since Cicero's theories of friendship were influenced by the lost work *On Moral Duties* by the Stoic Panaetius,[65] we may now consider Cicero's humane, civilised and inspiring ideas as

presented chiefly in the *Laelius* (or *De amicitia*) and in his own
De officiis, both of which were very influential on later writers
and in which he attaches great importance to friendship.

In the *Laelius* (6.20) Cicero gives the famous definition of
friendship as 'omnium divinarum humanarumque rerum cum
benevolentia et caritate consensio' (a relationship based on
agreement about all human and divine matters, together with
good-will and affection).[66] Another fundamental idea which is
often referred to by later writers is that there is nothing more
pleasant in life than to have a friend with whom one may talk
as if with oneself. In the same paragraph Cicero also mentions
that it is the nature of 'vera et perfecta (sc. amicitia)' (true and
perfect friendship) which is under discussion, which corresponds to Aristotle's ideal form of friendship just as Cicero's
description of the inferior kind corresponds to the relationships
based on enjoyment and utility in the *Nicomachean Ethics*.
Another important idea contained in this paragraph is the
popular one that a true friend is of benefit both in good and ill
fortune: with this may be compared for example what Aristotle
had written at *Rhet.*1381a 4, namely that a friend must be
someone who shares our happiness in what is good and our
pain in what is unpleasant for no other reason than for our
sake. Cicero can thus be seen to be mediating this, as so many
other philosophical ideas, from Greek to Roman civilisation
and it is in its role as transmitter of learned and popular ideas
about friendship (combined with information and examples
from Roman life) that the prime importance of this dialogue
lies, rather than for its contribution of original thoughts.[67]

If Cicero regarded true friendship as pertaining between
only a few people, perhaps at its best between only two, this is
not to deny that he was also influenced by the Stoic belief that
all men are united by nature by virtue of their common
humanity nor that he at times regarded *amicitia* in political
rather than personal terms as a network of alliances. Much has
already been written about the Roman concept of political
amicitia in the context of the study of ancient history,[68] while the
ideals of personal friendship have been relatively neglected, but
as Professor Brunt, for example, has shown, Cicero's view of

friendship was certainly not limited to political *amicitia*; indeed he would not have regarded it as the true kind of friendship[69] for he could see that such relationships were often based on usefulness and personal interest rather than on more stable values such as virtue or natural human tendencies.[70]

In the third part[71] of the *Laelius* Cicero moves on to more practical questions concerning the correct behaviour of friends, such as the need for careful choice of friends, the distinction between friend and flatterer, the benefits of frank speech, the problems of whether to desert old friends for new, what to do when the friends are not equal in status, whether one ought to help a friend if this involves contravening what is right or one's duty to the gods or one's country – questions which commonly occur in writings on friendship throughout antiquity.[72] And then in sections 16.56–60 Cicero refers to a number of popular answers to the problem of the limits of friendship, all of which he firmly rejects. What he writes here is of interest in that it shows what ideas were in circulation at the time regarding the limits of friendship, though unfortunately Cicero, as so often, does not mention his sources. The three alternative views he refers to are that we should have the same attitude to our friend as we do to ourselves, that we should love our friend as much as he loves us, or that a man should be valued by his friends in the same way as he values himself, but rejecting these Cicero gives his own positive answer at 17.61 as to the proper bounds to our love for our friends when he writes:

When the characters of friends are blameless, then there should be between them complete harmony of opinions and inclinations in everything without any exception; and even if by some chance the wishes of a friend are not altogether honourable, in matters which concern his life or reputation one should turn aside from the straight path, provided the consequence is not utter disgrace.

As well as ideas derived from the philosophical theories of the Greeks, Cicero included in his view of friendship as depicted in several of his writings a number of popular sayings, both Greek and Roman. In the *Laelius*, for example he refers to the proverb (6.22) about friendship being more necessary than fire and water[73] and later in the work (19.67–8) he approves the well-known proverb that 'men must eat many a measure of salt together before the claims of friendship are fulfilled', in connection with the idea that friendship takes time to mature.[74] In the speech in defence of Plancius (2.5) he mentions an idea which was to be frequently quoted in the form given it by Sallust, 'Idem velle atque idem nolle, ea demum firma amicitia est' (Stable friendship is based on common likes and dislikes,[75] which Cicero formulates less succinctly as 'Neque est ullum certius amicitiae vinculum quam consensus et societas consiliorum et voluntatum' (There is no surer bond of friendship than agreement and the union of thought and inclination). In the *De officiis* Cicero shows that he is aware of the proverbial nature of the statement that friends share everything, a saying to which he also alludes in the speech against Verres (II.2.36.89). In the *Laelius* he quotes a line from Terence's *Andria* which soon became proverbial, 'Obsequium amicos, veritas odium parit' (Flattery makes friends but the truth only breeds hatred): this rather cynical view of human relations was referred to by many writers in late antiquity, for example Lactantius, Ausonius, Sulpicius Severus, Rufinus, Augustine, Priscian and Isidore.[76] Although it is true that Terence was widely read in the schools of the period, it may be that the fact that Cicero quotes this line contributed to its great popularity. Occasionally he ventures to attribute a popular saying, as he does in the *Laelius* when he says that Bias is thought to have been the author of the dangerous idea that one should love a friend in the awareness that one might some time come to hate him; he also attributes the pithy saying 'amicus certus in re incerta cernitur' (a true friend is proved in adversity), this time to the epic poet Ennius. Twice Cicero mentions the idea that in friendship many friends form as it were one mind,[77] once attributing it to Pythagoras. This was of course one of the most common ideas to be found in both Greek and Latin literature on friendship. It is this which lies behind, for example, Horace's reference to Virgil as 'animae dimidium meae' (half of my soul). Equally common, as we have seen, is the related idea of the friend as a second self, mentioned by Cicero at *Lael.*21.80 and in a number of his letters.

It should be noted in passing that friendship to Cicero was not merely a subject for academic discussion but an essential part of his own experience. This is clear from his letters to his friends, especially those to his brother Quintus and to Atticus. In many ways the friendship between Cicero and Atticus, as presented in the correspondence, resembles closely the relationship between Scipio and Laelius as portrayed by Cicero in his dialogue. Theirs was a strong mutual affection based on their admiration of each other's virtue and tried and tested in adversity and by prolonged separation when they relied on letters to maintain their close relationship. As with Quintus, so Cicero shared with Atticus a deep interest in literature. It is to these men that he could speak as if to himself, confident of sympathy and support.[78] Atticus is referred to as Cicero's *alter ego* in III.15.4, implying unity, equality and harmony between the two friends. That the traditional picture of close friendship, inherited largely from Greek philosophy but enriched by peculiarly Roman elements, could be found to be relevant to the everyday experience of friendship must not be forgotten, especially when we consider the experiences of those living in an atmosphere of supposedly dry academicism and decadence at the end of the fourth century: if Cicero could sincerely feel the truth of the traditional sayings about friendship, why should not the friends of the later Classical world have been equally sincere despite their frequent adherence to received ideas?

It is now time to turn from a predominantly Stoic view of friendship to examine what their main rivals in the Hellenistic world, the Epicureans, said on the subject. Despite the paucity of the textual evidence and the cryptic nature of the remaining fragments relevant to the subject, it is evident that the Epicureans accorded to friendship a central position in their philosophical scheme, regarding it as intimately connected with the highest good – pleasure or the absence of pain, rather than virtue as in the Stoic philosophy. Lucretius speaks of the 'sperata voluptas suavis amicitiae' (the expected pleasure of delightful friendship) (*De rerum natura* 1.140) and in Torquatus' defence of Epicureanism Cicero writes (*De finibus* 1.20.65), 'Of all the means to happiness that wisdom has devised, none is

greater, none more fruitful, none more delightful than friendship', with which one may compare what Epicurus himself is
supposed to have said: 'Of the things which wisdom provides
for the happiness of the whole life, by far the greatest is
friendship.' It appears that friendship was regarded as beneficial in attaining a life of true happiness because, unlike sexual
love,[79] it provided a stable and peaceful atmosphere. In such a
life of *ataraxia* (freedom from passion) it was possible to avoid
such destructive forces as passion and rivalry, potential sources
of pain.[80]

Friendship was also to be sought for its own sake, as
providing pleasurable opportunities for intellectual intercourse
and mutual support and encouragement.[81] But although the
Epicureans might have agreed with the Stoic rivals on this
point, they seem to have confronted them head-on with regard
to the Epicurean belief that friendship developed out of a
need.[82] They have therefore been accused of proposing a purely
utilitarian view of friendship which excluded altruism. Certainly Cicero found such an idea of friendship based on utility
rebarbative and Seneca (Ep.9.8) expresses his pride that the
Stoics differ so radically on this point from the Epicureans.
Cicero found more acceptable the view (described as 'huma-
nius' at *De fin.* II.26.82) attributed to more recent Epicureans
that, although at the outset we desire a man's friendship for
utilitarian motives, yet when intimacy has developed we love
our friend for his own sake. In some form or other the problem
is likely to remain, as a consequence of making pleasure the
supreme good, but this does not compel the Epicureans to
concede that all altruistic actions are impossible and to deny all
sense of moral duty: indeed, friends were even expected to lay
down their lives for one another and certainly to endure great
pains on one another's behalf.[83] This resulted from the fact
that loyalty, as a stabilising factor, was so highly valued in
Epicurean circles. Further factors which moderated the apparently selfish aspect of utilitarianism were that the friend was
regarded as a second self and that the wise man was expected to
give more than he receives.

However, it had to be admitted that loyal and intimate

involvement with others might threaten the wise man's self-sufficiency and *ataraxia*; friends had therefore to be chosen with great care. It is unclear whether Epicurus recommended *polyphilia*: friendships were demanding and it might be argued that it was better to have only a few friends, but on the other hand, the more good friends one has, the more stable and secure life ought to be, if a positive view of friendship is adopted. Indeed, according to the advice given in a papyrus from Herculaneum,[84] a man should give as many people as possible the benefit of his good actions – hoping for benefits in return but not being motivated by this hope – and Epicurus himself, according to tradition, had many friends. But it seems that in practice the followers of Epicurus lived within a small group of friends who shared the same views, though their philosophy allowed also for a more universal feeling of phil-anthropy and even *philia* was generally regarded as extending beyond a one-to-one relationship to embrace a small com-munity. This aspect of Epicurean friendship is an important one: not only did such a community protect its members from the distractions inherent in normal daily life, but it also replaced traditional family and political groupings of society with the relationship between a wise spiritual leader and his admiring disciples. Wisdom was by no means to be pursued in solitude, but the ideal community for it was a private society withdrawn from the world,[85] enabling its members to live like the gods, for although man is not thought to be immortal, he can attain some form of divinity in this life by imitating the harmonious, peaceful and rational life of the gods.[86]

The popularity of the topic throughout antiquity is shown not only by its inclusion among the subjects for philosophical theorising, but also by the contribution made by a number of Greek and Latin authors whose views cannot be said to belong to any particular philosophical school, but whose statements about friendship – whether praise of the civilising influence of close friendships, advice about the behaviour of friends, or observations on the nature of friendship – added to the wealth of literature on the subject which was to continue to be influential for many centuries. Many of these works reached a

wide audience over the years because they were included in the
educational curriculum. Such was the case with a number of
the *sententiae* derived from the Latin mimes written by Publilius
Syrus in the first century B.C. Among these common sentiments
about friendship transmitted in memorable form, we find, for
example, 'amici vitia si feras facias tua' (If you put up with
your friend's faults, they become your own), 'Amico firmo nihil
emi melius potest' (There is nothing more valuable than a
reliable friend), 'Amici mores noveris, non oderis' (You should
know your friend's habits, not hate them), 'Cave amicum
credas nisi si quem probaveris' (Do not trust a man as your
friend until he has been tried and tested) and 'Peccatum amici
veluti tuum recte putes' (Consider your friend's mistakes as
your own).[87]

A more coherent essay on friendship is provided by a chapter
'De amicitia' in the handbook of illustrative historical and
rhetorical examples composed by the historian Valerius Maximus who wrote his work (*Factorum et dictorum memorabilium libri
novem*) under the emperor Tiberius.[88] In the general introduction to this chapter we find such familiar ideas as that true
friends can best be recognised in adversity, as exemplified by
the story of Orestes and Pylades, and the distinction between
family and friends which was an essential element in the
Roman view of friendship. In accordance with the nationalistic
spirit of the work, Valerius goes on to provide examples of
various Roman pairs of friends who also proved their constancy
in adversity, friends such as Ti. Gracchus and Blossius or
C. Gracchus and Pomponius and Laetorius,[89] though he later
refers also to the famous Greeks, Damon and Phintias. The
conclusion drawn is that friendship has such great power that it
is able to inspire men with a contempt for death, moderate the
force of cruelty, turn hatred to love and repay punishment with
kindness.

Although Plutarch's discussions of different aspects of friendship, enlivened by imagery and illustrations, bear the imprint
of certain Greek philosophical attitudes to the subject, especially those of Aristotle, yet they are more concerned with

practical problems than with any theory of the nature of friendship. In his role as popular, if scholarly, moralist he discusses, for example, the problem of distinguishing the flatterer from a friend, saying that a degree of frankness is a *sine qua non* for true friendship, but difficult for the flatterer to practise. In the same essay he refers to the proverb about friendship being more useful than fire and water, admitting that pleasure and usefulness are important constituents of friendship: true friendship has three aims in particular, virtue which is good, intimacy which is pleasurable and advantage which is necessary (94B) – an interesting variation on the threefold division of friendship. As the basis of true friendship Plutarch proposes that there should exist a similarity of character and interest. This is one of the reasons why he rejects the possibility or desirability of friendship with many, for such intimacy and harmony is only rarely achieved,[90] as he illustrates by reference to a few pairs of friends, familiar from other writings on the subject. Another reason for rejecting *polyphilia* is that friendship with many has overtones of purely utilitarian motives, and such a relationship he regards, following Aristotle, as inferior to true friendship. In the essay on brotherly love the advice on how to behave towards brothers contains some things relevant to friendship. At 478D he suggests that need is the basis for all human relationships: it is this which 'welcomes and seeks friendship and companionship and which teaches us to honour and cherish and protect our family, since we are unable and unfitted by nature to live friendless, unsocial lives'. Here, as in the work on flatterers and friends, Plutarch says that friendship develops naturally from what is advantageous and is a reflection of close family ties. In these three works Plutarch refers to many popular sayings and some which he specifically attributes to such philosophers as Pythagoras and Theophrastus,[91] but his general view of friendship is very much his own: he regards it as a pleasant and useful part of life which ought to be conducted according to certain moral principles; he does not place as much emphasis as one might expect on the connection between friendship and virtue, but friendship is certainly considered a fundamental component of social morals in many areas of human life.

While Plutarch's interest in a wide range of moral issues makes it unsurprising that he should have discussed *philia* in a number of works, it may seem strange that Lucian should have devoted one of his works, the *Toxaris*, to the subject, and set his discussion in the unusual context of a dialogue between a Scythian, Toxaris, and a Greek, Mnesippus. Toxaris explains that the memory of Orestes and Pylades is rather unexpectedly honoured in Scythia because his countrymen regard them as models of loyal friendship which they value highly. Mnesippus defends the Greeks against the charge that they are better at praising friendship than at practising it: he does so by relating five stories to illustrate Greek loyalty in friendship while Toxaris counters with an equal number of stories about Scythian friends. The result of the dispute is predictably a draw which provides the basis for a close friendship between Mnesippus and Toxaris. The dialogue does not aim at providing serious philosophical discussion but includes some interesting statements about friendship, echoing the popular Classical attitudes, with mention not only of Orestes and Pylades but also of Achilles and Patroclus, Theseus and Peirithous, as well as offering an unfamiliar set of examples of the theme of fidelity in friendship.

More closely akin to the approach of Plutarch is that of the second-century Greek writer Maximus of Tyre, among whose forty-one extant philosophical essays are two which touch on friendship – the fourteenth on the question of how to distinguish a flatterer from a friend and the thirty-fifth on how one ought to go about making friends. In the fourteenth Maximus adapts Prodicus' fable about Heracles faced at the crossroads by Virtue and Pleasure,[92] replacing these two goddesses by a friend and a flatterer respectively. Characteristics of friendship which he offers in his discussion are that it involves pleasure, it makes the friends willing to share their possessions with one another and to keep one another company in prosperity and adversity alike. Friendship is increased, flattery confuted, by time. It is more likely to be found among aristocrats, while flattery and democracy go hand in hand; here, as often, Maximus reveals the influence of Plato. His thirty-fifth essay is likewise full of examples from Greek literature, especially Homer, and from history, illustrating the fact that genuine friendships among mortals are rare and must be based on the principle of like to like.[93] Maximus treats this popular theme with some originality and strong feeling. He expresses doubts, considering the depravity of human nature, that it was possible for friends to hold everything in common as they are said to have done both among Greeks and barbarians. He points out that even Homer could tell of only one instance of true friendship in the whole Greek army at Troy. No, history is full of hatred, destruction, corruption and avarice which are wholly inimical to friendship. Maximus concludes that there can be no friendship while men are dazzled by gold or human beauty or public acclaim; all these must be despised if friendship is to be allowed to develop, a possession more admirable than wealth, more long-lasting than beauty, more secure than glory, more true than honour. He warns that true friendship, as opposed to flattery, will not be found unless man realises that friendship, though attended by reward, does not consist in reward. To conclude, Maximus invokes philosophy to bring peace to men's souls, without which friendship is sought in vain.

The connection between the philosophical life and friendship is even more prominent in the attitude of the Neoplatonists to *philia*, as far as this attitude can be deduced from the scanty and problematic evidence surviving. Since Neoplatonism was to be so influential in the Christian circles of the fourth century which we shall be considering in a later chapter, some mention should be made of the place accorded by it to friendship. What part did friendship play in the lives and thought of Plotinus, Porphyry or Iamblichus? Anything we can learn on this subject must be gleaned from the *Enneads*, from Porphyry's biography of Plotinus and from Iamblichus' of Pythagoras. As far as Plotinus is concerned Porphyry tells us that when Plotinus came to Rome he was surrounded by a circle of close friends from all over the Roman Empire. Among these were a number of women devoted to him in a manner similar to the aristocratic Roman women who attached themselves to Jerome during the late 370s and early 380s, adopting him as their spiritual and intellectual guide. These friends were Plotinus' disciples who learned from him and helped him either by providing accommodation or by assisting him with his philosophical work. Plotinus apparently believed that a man could do nothing better for his friends than to teach them, and yet he also believed that a man's primary concern must be with his inner self and with the return of his own soul to the One. Man must reach upwards towards the higher world of the intellect rather than involving himself in the world of the senses and of everyday life. How could such an aim be reconciled with a commitment towards one's friends? It is true that Plotinus in the *Enneads* denies that the wise man is unconcerned with friendship (1.4.15.21) and in the first *Ennead*, after making a distinction between man as a joint entity of soul and body and the inner man consisting only of soul, he asks to which of these two friendship will belong, to which the cryptic reply is given, 'Some to the joint entity, some to the inner man'. This suggests perhaps that some close relationships might not hinder the philosopher in his progress towards the One, although it is still unclear why the philosopher should not strive to detach himself completely from other men, since Plotinus appears to have had no sense that the philosopher might need others for the attainment of the highest good. It may be, as Rist has suggested,[94] that he believed that the closer man's soul comes to the One, the more it will concern itself with the rest of creation, seeing that creation is of the One and as the One loves itself, in this sense it can be said to love what belongs to it. Here we have a development of the Platonic idea of *oikeiosis* which appeared in the *Lysis*. Another possibility is that Plotinus held a view similar to that of Plato in the *Republic*, whereby the philosopher who has gained a vision of the truth has a duty to return to his fellow citizens to instruct them about the truth.

Iamblichus' biography of Pythagoras contains several sections dealing with what was considered to be the Pythagorean doctrine of *philia* and it is possible that the Neoplatonists were attracted by the Pythagorean attitude to friendship; certainly the circle of friends around Plotinus bore some resemblance to a Pythagorean community of friends devoted to the philosophical life. It may be that such a view of *philia* was transmitted to the educated Christians of the fourth century by means of Iamblichus' work on Pythagoras, though there were of course other available sources for what had become commonplaces about the nature of friendship attributed to Pythagoras in antiquity. But certain writings of Basil and Augustine, for example, undoubtedly contain ideas very similar to those found in this work of Iamblichus which suggests that they were familiar with it at first hand.

Furthermore, it may be significant that later Neoplatonists seem to have had a special interest in the topic of friendship, thereby following in a Classical philosophical tradition. There is evidence that Hierocles in the early fifth century wrote on the subject, albeit briefly, and Simplicius in the mid-sixth century writes at some length about it in his commentary on Epictetus when expounding the thirtieth chapter of the *Enchiridion*, concerned with family relationships rather than close relationships between non-family members.

Simplicius mentions the old saying that a friend is a second self and offers a variation on the idea that friends form one soul in two bodies when he writes that each of the friends will have two souls and two bodies. He also alludes to the saying *koina ta ton philon* and implies that friendship is a source of many great benefits. It may well be, therefore, that we must attribute our inability properly to appreciate the part played by friendship in Neoplatonism to the lack of evidence rather than being tempted to rush to the conclusion that the subject was only of marginal importance.

Here we must end this survey: much more could be said on so many aspects and so many authors, especially on Aristotle, Cicero and Seneca. As has been seen, certain questions relating to the nature and practice of friendship recur frequently in discussions and certain sentiments concerning friendship become crystallised in the form of proverbial statements, concisely expressed, which appear in various kinds of writings:

drama, letters, philosophical works and poetry. Such commonly found sentiments are *isotes philotes, koina ta ton philon,* the idea of two friends forming one soul or the friend as a second self, the warning not to form friendships rashly, the sceptical observation that friends are in abundant supply only in times of good fortune, that flattery destroys friendship while gentle rebuke is beneficial, that it is necessary to associate closely with one's friends and that friendship is based on similarity of character and interests. These are not necessarily profound statements but they are based on realistic human observation and regardless of their apparent banality they do occur frequently, even in the writings of philosophers and highly educated writers: together they form the essence of Classical thought about friendship and human relations in general as it is transmitted and developed down the centuries.

CHAPTER 3

Some problems of Christian friendship

If it is undeniable that friendship was an important concept in both Greek and Roman social thought, offering one of the highest ideals for human life, the picture seems at first sight very different when we turn to Christian attitudes, for the common view appears to be that the arrival and spread of Christianity in the ancient world pushed this ideal out and made it redundant: Christian *agape* and Classical *amicitia* were not compatible. As Kierkegaard expresses it, 'Christianity has pushed earthly love and friendship from the throne, the impulsive and preferential love, the partiality, in order to set spiritual love in its place, the love to one's neighbour, a love which in earnestness and truth and inwardness is more tender than any earthly love... The praise of earthly love and friendship belongs to paganism', and this view is echoed by many.[1] It may be argued that such a radical contrast is misleading, for in its finest forms even earthly love and friendship can be virtuous, spiritual and intent on truth, as many Classical writers have shown; however, there is a problem in the apparent difficulty of reconciling the Biblical commandment to love your neighbour, so central to Christian ethics, with what seems to be an essential characteristic of friendship, namely exclusivity and partiality in our love for others. Later in this chapter we shall consider how this problem was handled by some of the early Christian writers.

And yet Kierkegaard's response is not the only one; other writers have reached more positive conclusions. J. H. Newman, for example, in attempting a reconciliation between the two approaches to loving our fellow human beings, maintained that

'The best preparation for loving the world at large is to cultivate an intimate friendship and affection towards those who are immediately about us' for 'by trying to love our relations and friends, by submitting to their wishes though contrary to our own, by bearing with their infirmities, by overcoming their occasional waywardness with kindness, by dwelling on their excellences and trying to copy them, thus it is that we form in our hearts that root of charity which, though small at first, may, like the mustard seed, at last even over-shadow the earth'.[2]

As far as the early development of a positive Christian attitude to friendship goes, it has also been suggested that the best elements in Classical friendship were in fact transformed and absorbed into Christianity and one might say that friendship is indeed compatible with friendship as long as *amicitia* is tempered by *agape*, maintaining some of its characteristics as defined by the Classical writers but being transposed to a higher plane which takes account of the divine dimension.[3] Recently theological attention has focussed on the apparent dichotomy between *eros* and *agape*,[4] a dichotomy regarded as fundamental to the development of early Christian thought, and on the attempts by various writers to combine, if not reconcile, these opposing forces of love. In this study we shall be concerned rather with the combination of certain characteristics of *agape* with those of *philia*, the traditional partner of *eros* in the Greek philosophical vocabulary of love.

But it must not be forgotten that, if any positive evaluation of friendship was to develop within early Christian thought, it had to be firmly based on Scripture. It is therefore essential to consider first the Biblical evidence to see how friendship is portrayed in the Old and the New Testaments and then, from the evidence of the writers who form the subject of this study, which specific Scriptural texts were generally used in Christian discussions of friendship.

The Greek Septuagint translation of the Old Testament uses the word *philos* for a number of different, related Hebrew words such as 'neighbour' and 'fellow countryman' because Biblical Hebrew has no exact equivalent for the word 'friend'.[5] In general friendship as a valuable social or theological concept is not often found in the Old Testament, though there is of course the famous example of the ideal friendship between David and Jonathan which became legendary, on a par with those of Achilles and Patroclus or Orestes and Pylades. In 1 Sam.18 it is said that 'the soul of Jonathan was knit to the soul of David and Jonathan loved him as his own soul' and there is also a description of the ritual which the two young men perform to cement their friendship which is reminiscent of the encounter between Glaucus and Diomedes in *Iliad* 6. And David's lament for Saul and Jonathan in 2 Sam.1 was to haunt later literature, as for example in Peter Abelard's *Planctus* on this theme.[6]

Apart from this vivid story, mention of friendship in the Old Testament is largely restricted to occasional complaints of the treachery of friends. It is only in the so-called Wisdom litera-ture that friendship has a more obvious place, in such books as Proverbs, the Wisdom of Solomon and Ecclesiasticus. Here a concept which is basically foreign to the Old Testament world comes to the fore possibly under the influence of Hellenistic culture which provided the background against which these books were written. At Sir.6:5–17, for example, we find a number of statements about friendship closely resembling those to be found in Classical Greek and Hellenistic literature, both the wary, negative comments of Theognis[7] and the positive praise of the value of friendship, but connected in the Old Testament text with a God-fearing attitude, as in verses 14–16: 'A faithful friend is a sure shelter, whoever finds one has found a rare treasure. A faithful friend is priceless, there is no measuring his worth. A faithful friend is the elixir of life and those who fear the Lord will find one.'

Hellenistic evidence is more obvious in the writings of Philo the Jew who even quotes the Greek proverb *koina ta ton philon* and the Stoic definition of benevolence as the desire that good should befall your neighbour for his own sake.[8] It is possible that Philo in turn influenced early Christian writers on the subject of friendship for in his writings they could find a kind of friendship familiar to them from their knowledge of Greek culture but integrated in an acceptable theological perspective.

For example, a recurring idea in Philo's writings[9] is that men are brought together in friendship and harmony, indeed, bound together by an indissoluble bond, if they worship and love God together; the best kind of friendship between men is based on a shared, and close, relationship with God.[10]

It might seem that friendship is accorded even less value in the New Testament than in the Old. It is true that the word *philia* occurs only once, at James 4:4, and the verb *philein* is far less common than *agapan*, though there is hardly any distinction between the words except that *philein* is never used of love of God. The group of words *philos*, *philein* and *philia* are found more frequently in the Gospels of Luke and John, especially the latter: Luke here possibly betrays his Greek background while for John, both in the Gospel and the Epistles, love is of central importance and the use of these words is therefore more understandable. It is certainly possible to derive some idea of friendship as part of the daily life of the society depicted in the New Testament, as from the parables at Luke 11:5–8, 15:6, 9 and 29, but this would hardly be sufficient to recommend friendship as a positive virtue to a Christian. For this, certain passages of St John's Gospel are crucial. It is true that there are several places in the Gospels where Jesus appears to condemn friendship, as at Luke 14:12 and Matt. 5:46 where it seems that friendships based on mutual benefit and exclusiveness are rejected, for are not Christians to imitate their God who loves freely and without partiality? Jesus breaks through the exclusivity of family and friends, contradicting forcibly the ancient values.

Furthermore, Christian emphasis on the eschatological element in its theology and the belief that the end of the world was at hand deprived friendship of much of its importance by undermining the value accorded to the traditionally accepted benefits of this life and radically altering the perspective on life. And yet Jesus' disciples are referred to as friends as well as brothers, possibly indicating that they have a share in the eternal life brought by Christ, and Lazarus is said by Jesus to be 'our friend' for whom he shows his love by weeping at his death (John 11:35–6). And did not Jesus regard John as his favourite disciple whom he loved more than the others? In fact, the passage in which Jesus speaks of the disciples as his friends, in the fifteenth chapter of John, is crucial for our understanding of the love which is the essence of the life of God's people and which, it is clear, is as much a love between men as between man and God; that Jesus should here refer to his disciples as friends is significant. His words here could provide some model for a view of friendship which is created by Christ and which involves both love for our fellow men and an intimate relationship with Christ himself, a friendship in which the participants strive to attain that love with which Christ sacrificed his life for his friends. By taking the Scriptural texts of John 15:12 and 15:14 together one can see how closely connected are the love of those we hold dear and complete intimacy with Christ. Although Jesus' words here in no way deny the call to love our enemies and to extend our love beyond a close circle of friends and relatives, they do show that a mutual love among members of a small group, as of his disciples, is also valid, even essential to the perfect Christian life, as long as it is at the same time a love whose aim it is that God should be all in all. With these verses should be taken closely St John's words in the fourth chapter of his first Epistle, especially 1 John 4:7 and 4:11–12, for thus it can be seen how mutual love may legitimately be regarded as at least part of the general commandment to love one's neighbour on which Christ placed so much more emphasis than the Jews had done.

Along with these Johannine texts, Acts 2:44–5 and 4:32–5 stand as perhaps the chief Biblical texts which became important in discussions of friendship: 'And all who believed were together and had all things in common; and they sold their possessions and goods and distributed them to all, as any had need'; 'Now the company of those who believed were of one heart and one soul, and no one claimed any of the things as his own, but they held everything in common.' This may at first sight seem surprising as these short texts have little to do with friendship, but the description of the early Christian community at Jerusalem was interpreted as implying that there had existed a form of friendship among its members because of the connection provided by the idea of *koina ta philon* between the Classical view of friendship and this Christian way of life: if the mutually loving members of the harmonious community at Jerusalem held all their property in common as Acts 4:32 tells us, then they must have been friends for did not friends hold all things in common? These texts were also taken by Christian writers in support of the ideal of *unanimitas* (like-mindedness) in friendship, an ideal already put forward by the ancients.[11]

However, these were not the only Scriptural passages repeatedly referred to by Christians as relevant to their view of friendship. A certain number of texts, drawn both from the Old Testament and the New, became as it were substitutes for, or Christian equivalents of, the Classical proverbs concerning friendship, often used to express much the same ideas even though the Biblical texts often had no obvious connection with the topic. Conversely, pagan proverbial statements seem occasionally to have been accorded the authority due to a Biblical text: Augustine, for example, says that Cicero's famous definition of friendship was absolutely correct and made in a most reverent spirit.

One verse which is commonly cited from the Old Testament is Ps.54(55):7, 'Who will give me the wings of a dove and I will fly and be at peace?' This is usually found in letters from one Christian to another, expressing the writer's longing to join his friend.[12] An interesting comment on such uses of this verse is provided by Augustine's interpretation of the wings as our love for God and for one another which carries us up towards God.[13] Another psalm verse apparently unconnected with friendship but which is often quoted in discussions of the benefits of community life and companionship is the opening of Ps.132(133), 'Behold, how good and pleasant it is when brothers dwell in unity.' Occasionally, as in the commentaries by Jerome and Augustine, the whole psalm is taken as recommending communal life in opposition to the life of the ascetic recluse.[14]

The amount of relevant material in the Wisdom literature has already been referred to and indeed texts such as Prov.27:6, 'Better are the wounds of a friend than the deceitful kisses of the enemy' and Eccles.4:9–10, 'Two are better than one ... for if they fall, one will lift up his companion' are frequently cited in discussions of friendship or in personal letters. The latter text was seen to bear implications similar to those of St Paul's exhortation at Gal.6:2 where he says, 'Bear one another's burdens so that you fulfil the law of Christ' which is also quoted in similar contexts where the idea of friendship as a source of support and comfort is in the foreground.[15] Both the text from Ecclesiastes and that from Galatians foster the notion of friendship as a mutual relationship and can be taken as recommending fraternal rebuke and correction when necessary.

With regard to the striking passage in the sixth chapter of the apocryphal book Ecclesiasticus, in which friendship is praised as more precious than gold or precious stones and is called 'an elixir of life', it appears surprisingly rarely in such contexts. Gregory of Nazianzus does however refer to it extensively, together with phrases from Ps.18:11(19:10) and Song of Songs 4:12 which he applies to friendship, at the beginning of his eleventh oration addressed to Gregory of Nyssa, his best friend's brother. In his tenth oration he quotes Jerem.9:4, 'Let everyone beware of his neighbour and put no trust in any brother, for every brother is a supplanter and every friend goes about as a slanderer', in complaining of Basil's treatment of him and expressing his bitterness at the state of their famous and much-admired friendship. An even more negative attitude to friendship is expressed at Micah 7:5 where the prophet warns that a friend should never be trusted. It is perhaps not surprising that it is Jerome, with his pessimistic view of the possibility of forming faithful friendships who, as we shall see, chooses to expound this verse in some detail, taking it as a starting-point for his fullest discussion of the subject of friendship, a discussion in which he also quotes Jerem.9:4 in support of this view.

As for the New Testament, the central importance of the twofold commandment, of Jesus' words to his disciples at the Last Supper and of the description of the apostolic community at Jerusalem for the development of a Christian ideal of friendship, has already been mentioned. Another frequently quoted text which is sometimes applied to this subject is Matt.24:12, Jesus' prophecy that because wickedness abounds, the love of most men will grow cold. This is of course found mainly in pessimistic contexts as when Basil laments the lack of harmony and friendship within the Church in his day, plagued as it is by heresy and schism, or when Augustine writes to Jerome lamenting the rift in the friendship between Jerome and Rufinus which, like that of Basil and Gregory of Nazianzus, had been famous and much-admired.[16] The words of St Paul to the Corinthians, 'Love does not insist on its own way' (1 Cor.13:5) and to the Romans, 'Love does no wrong to a neighbour; therefore it is the fulfilment of the law' (13:10) are also often found in personal letters and in discussions of the nature of friendship between Christians. Basil resumes his correspondence with Atarbius after a period of coolness in their relations, quoting the passage from the Epistle to the Corinthians and saying that 'In matters of friendship defeat has the force of victory . . . for he who subjects himself to his neighbour in a spirit of charity is not humbled.'[17]

Although Jesus had given the demanding commandment to love your neighbour apparently without discrimination, it seems to have been generally admitted that love for fellow Christians would be stronger than for those outside the faith. Did not all Christians by virtue of their fellowship in Christ form one body and one spirit? Such a spiritual intimacy, though spread among all Christians, might appear to resemble the intense intimacy experienced by friends: such expressions as 'one body and one spirit' and 'all those who believed were of one heart and one soul' would remind many of the popular Classical expression 'one soul in two bodies' referring to close friendships. In fact it has been suggested[18] that such texts as Acts 2:44, 4:32, Gal.6:2 and Phil.1:27 were themselves influenced by such well-known maxims as *koina ta ton philon* and 'one soul in two bodies'.

That close spiritual relationships are essential to the truly Christian life is sometimes taken to be the import of Col.1:8 where St Paul writes that Epaphras 'has made known to us your love in the Spirit'. John Chrysostom, for example, in his commentary on this Epistle takes this verse as his starting-point for a long discussion of the various types of friendship and their causes, whether wicked, natural or social, all of which are inferior to the friendship inspired by spiritual love which does not grow out of mutual benefits and is not destroyed by injuries; it has nothing earthly about it but is sent from heaven.[19] It is interesting to note in passing that Chrysostom here mentions Jesus' words at Luke 14:12 referred to above but interprets them as applicable only to relationships formed between table companions, one of the inferior types of friendship, and not to friendships which are of the spirit and which gain their reward in heaven, producing friendship with God.

The idea that spiritual friendships are a gift from God, transmitted to men through the agency of the Holy Spirit, is confirmed by reference to Rom.5:5 where St Paul writes that God's love has been poured into our hearts through the Holy Spirit which has been granted to us. This idea sharply distinguishes the Christian from the Classical view of friendship as founded on rational choice, natural human feelings and human virtue. It is significant that, as we shall see, Augustine is especially fond of quoting this text, considering the emphasis in his thought on divine grace and man's inability to instigate anything good without God's help.

It is clear, therefore, that although the number of direct references to friendship in the Bible were few and it might seem that Jesus' insistence on love of neighbour extending beyond our immediate circle to include even our enemies would exclude friendship in its traditional form, this does not mean that Christians felt they needed to reject friendship in any and every form. As seen in the introduction, this was especially true of the Christians of the fourth century who, despite the climate of wariness of, if not outright hostility towards, pagan ideas and culture, were able to accept certain of the traditional theories regarding friendship as either true in themselves or capable of adaptation, in various ways, to Christian doctrines. The use of the concept of friendship did of course vary from individual to individual, as did the terminology used and it is therefore difficult to draw definite conclusions about the relative frequency with which such words as *philia* and *amicitia* occur from writer to writer. Some linguistic studies of these words in the early Christian era have already been produced[20] but they are often vitiated by the scholar's desire to make a particular point without allowing the facts to speak for themselves. To be too categorical about usages of particular words is dangerous and can prove misleading. It seems, for example, to be generally accepted that there is a radical distinction between the use of the word *philia* by Basil and by Gregory of Nazianzus: Basil is regarded as having adhered to Biblical language and therefore to have avoided *philia* in favour of *agape*, while Gregory apparently remains trapped by his Classical education and cannot help using *philia* constantly. In fact, although Basil does use *agape* more often than *philia*, it is not true to say that he never uses the latter word in a positive context. Too great a concern to drive a wedge between Christian *agape* and Classical *philia* may also lead to inaccurate conclusions, for in reality the two terms not only overlap in meaning to a large extent but are often used interchangeably by Christian writers. Thus, in a homily on the second Epistle to Timothy, Chrysostom substitutes the Classical term for the Christian in referring to Matt.22:40 when he writes that *philia* is the basis of all good things and that on this depend all the law and the prophets. Augustine, in describing the relation between the three persons of the Trinity, considers *amicitia* to be the most appropriate word to express this relation, but chooses to use *caritas* instead, presumably under the influence of 1 John 4:16.[21] In short, it must be remembered that at this period the Classical terminology of friendship was not necessarily restricted to an inferior, worldly, purely human relationship.

Despite the difficulties involved in pinning down the usage and precise meaning of these words, I shall attempt to point to certain general characteristics of the Christian view of friendship as developed in the fourth century, in the hope that this will provide some idea not only of how Christian *agape/caritas* differed from Classical *philia/amicitia* but also of how the two appear to merge in certain respects, with the result that friendship could be regarded as part of love of God rather than love of something merely mortal.[22]

First of all, what might be said to be the distinctive characteristics of the traditional view of friendship? A fundamental belief in reciprocity as a *sine qua non* of friendship, a high degree of intimacy between two or at most a few persons which made it possible to think of a friend as a second self; the idea that a friend ought to possess some reason for being loved, which in the case of good men would be their virtue, and that friends should share material things and have interests in common. Furthermore, it was generally admitted that, although there was only one true kind of friendship, that which was devoted to virtue above all else, there were other inferior kinds; *agape/ caritas*, in contrast, was never divided up in this way. Other elements considered to be indispensable to true friendship were a need for some kind of equality between friends, as well as a concern for justice.

Agape/caritas, on the other hand, which flows from God to man, lacks certain of these distinguishing characteristics. Reciprocity was not necessary for this form of love and it could therefore extend even to those who hate you. Consequently forgiveness towards those you love is an essential element. This love did not make you seek earnestly for objects worthy of your love for Christians were supposed to love any other fellow human *qua* human whether he merited your love or not, and even to be willing to sacrifice themselves for anyone as Christ had sacrificed himself for mankind. This love was no respecter of persons and Christians were expected to imitate God's love for man: does not God allow his sun to rise on the wicked and the good alike? As with God's love, man's love for others has a creative element: by loving, a man may bring others to love. And by taking God's love as his model, a man is brought closer to God as well as to his fellow men.

Another important element in Christian love, which appeared in the writings of certain writers, was the eschatological perspective lacking in the Classical view. Not only is all love closely related to God, it is also related to the future fulfilment of God's kingdom where the love will be perfected and man will attain knowledge of God – this characteristic was to be of central importance in Augustine's development of a Christian ideal of friendship.

Certainly *agape/caritas* did allow for love of one's fellow humans but it seems that the early Christians felt a need to supplement this love or to explain it in terms of certain of the characteristics traditionally associated with *philia/amicitia* as summarised above. This is not to suggest that such a combination of different elements was made as a result of a conscious decision but rather it happened as a natural result of these men being educated in the way they were and living in the particular form of Christian society in which they found themselves, together with a natural human belief in the value of mutual love and an intimacy which seems only to be realised within a reciprocal relationship. It is surely not surprising that these men valued the fact that they had common interests and aims, one of the most basic motives for friendship, considering that these aims were so important to them at a time when their interests and beliefs were threatened on all sides, whether by pagan attacks or by schisms tearing the Church apart from within.

The men of antiquity who had observed that these characteristics of *philia* were natural to men had been perceptive and their observations held good for Christian society, too, despite the differences such as the Christian's theocentric viewpoint and eschatological perspective. Equally perceptive were the Church Fathers who appreciated that *philia*, implying a mutual relationship of a high degree of intimacy, could enrich the Christian view of love, though they regarded it as having its source in God rather than in nature. Thus the best in Classical friendship was transformed and found a secure purpose in Christianity, which offered many favourable conditions for the development of friendship. Not only could the Christians' common faith and devotion to God provide a similar basis for friendship as shared interests and a devotion to virtue or truth had done for the men of antiquity, but also, for example, the belief that all men are equal in the sight of God meant that Christian friends could feel free in some sense from the problems which were traditionally regarded as arising if the friends were unequal, socially or morally.[23] The emphasis placed on unity in Christ among all Christians encouraged men to come together in a high degree of spiritual intimacy resembling, even surpassing, the intimacy held to be the prerogative of perfect friendships in antiquity. Furthermore, the fact that friendships were believed to spring from the love of Christ meant that they were, at least in theory, divinely endowed with a stability and permanence which would have made the pagans of antiquity envious.

But if Christianity provided certain conditions favourable to the establishment of perfect friendships, the Classical theories also offered much to Christian writers on friendship which helped them to express their view of Christian love and which inevitably influenced their views. Many of them were attracted by the idea that there existed different kinds of love and friendship, of which only one was perfect and that was, of course, love in Christ. Also, the value attached to reciprocity by the pagans appears to have encouraged Christians to emphasise the importance of Jesus' words to his disciples at John 15:12.

In considering the ways in which some of the fourth-century writers responded to the Classical ideal of friendship, we encounter several potential problems which need to be outlined here, problems which are to some extent caused by a lack of understanding in modern attitudes to the theory and practice of Classical friendship. It is true that the question of whether friendship and Christian love of neighbour conflict is a fundamental one. There does indeed appear to be a basic difference between these two forms of love, for love of neighbour is specifically supposed to include our enemies while in friendship to be our enemy's friend is a contradiction in terms. And yet perhaps the two are not completely incompatible. In the words of Burnaby, '... we may be certain that Christ did not mean either that it is better to have enemies than friends or that any outward act of beneficence can be a substitute for the inward disposition of heart which would make a friend out of the enemy'.[24] It is perhaps not so much that the Christian must eschew any love which bears with it the comfort and fulfilment offered by reciprocity, but rather that he should not be content to love only those who love him but go beyond that, attempting to bring others, even his enemies, into the satisfying relationship of mutual love. Is it not possible to regard friendship as the most intense and perfect form of love of neighbour? If the Church Fathers spoke negatively about friendship at times, it was not of something necessarily in conflict with love of neighbour but of that kind of friendship which was based on human values rather than being part of a theological scheme of love. In fact the question of a conflict between the two seems not to have exercised the Fathers greatly because they were able to regard *philia* as a predominantly spiritual relationship, independent of material benefits. Indeed, it often seems to be the case that these Christians assumed that friendship and love of neighbour were virtually identical. In his Ep.56, for example, Basil associates closely the duties of friendship with Jesus' command to love your neighbour when he defends himself against a charge of being forgetful of his friends and shows that he takes Jesus' command to involve care of friends, too. In Ep.204 he writes that there have always existed strong reasons for 'the highest friendship and union' between himself and the Neocaesareans, the strongest reason being the commandment of the Lord at John 13:35 that his disciples should love one another as he has loved them.[25] Augustine, in his Ep.258, similarly associates the twofold commandment with friendship when he applies Cicero's definition of *amicitia* to love of God and neighbour, concluding significantly with the advice, 'If you hold firmly to these two, then our friendship will be true and everlasting and will bring us close not only to each other but also to the Lord.'

Another problem which is often mentioned in connection with love and friendship is that of the place of self-love, a concept which has usually appeared repugnant but which paradoxically seems to be encouraged by the commandment to love your neighbour as yourself. Yet only Augustine among the fourth-century Fathers seems to have considered the question in some depth, developing a distinction between a proper self-love, morally neutral, and a reprehensible one which produced selfish behaviour. Augustine's treatment of the problem has been discussed by O'Donovan[26] and it is therefore unnecessary to consider it in detail here. Suffice it to observe that the formulation of the second part of the twofold commandment may even have served to bring the traditional view of friendship and Christian love of neighbour closer together: if love of neighbour was regarded as being in some way based on regard for self, it might be remembered that true friendship, too, in Aristotelian terms, was founded on a certain positive self-love. Moreover, one factor which protected the Christian view of friendship from the charge of selfishness was the belief that friendships were created by God's grace rather than by any conscious attempt on the part of a Christian to create something conducive to his own salvation. Only if it is believed that Christians never perform good works or love others except for the sake of the reward promised them, rather than as a result of God's love overflowing in them, can one accuse them of forming friendships for purely selfish reasons.

What about recent allegations that Christian friendships at this period were homosexual relationships?[27] It is true that the friendships usually existed between members of the same sex and usually between men but to imply that all close friendships between members of the same sex are homosexual is absurd, an unfortunate consequence of modern attitudes to friendship. Even if these friends wrote to one another in warmly affectionate terms there is no evidence that men such as Basil and Gregory or Paulinus and Ausonius were homosexuals as has been alleged, for the erotic attraction implicit in such a term was almost certainly lacking. Not only is there no reason to take such allegations seriously, they are in fact of no relevance to the writings of these Christians or to the view of friendship which they held and which goes beyond such considerations. The only context in which we do find this a recognised problem as a canker destroying the necessary harmony is that of the monastic life, where its devotees were subject to particular pressures, living in close and constant proximity and isolated from society.

To summarise: it would seem that *philia/amicitia*, for a number of reasons, regained in the fourth and fifth centuries a large measure of the importance that these ethical and social concepts had enjoyed in earlier antiquity before the coming of Christianity began to effect changes in Classical society. The similarities between the Classical theories of friendship and some of the ideas developed by Christian writers is very striking.[28] They can be partially explained by the continuity of the cultural heritage made possible by the forms of education and government which these men experienced, but it must not be forgotten that these concepts did in large measure undergo a transformation under the influence of the Christian doctrines with which these men were so concerned. It was as a result of such transformation that friendship was elevated to a higher level of significance, often gaining profound theological and ecclesiological implications in the thought and writings of these eminent Christians.

CHAPTER 4

Friendship in the lives and thought of Basil and of Gregory of Nazianzus

In the preceding chapters I have given some idea of the Classical and Christian material on the subject of friendship which was available to the writers of the fourth century and which inevitably would have affected their views to some extent. It is now time to consider how these Christians experienced friendship in their own personal lives (as documented primarily by letters between the friends) and to try to see how this experience and their knowledge of earlier theories on the subject influenced their own ideas about the nature of friendship and its role in a life lived strictly according to Christian ideals.

The fact that two of the leading Christian writers and Church men in the Greek East during the fourth century, St Basil the Great who became bishop of Caesarea, and St Gregory of Nazianzus, later patriarch of Constantinople, had a long-lasting and close friendship is well-known, but this fact might lead one to suppose that there was complete agreement between them, whereas actually it is clear that they held rather different views about the way a devoted Christian could best serve Christ and had different expectations about their friendship and where a Christian friend's priorities should lie. In attempting to chart the course of their friendship as it developed at Athens and in Cappadocia over a period of almost thirty years, it is necessary to bear in mind that our knowledge of it is derived almost exclusively from the writings of Gregory, so that Basil's view of it, especially in its early stages, is sometimes unclear, or at least seen only through Gregory's reaction to what Basil says. The primary sources are their letters to each other, Gregory's autobiographical poem *De vita sua* and his forty-third oration, the funeral speech which he wrote for his friend after Basil's death in 379.[1] Later in this chapter we shall be able to see what Basil's own ideas about friendship were from the evidence of his letters in general and from his theological and ascetic writings.

It appears that Basil and Gregory's acquaintance went back to their school days in Caesarea, although their friendship only developed when they were studying in Athens. It is in Gregory's funeral oration to Basil that the fullest account is given of the beginnings of that relationship, for Gregory digresses at length to relate how these two young men, one the son of a bishop, the other of an eminent Christian professor of rhetoric, came to be friends. Their affection for each other was apparently roused by two incidents which occurred shortly after Basil's arrival in Athens, in which Gregory detects God's providential work. In the first instance Gregory, with some experience of student life and impressed by the newcomer, persuaded a group of students to refrain from submitting the unsuspecting Basil to the traditional initiation trick. And secondly, Gregory supported Basil in an argument with a group of contentious Armenians, jealous of his reputation, for which Basil was again grateful to Gregory: it was this gratitude which helped to fire their friendship.[2]

Their mutual dependence increased as they began to seek advice and consolation from each other and thus gradually came to know each other intimately. They realised that they were both seeking the same ideal and that this set them apart from many of their fellow students who had come to Athens from all over the Mediterranean: their deepest desire was for a life of the spirit, of asceticism and contemplation and even at this stage, when they were absorbed in the study of pagan philosophy and rhetoric, their ideal was a Christian one, aimed at making themselves better followers of Christ. Sharing this ideal it was natural that they should also share everything else, living side by side and providing mutual encouragement, so that it was as if they had but one soul between them. Gregory writes of his friendship with Basil:

In studies, in lodgings, in discussions I had him as companion. We made a team, if I may boast a little, that was celebrated throughout Greece. We had all things in common and a single soul, as it were, bound together our two distinct bodies. But above all it was God, of course, and a mutual desire for higher things, that drew us to each other. As a result we reached such a pitch of confidence that we revealed the depths of our hearts, becoming ever more united in our yearning. There is no such solid bond of union as thinking the same thoughts.[3]

Such a friendship was, in Gregory's eyes, very unusual. As a spiritual relationship with its foundation in God it was more lasting and intimate than the kind of 'physical' friendships, motivated by utility or pleasure, which Gregory compares to spring flowers because of their lack of permanence;[4] to this we may liken another comparison of friendship to flowers made by John Chrysostom in his second homily on St Paul's first Epistle to the Thessalonians where he writes, 'True friendship is like a rare Indian plant: however hard I tried to describe it, I would be unable to convey a proper understanding of it to someone who had no experience of it'.[5]

It is clear from Gregory's Ep.1 that they both hoped that this life, in which they held everything in common, would continue after they left Athens; in this letter to Basil he promises that he will at some stage join his friend in ascetic retirement, in the continued belief that they can both draw closer to God more effectively together and by means of each other. But Basil left Athens before his friend, at the end of 355 or the beginning of 356, returning to the Pontus and then to Caesarea where he became professor of rhetoric for a time. Gregory was devastated by this separation and felt that he had been cut in half;[6] he compares his feelings to those of two oxen which have been brought up together and have drawn the same yoke and are then separated – a comparison similar to that found at *Iliad* 13.703 applied to the two Aiaces.[7] Gradually, however, they became accustomed to separation which, despite their desire to be together, was to last for most of their lives. Although Gregory left Athens shortly after Basil and Basil invited him to come to the Pontus so that they could share a life of Christian philosophy, searching for the true wisdom as they had planned, he did not initially rejoin his friend but returned to Nazianzus to be with his parents. These familial commitments were to keep them from seeing each other for many years, apart from a brief period when Gregory did indeed join Basil in the remote, ascetic life he had chosen to practise.

His letters 4–6 are addressed to Basil after this experience of a common life of prayer and Scriptural study in an atmosphere of intense friendship; at times he playfully teases Basil about his harsh existence in that desert-like spot, at others he seems seriously to regret his departure and especially his separation from his friend, and he ends Ep.6 by saying that he is more dependent on Basil for life than on the air he breathes and that he can only be said to be alive in so far as he is joined to Basil, either when they are really together or, when separated, they are together in their thoughts. He begs Basil for support, even if they cannot be together: 'Help me and strive with me for virtue, and if we together gained any benefits in the past, help me to preserve them through your prayers, lest we gradually dissolve like a shadow at night-fall.' He may have left his friend but it is clear that they still long to be together as at Athens, some five years earlier, and that they still share such ideals as a desire for retirement from the world. Basil, too, repeatedly expresses his disappointment that they are unable to live together and there is even a note of disillusionment detectable in his Ep.14 when he writes that he has with difficulty renounced the vain hopes or dreams which he had once placed in his friend.

While they were separated both friends were ordained, both apparently against their will, Gregory in 362 and Basil at Caesarea two years later, during the period of upheaval and uncertainty during and after the emperor Julian's brief reign, and priestly duties kept them in Nazianzus and Caesarea respectively. In a letter addressed to Basil after his ordination (Ep.8), Gregory exhorts his friend to act responsibly in his new office but expresses his regret that they are now unable to lead a shared life of ascetic retirement: it had never been their wish to rise to positions of public responsibility within the Church. As it turned out Basil was to come to terms with these changes, and his subsequent rise to eminence, much more easily than Gregory, whose inability to accept what had happened was to put a great strain on their relationship. Already in Ep.8 Gregory seems to foresee that there would be problems when he writes that perhaps it would have been better if this had never happened, but at this stage he does more or less accept the change in their status, putting his trust in the workings of the Holy Spirit and expressing his belief that they have a duty to endure the new responsibilities and take part in the struggle against the heretics. Later he was not to find these arguments so convincing when he came to see their change of status and the gradual relinquishment of their early ideas as the cause of what he regarded as the breakdown of their friendship. Indeed, Vischer explains this breakdown as due to Gregory's inability to transform his view of friendship in the way Basil did, placing the Christian's duty to serve God above all else while still maintaining a friendship subordinated to, or focussed on, this ideal.[8] The blame cannot however be attached solely to Gregory.

In fact it was not until after 370 that the tensions in their friendship surfaced as a result of two major incidents.[9] Gregory's writings reveal that he felt that Basil was to blame for these troubles, both in the case of Basil's election as bishop of Caesarea in succession to Eusebius and in the case of Gregory being forced by his friend to become bishop of Sasima as part of Basil's ecclesiastical policy in fighting the Arian heresy. In 370, after the death of Eusebius, Basil wrote to Gregory, as we learn from Gregory's Ep.40, asking him to come to Caesarea, saying that he was very ill and wished to see his friend before he died. But it seems that his true reason for inviting Gregory was to get his friend's support in his bid for the episcopate of Caesarea, a very influential position. Gregory therefore felt strongly that he had been deceived and their God-given friendship betrayed, as well as having been deeply distressed at the news that Basil was dying. But if Gregory himself refused to help his friend in this matter, his father, bishop of Nazianzus at the time, did make an active effort to support Basil. Gregory's Ep.41 is addressed to the Church at Caesarea on behalf of the elder Gregory, making known his desire for Basil's election and speaking of him in glowing terms. Basil was indeed duly elected but the incident left scars on their relationship for Basil may have felt that Gregory had betrayed the duties of friendship in not coming to Caesarea when Basil needed him, while Gregory, in his Ep.45 to Basil, hints at the belief that Basil's election has destroyed the necessary equality between the two friends and that Basil's pride is proving detrimental to their friendship. His bitterness comes out perhaps most forcibly when he ironically associates himself with the crowd of Basil's supporters rather than referring to himself as Basil's friend.

Indeed, things seem to have gone from bad to worse at this point. Although Basil's reply to Ep.45 is lost, we can infer the substance of it from the reaction with which Gregory meets it in Ep.46. Now Gregory is openly bitter and protests angrily that he does admire Basil; perhaps his expression of admiration contains a hint of irony for Gregory may well have felt that such effusive flattery was what Basil now demanded. At the end of the letter he makes it clear that he feels that his and Basil's values are now incompatible and indignantly defends the ideal he has held since his student days, that of the philosophical life, an ideal which he feels Basil has now betrayed.

It seems, however, that Gregory's passionate resentment of Basil's move up from the presbyterate to the episcopate did die down for a time, for his next letter (Ep.47) to Basil, written in early 372 and concerned with the division of Cappadocia by the emperor Valens in order to check the influence of Basil as an orthodox and fervently anti-Arian bishop, contains nothing but friendly exhortation, encouraging him to rise above his troubles: 'I am confident that it is now in particular that my dear Basil will reveal himself and that the philosophy which you have been gathering for a long time will show itself and that you will rise superior, as if on a high wave, to these slanders, remaining unshaken while others are thrown into confusion.' He even offers to join Basil in Caesarea to help him act in a calm and restrained manner at this difficult time, when Basil is being calumniated on all sides.

But a few months later the second dispute between the friends flared up as a result of Basil's action. In dividing Cappadocia into two, Valens had made the city of Tyana the capital of Cappadocia Secunda and wanted to install Anthimus as its bishop. In answer to this move on the part of the Arian emperor, Basil decided to institute a number of new bishoprics in which he would place his own partisans to support him in the power struggle against Anthimus. At Nyssa he placed his brother Gregory and at Sasima in Cappadocia Secunda he placed his friend Gregory. Sasima was an insignificant town in itself but of great strategic importance for Basil. Gregory describes the place as he saw it in his autobiographical poem, *De vita sua* (439–62): he refers to it as a 'staging-post ... without water, without trees, offering nothing to a civilised person, full of dust and noise and carriages, a place devoid of native inhabitants'. He might as well have been made bishop of a town in the Wild West: clearly his and Basil's views of it did not coincide, though Basil did admit that there were places more worthy of his friend. Once again it was Gregory's father who came out in support of Basil and insisted that Gregory submit to consecration at Basil's hands, although Gregory then refused to take up his position at Sasima and remained at Nazianzus. As a result he was reproached by Basil which angered him even more![10] In Ep.48 Gregory defends himself against Basil's reproaches: he says he is not aware of any wrong on his part; all he knows is that he has been deceived and that he has heard men say that Basil has ill-treated him, discarding him when he has no more use for him like the supports on which a vault rests while it is being constructed but which are no longer needed once the builders have finished. At the end of the letter he expressed his disillusionment with friendship, begging Basil to grant him the peace and quiet necessary to his way of life. In this request there is more than a hint of bitterness for it also contains an implicit reminder that once the two friends had shared a longing for peace and quiet, but now their paths have radically diverged, according to Gregory who concludes sarcastically that he has at least learnt one thing from his friendship with Basil, namely that one should not put one's faith in friends.

It was hard to learn from your best friend the lesson that men are fickle. Indeed, what Gregory regarded as Basil's betrayal of their friendship left a deep scar, for even ten years later, when Gregory wrote the funeral oration for Basil in which he otherwise speaks of his friend in the highest terms, this is the one instance in the account of their relationship where Gregory criticises Basil and it is clear that he felt that the worst thing about the whole incident was that their friendship had broken down.

In another letter, written at about the same time as Ep.48, Gregory is more concerned with self-defence than with accusation, but the tone is similar. We do not know how strongly Basil had accused Gregory of laziness and indifference in not taking possession of Sasima, but certainly Gregory's reply in Ep.49 is hardly gentle. He asserts his independence over against Basil by stubbornly clinging to his ideal of inaction which would leave him free to devote himself to the contemplative life and he implies that if everyone followed his example the Church would not be rent by personal quarrels – here he is getting at Basil and his commitment to working for the reunification of the Church by means of politics and involvement in public affairs.

Ironically the boot was soon to be on the other foot, for a further development led to Basil feeling that Gregory had betrayed him. In reaction to the increased pressure put on him to go to Sasima, Gregory had fled to the mountains and could only be induced to return to Nazianzus by his father's anger. There both the elder and the younger Gregory were visited by Anthimus who attempted to win them over to his side and although they both stood firm in their support for Basil they did agree to try to effect a reconciliation. This move on their part was what induced Basil to write a letter (now lost) to Gregory expressing his anger and disappointment, to which Gregory replied in Ep.50, again expressing his belief that the inequality in their positions meant that intimate friendship was now impossible. No doubt Gregory was not only angered by the fact that Basil had tried to use him in his politicking and to draw him away from the life he wished to lead, but also by the fact that he had been made bishop of a one-horse town like Sasima.

Basil, on the other hand, felt that the problem in their friendship stemmed from the fact that they saw each other so rarely, which he presumably regards as largely Gregory's fault. It is clear from his Ep.71 that Basil had not forgotten their old friendship and all that it involved. Here he speaks not in anger or pride but with sorrowful pleading for Gregory's support, deeply aware that he himself must suffer for the Church but that he cannot abandon it.

It is commonly assumed[11] that Basil and Gregory remained unreconciled, at loggerheads because of their conflicting characters, attitudes and ideals, but Basil's Ep.71 is full of tenderness and the last three letters we have from Gregory to Basil (Epp.58–60) are also lacking in bitterness; in them he returns to his former expressions of devotion and admiration, now without irony, 'I have always regarded you as my mentor in life, my teacher in the faith and everything admirable anyone might name, and I still regarded you as such ... The greatest benefit which life has brought me is your friendship and my intimacy with you.' He offers Basil support and consolation, though his mother's illness and his duties to the Church at Nazianzus prevented him from fulfilling his desire of rejoining Basil at Caesarea. Further evidence supporting the view that their friendship continued after the problems of 372 is provided by the letter (Ep.53) which Gregory wrote to his great-nephew Nicoboulos at some point during the years 384– 90, some years after Basil's death. Here he says that he has always loved Basil more than himself even when Basil was of a different opinion and that is why he has put Basil's letters before his own in his collection. There is no reason to believe that this profession is insincere since it is written not to Basil himself but to a close relative of Gregory to whom he can speak as to himself. And in the funeral oration[12] for Basil Gregory expresses his personal sense of loss after Basil dies, his feeling of being but half-alive, cut in two and haunted by thoughts of his friend – feelings which are reminiscent of the trauma Gregory

experienced when Basil left Athens after their student days
together. Such a strong and vivid grief does not belong to a
friendship which has faded into nothing or even turned to
enmity, as their relationship had threatened to do in the early
370s.

We must now move from a sharp focus on the friendship
between Basil and Gregory to a more general consideration of
their attitudes to friendship and their use of Classical and
Christian ideas on the subject. That Gregory did value friendship highly, not only in his relations with Basil, is clear from a
number of passages in his writings. In Ep.94 to Amazonios, for
example, Gregory writes that his weak point is friendship and
he begins a letter to Palladios (Ep.103) with the words, 'If
anyone were to ask me, "What is the best thing in life?", I
would answer, "Friends".' The eleventh oration, addressed to
Basil's brother Gregory of Nyssa, opens with a eulogy on
friendship based on a number of Scriptural texts, including the
popular Ps.132(133), as well as Sir.6:14–15, 'A trustworthy
friend is a powerful protection' etc. At other times Gregory's
eloquent expressions of the pain involved in separation from
one's friends shows how much he valued the company and
support of friends. 'Now that we are separated', he writes to
Victor, a friend who held a high military position, 'please
continue to show me the favour you showed when we were
together and do not hesitate to write to me, to console me for
the pain occasioned by our separation.'[13]

In discussing the nature of friendship or his personal relations with his friends, Gregory often alludes to pagan writers
and Classical proverbs on the subject. The proverb expressing
the idea that a friend is a second self may, for example, be at the
back of Gregory's mind when he writes to Olympus, governor
of Cappadocia Secunda, in Ep.146, 'If it is true that my friends'
problems are my own problems . . .' And in Ep.31 to Philagrios,
a friend of long standing, he refers to the proverbial phrase
koina ta ton philon, as well as to the idea of a law of friendship
which prescribes certain duties, while in Ep.88 to Nectarius, his
successor as bishop at Constantinople, Gregory congratulates
Nectarius on his appointment, saying that, since friends share

all their possessions and experiences, he shares not only Nectarius' joy but also the honour accruing to him through his
appointment. Gregory is clearly not afraid to allude to
proverbs of pagan provenance in letters to Christian friends. In
fact, there is no need to make a sharp distinction between
pagan and Christian as is shown by the fact that in Ep. 168 the
idea of *koina ta ton philon* is expresséd in Biblical terms: Gregory
quotes Luke 15:31, where the father says to his prodigal son,
'All that is mine is yours', and says that friends share everything
because of the fellowship (*koinonia*) of the Spirit and because of
the *agape* which unites them.

A distinctive feature of Gregory's discussions of friendship
is his frequent references to Classical literature. In Ep. 13 he
quotes Theognis, lines 643–4, approving the poet's recommendation of a friendship which is supported by deeds rather than
the sort which is based merely on pleasure. This idea recurs in
an important passage in Ep. 230, this time with reference to
Homer: Gregory writes to Theodosius that there exists between
them a pure friendship, free from guile, which is rare indeed;
they are united neither by blood relationship nor by their
common nationality nor by what Homer refers to as the
affection between those of the same age, but by the similarity of
their interests. The Homeric phrase, 'delightful companionship', applied here to a relationship placed on a lower level
than the friendship between Theodosius and Gregory recurs in
a more positive context in Ep. 30 to Philagrios in which Gregory
recalls nostalgically the elements of their early friendship
initiated at Athens, and Homer is also referred to in a letter to
Eutropius (Ep. 71) whom Gregory exhorts not to allow his
governmental duties to obstruct his attentions to his friends but
to imitate the young warriors in the *Iliad* who managed to
practise friendship in the midst of war. And Gregory twice[14]
refers specifically, in the context of close personal friendships, to
two such warriors, the twin sons of Actor, as a model of
intimacy and solidarity in friendship.

Another Classical author referred to by Gregory is Hesiod.
In a letter written towards the end of his life (Ep. 195) he quotes
Hesiod's *Works and Days* 25–6, disagreeing with its implication

that men who have the same interests or profession cannot be friends. Euripides, too, is cited in connection with friendship.[15] It is interesting to note that the pagan orator Themistius, to whom the Christian emperor Theodosius entrusted the education of his son Arcadius and to whom two of Gregory's extant letters are addressed (Epp. 24 and 38) composed a speech on friendship which Gregory may have read and which contains allusions to Homer, Theognis, Euripides and to the same two lines of Hesiod as Gregory quotes in Ep.195.

Despite his readiness to refer to Classical proverbs and literature, Gregory did often speak of friendship in Christian terms, as has already been mentioned in connection with Ep.168. This is particularly true in the case of his friendship with Basil but is also evident in other letters, showing that Gregory's view of friendship was not a strictly pagan one. In Ep.11, probably addressed to Basil's brother Gregory of Nyssa, Gregory outlines one aspect of his theory of Christian friendship when he writes in the opening paragraph that all who live according to God and who follow the same gospel are friends and relations. It has already been seen that Gregory believes that it is God who creates friendships and the same idea occurs in a number of other letters, such as Ep.56 to Thecla to whom he writes that they belong to each other, joined by the Holy Spirit. Even his belief that it was possible and legitimate to love some men more strongly than others is expressed in Christian terms and he appears not to have seen any conflict between man's duty to love all men and his desire for close friendships. In Ep.147 he justifies his special love for Nicoboulos by saying that he is following God's example, for did not God, the creator of all, choose one race as his own but was not deemed unjust for so doing? Such special love could co-exist with a more general, extensive philanthropy which the very nature of Christ, the members of whose body all Christians are, teaches us to practise.[16]

Although Gregory frequently speaks of the only true friendship being that which is founded on virtue, his view of virtue is not unchristian for he sees it as closely connected with a man's devotion to God and his desire for intimacy with the divine, as well as with rejection of attachment to earthly things. The focus of the virtuous man must be God: this is on the whole a view which is foreign to the Classical idea of the relation between virtue and friendship. Gregory's view is perhaps closest, in pagan thought, to the Neoplatonic ideal which seems to have permitted human friendships while directing the sage first and foremost up towards the One, away from the things of this world. But even if there are traces of Neoplatonic influence here – and the use of the term *oikeiosis* might be taken to confirm this[17] – Gregory's view is by no means incompatible with orthodox Christianity.

So far we have concentrated almost exclusively on Gregory, largely because he is our primary source for the course of the friendship between Basil and himself, but this is not to say that Basil does not have a developed view of friendship of his own. Indeed, it is possible to chart a development in his view from that of his student days to a more mature and original Christian theory of friendship held in his later years. It seems that Basil began by sharing Gregory's idea that it was essential for friends to share everything, as is revealed by a letter (Ep.271) written towards the end of his life to Eusebius who had been a fellow student of theirs at Athens; Basil writes that he wishes he could have seen this dear friend again and relived the days when they shared the same home and the same teacher, as well as their study and leisure and both luxury and poverty. It is clear from this and other letters written late in life that Basil not only experienced a number of close friendships from his earliest youth but that he was also able to maintain them over many years, continuing to value friendship highly.

As will be seen, Basil's view of friendship did become increasingly influenced by his Christian beliefs, but it remains undeniable that it also retained certain elements apparently derived from his knowledge of Classical philosophy and literature but which did not conflict with his strongly held Christian beliefs. It appears that, like Aristotle, he believed friendship to be a virtue.[18] He also takes for granted that it will be a long-lasting relationship if it is based on virtue, though virtue is to some extent replaced by the common faith held by Christians, providing a firm basis for their mutual love. Like Aristotle, too, Basil differentiates between various kinds of friendship, without using the same categories as Aristotle. Instead he draws a distinction between earthly or bodily friendship and spiritual friendship,[19] the latter being a rare and superior relationship closely connected with the workings of the Holy Spirit and of divine grace.

A further allusion to an idea of Classical provenance is to be found in Ep.83 where the famous phrase about a friend as a second self is specifically referred to by Basil as a wise saying. In Ep.36 he speaks of those friends for whom he is begging assistance as 'those whom I regard as my own self' and in Ep.322 he writes to an anonymous friend, 'It is impossible for me to forget you even for the briefest moment – I would sooner forget myself.'

Another sentiment commonly expressed by Classical writers which is echoed by Basil on a number of occasions is the idea that flattery is destructive of friendships. Basil concludes his Ep.20 to Gregory in the form of a maxim, 'For a friend particularly differs from the flatterer in this way: the flatterer speaks to give pleasure while the friend refrains from nothing, even that which causes pain', and to Sophronius (Ep.272) he writes that just as mildew destroys the grain, so flattery is a blight upon friendship.[20] A more specific reference to a Classical author is made in a letter to the governor of Neocaesarea where Basil quotes one of Euripides' many sayings on the subject of friendship in a form otherwise unattested;[21] he opens the letter with these lines, 'I regard the wise man as my friend even if he lives in a distant place and I never see him with my eyes', to explain, in a learned and complimentary manner, why he should feel that his addressee is his close friend despite the fact that they have never met.

More characteristic of Basil's use of Classical sayings and theories about friendship than mere reminiscences of Classical texts is his ability to transpose the Classical into a Christian context and to broaden the application of what was originally applied to personal friendships or to choose those theories which are more concerned with *philia* in society at large, for in general his interest lies more in the community than in the individual. As he came to assume greater responsibilities within the Church and to realise the problems afflicting it at the time, he became increasingly attracted by the principle of *koinonia* which had figured as one aspect of friendship in Aristotle's theories and been developed by the post-Aristotelian philosophical schools. This concept was to prove central to the two main areas in which Basil's influence was felt, that of Church politics and that of the development of coenobitic monasticism. In both cases Basil often speaks of the need for friendship and peaceful harmony: each member of society needs harmony around him and the support of the other members in order to be able to function properly within his society. Basil is constantly looking beyond the individual and particular to what he regards as the overwhelming benefit of building up an extensive system of mutual dependence in a spirit of love.

Our knowledge of Basil's use of theories of *philia* in the context of ecclesiastical politics is largely derived from his numerous letters, many of which he wrote in pursuit of his aims of restoring unity to the Church, riddled with schism and heresy. He remained indefatigable in tackling this task, though a strong current of pessimism underlies his efforts at reconciliation and the establishment of orthodoxy based on the decisions of the Council of Nicaea, as illustrated by the frequent allusions to Matt.24:12, 'And because wickedness increases, the love of many grows cold'[22] and his repeated lament that the essential harmony of the Church, based on love, is being destroyed by the theological quarrels of those who ought to be of one soul.

Central to the belief in the primary importance of harmony and unity is the concept of the body of Christ on which Basil's theory of *koinonia* rests. In Ep.156 to Evagrius of Antioch Basil says that the union of the members of the body of Christ is the greatest good. The fact that all Christians are members of the body of Christ, united by spiritual love, means that there should exist a unity despite the fact that they are physically separated from one another, scattered throughout the Empire.[23] A further consequence of the belief in the Church as

the body of Christ which Basil stresses is the profound inter-
dependence of its members who need one another and are so
closely involved with one another that they will experience
deep sympathy for one another's joys and sorrows. For this
aspect of Basil's theory of *philia* it is likely that Classical ideas
about the sharing of feelings were less influential than the text
of 1 Cor. 12:26 where Paul writes, 'If one member suffers,
all suffer together; if one member is honoured, all rejoice
together'.[24]

Alongside the concept of the body of Christ we find that the
key words in such contexts are *henosis* (union), *symphonia*
(agreement), *homonoia* (concord) and even *philia*, all associated
with *koinonia* (community). It is interesting to note that these
three last terms are discussed together by Aristotle in the
Nicomachean Ethics when he explains that all *philia* involves
koinonia, while *homonoia* is defined more specifically at 1167b 2 as
friendship among fellow citizens, a friendship which can exist
only between good men. *Homonoia* also occurs in Plato's
Alcibiades where Socrates identifies it with *philia*.[25] Once again
we see that a Classical term or idea connected with friendship
has been removed by Basil from its original context, whether
personal or political, and applied to the loving and harmonious
relationship between members of Christ's Church. In fact, the
word *homonoia* occurs very frequently in Basil's writings after he
was made bishop of Caesarea in 370. In Ep.203, for example,
Basil refers to this concept in connection with the text of Matt.
24:12 and the need for Christian fellowship, in a letter in which
he also makes much of Christ's commandment to his disciples
that they should love one another, referring explicitly to John
13:35 and then going on to say, 'I am unable to persuade myself
that without love toward one another, and without, as far as I
am concerned, being peaceful toward all, I can be called a
worthy servant of Jesus Christ'.[26]

Similar terms used by Basil in connection with the various
problems of heresy and schism are *homophron* (in agreement),
homognomon (like-minded), *homodoxia* (unanimity) and *homopsychos* (of one mind), of which the last is by far the most
frequent. *Homodoxia* is mentioned by Aristotle when he says that

philia is identical neither with *homonoia* nor with *homodoxia*, for even people who do not know one another and are therefore not friends might hold the same opinions. *Homodoxia* was clearly an important concept to Basil, always associated in his writings with the unity among Christians.[27] The term *homopsychos*, though it does not occur in this form in Aristotle's discussions of the nature of friendship, is reminiscent of the phrase *mia psyche* (one soul) which is quoted as a proverb by Aristotle at *Nicomachean Ethics* 1168b 7–8 in support of the argument that all friendly feelings towards others are an extension of the benevolent feelings a person has towards himself. In Basil's writings the word is primarily used with reference to communion within the Church, rather than to personal friendships. In Ep.67 he speaks of his fellow bishops in the West as *homopsychoi*, while to Eustathius of Himmeria he writes in an unknown but possibly more personal context when he says that since discourse between those of like minds is a consolation for every grief, Eustathius should write to him as often as possible so that they may give each other mutual support.[28] The application of such words to the context of Church politics reflects Basil's desire to restore the Church to a kind of friendship where all the members of Christ's body are united as close friends dedicated to serving God according to the true faith. His aim is well illustrated by his exhortation to Amphilochius, bishop of Iconium in Ep.191 to call together men of like mind so that by meeting together they may then be able to govern the churches by the old kind of love, communicating with one another as with intimate friends. In this letter Basil also refers to Matt.24:12 and to John 13:35: by loving one another as friends Christians not only show themselves to be faithful followers of Christ but also maintain the unity of the body of Christ. Ideally mutual love among men and universal allegiance to the true faith would combine so that the Church would form a perfect realisation of the body of Christ but, as it is, many men fail on one or both of these scores (and neither is of value without the other) and this explains, according to Basil, the lamentable state of the Church in his day.

In the case of a more universal spiritual union as well as in

more personal attachments Basil emphasises the importance of
letters for maintaining unity because letters can act as surro-
gates for the friend's presence,[29] regarded as essential to friendship by certain Classical writers. Letters can communicate the
friends' most intimate feelings as a personal conversation might
do and accurately reveal a man's true character,[30] as well as
providing proof of the friends' affection for one another, an
important function when they are separated by such great
distances and for such long periods. In Ep.163 Basil urges the
otherwise unknown Jovinus to write to him again, since his last
letter was such a success in making Basil feel close to his friend.
He writes:

I saw your soul in your letter, for truly no painter can grasp so
accurately the characteristics of the body as words can portray the
secrets of the soul. When I read your letter, its words adequately
delineated to us the soundness of your character, the genuineness of
your worth, and the integrity of your mind in everything; and so it
brought to us great consolation for your absence.

We have already seen Basil express the idea that letters offer
consolation to those who are separated; they can also provide
spiritual nourishment to those who are unable to profit from
one another's spiritual gifts in person. The opportunity for such
communication is itself a gift from God, as is friendship itself, as
Basil writes in a letter (Ep.197) to Ambrose of Milan.

Basil's own letters reveal clearly how his idea of friendship as
an intimate, spiritual relationship between a small number of
people dedicated to contemplation and the service of God,
which he held in his youth, developed into a vision of the
Church, its members united by love founded on a common
faith in a relationship resembling a kind of extended, divinely
endowed friendship which could provide the peace necessary to
the fulfilment of the truly Christian life. It was to this end that
Basil advised Christians to rebuke one another (as friends were
traditionally expected to do for the sake of virtue) and to pray
for one another. Despite the fact that the idea of community
came to dominate Basil's thought on the Church and on
monastic life, it appears nevertheless that he remained faithful
to the belief expressed in Ep.2 to Gregory that it must be the

ultimate aim of each Christian to gain personal knowledge of God through contemplation. Perfect contemplation will be achieved only in the kingdom of God when man shall pass from material knowledge to immaterial contemplation[31] but in the meantime one must strive to imitate Christ and purify the soul. The influence of Plato is likely here.[32] However, such a view of the importance of the individual's relationship with God is not completely divorced from the more social perspective, for even in the context of spiritual self-purification letters and friendship are regarded as helping the Christian in his search for God, for they give him the opportunity to devote himself to Christian thoughts and actions by which means he may draw closer to God.[33]

So far our knowledge of Basil's use of the ideas connected with friendship has been derived from his letters. However, when we turn to consider the relation between friendship and his theories on monasticism, our conclusions are largely drawn from the *Moralia* with its double prologue *De fide* and *De iudicio Dei*, and the two sets of Rules, namely the *Regula fusius tractata* (The Long Rules), a collection of general precepts for the ascetic life (henceforth referred to as the *RFT*) and the *Regula brevius tractata* (The Shorter Rules), a collection of a large number of questions arising out of specific situations in the everyday life of the monastic community (*RBT*), works which are generally accepted as genuine. As for the other works collected in PG31, they are considered likely to be genuine by Amand de Mendieta, though not by E.F. Morison: these are the *Introduction to the Ascetic Life*, and the discourses *On the Renunciation of the World* and *On Ascetic Discipline*.[34]

In these works, too, there is evidence of the possible influence of Classical philosophical, humanist ideas, although Basil's chief inspiration is undoubtedly the Bible. Most obviously, there is the concept of *koinonia* which provides the basis of his monastic theories as well as being important in his view of the Church as a whole. But if Basil's familiarity with the term from Platonic, Aristotelian and Stoic circles was influential in the development of his ideal of coenobitic monasticism, with its underlying belief that it is natural for human beings to

associate with one another,[35] it is also true that he could find
this concept referred to frequently by St Paul.[36]

It seems that Basil, after returning from Athens and being
appointed to the chair of rhetoric at Caesarea, was persuaded
by his sister Macrina and by his friend and spiritual father
Eustathius of Sebaste to devote himself to the ascetic life and to
explore more deeply a way of life which had attracted him even
during his student days at Athens. As a result he undertook a
tour of Egypt, Palestine, Syria and Mesopotamia while still in
his twenties, a tour which was undoubtedly also influential in
the development of the theories of this man who was to become
'the Benedict of the Oriental Church'.[37] In a letter (Ep.223)
written late in life against Eustathius, relations with whom had
unfortunately turned sour, Basil explains that he made this
two-year long tour in the hope of finding men who lived in
strict accordance with the gospel with whom he might live. On
his return to Cappadocia, however, it was not the strictly
eremitic life of the desert monks which he adopted, but an
ascetic life spent in prayer, manual work, reading of the Bible
and fasting within a small community, first among family and
friends in the Pontus and later in a larger community in
Caesarea. His belief in the importance of the ascetic life was
inspired by no fanatical hatred of the world but by the idea that
it was within a monastic community that men and women
could best reject those values and elements of normal society
which conflicted with their duty to God.

Biblical support for his ideas was to be found in a number of
texts which are repeatedly referred to in his writings, such as
Christ's exhortation to sell everything and to follow him
(Matt.16:24, 19:21); many of them are texts used by Christians
of this period when writing about friendship, most prominently
perhaps the description of the community life practised by the
apostles in Acts 2:42–7 and Acts 4:32–5, while at *RFT* 7.4 we
find an allusion to the opening of Ps.132. Above all it was
Christ's commandment to love your neighbour as yourself,
supported by Paul's words to the Galatians (5:14) which lay at
the centre of Basil's monastic theories. This is where the
emphasis should be placed rather than on the elements of

celibacy and renunciation. It was clearly his belief that this must be a Christian's prime concern if he is to serve God properly. Although in *RFT* 5 Basil says that it is important not to allow human concerns to deflect one from the intention to serve God, this does not imply that one should therefore live apart from one's fellow men but that one must focus on divine matters rather than on the things of this world if one is to love God and neighbour rightly. The communal life has the benefit of providing the best conditions for love of neighbour, in spiritual and practical terms, and also of offering a continuation of the apostolic life as portrayed in Acts. These texts from Acts were used to give authority to various details of the ascetic life, as for example the holding of things in common in an equitable way and the importance of unity and harmony.[38] In the *RBT* there are several occasions on which Basil cites these texts: in question 85 he mentions Acts 4:32 in trying to prove that it is wrong for any member of the *koinonia* to own anything of his own; he combines this text with a reference to John 13:34, thereby using Christ's words about laying down one's life for a friend to give added support to his plea for monastic poverty and communism. And in question 193 Basil returns to the idea of Christian unity, here linking John 17:21 and Phil.2:2 with Acts 4:32.

As in his writings on the state of the Church, the important concept of *koinonia* was closely associated with the doctrine of the Christian community forming the body of Christ which had clear implications for the coenobitic way of life. One of these was that the members of the community would be mutually dependent, needing one another and able to offer one another much, both in the way of material needs and so as to be surrounded by people of like minds whom they would trust and who would rebuke them justly for the sake of their moral progress[39] but also feel deep sympathy for their problems. Such a view of the benefits of community life has much in common with the Classical view of friendship with its emphasis on a shared life, rebuking your friends for their own sakes in a spirit of gentleness and always being ready to offer sympathy and support. According to Basil, this way of treating those around us would be inspired by true love for them as fellow members of the body of Christ.[40] Furthermore, in the monastic community people's different talents can be used in the best way, for all, though insufficient in themselves, are needed for the perfect functioning of the whole, as in the case of the human body.[41] As a result all the members would share the benefits as if they were a group of close friends and this situation would necessarily involve a degree of equality and justice such as we might expect to find in discussions about the nature of true friendship. A belief in the importance of such equality is also supported by reference to John 13:34 and John 15:13, texts which are often found in connection with Christian ideas of friendship at this period; Basil appeals to these texts at *RBT* 98 in advising the superior of the monastic community not to treat the monks as his subordinates but as his closest friends, in imitation of Christ's love for his disciples.

In connection with Basil's stress on unity within the community should be noted his views on what he regards as a negative aspect of close-knit communities, an aspect which tends to destroy the harmony necessary for the truly spiritual life. Such a threat comes from the formation of particular friendships, the development of preferences for certain fellow monks over others, which will lead to a loss of equality among the members of that community and a consequent growth of mistrust and jealousy, even of hatred. That Basil felt the need to combat such feelings is shown, for example, in *RFT* 34 where he starts from the practical question of what sort of men ought to be entrusted with the distribution of everyday necessities to the other monks, the answer being, 'Those who can imitate the behaviour of the early Christians as described in Acts 4:35'. These men must be free from all feelings of partiality (*prospatheia*) lest they be tempted to distribute things unfairly which would cause dissension among the monks, distracting them from their spiritual goals. In the first of the two short Ascetic Sermons Basil, if he is the author,[42] explains his disapproval of particular friendships by saying that the law of love does not allow such friendships in a community because they are seriously detrimental to the common harmony which is fostered by all the members feeling equal affection for all the others; if somebody has a particular affection for another monk it must mean that he is guilty of feeling less than perfect love for all the others. Perfect love must be impartial in imitation of God's love for men – here Basil refers to Matt.5:45. Although these works may be spurious, the same views are repeated in the *RFT* whose authenticity is not doubted. He is constantly aware that love must be equal and extended to all in the community for the sake of peace and obedience to Christ's commandment.

Related to the question of *prospatheia* is the problem of the possible development of homosexual relationships within the community – and Basil does regard it as a problem, though it is mentioned explicitly only in the sermon on the renunciation of the world, another work of dubious authenticity. In this he warns the potential young ascetic, in forceful terms, to flee *syndiagoge* (intimacy) with those of his own age, to run from them as from a fire, for the devil has consigned many to the fires of hell. He goes on to give more practical advice on how to avoid these dangers: the young man ought not to sit or sleep close to another young man and when he faces you in conversation or psalm-singing, you should not look at him lest the seeds of desire are sown. The possible dangers for the monks arising from close association with young men are also hinted at in the first Ascetic Sermon when Basil says that it often happens that however self-controlled people are, the beauty of a young person can prove attractive and be an inducement to passion, so someone who has the physical beauty of youth has a duty to conceal it; and in *RBT* 220 he writes that a monk ought never to be alone with another man without permission nor with a woman – in this context he quotes Eccl.4:10 in support of his belief that unsupervised meetings between two people can be dangerous. Whether some of these works are authentic or not, it seems likely that Basil was aware of some of the possible problems for the community resulting from such relationships and that he wished only to encourage such friendships as were compatible with the monastic spirit as he envisaged it.

In conclusion: we have seen how Basil based his view of monastic *koinonia* on Christ's commandment to love one's neighbour, on the concept of the body of Christ which held certain implications for the mutual relations within the community, and on the brief description of the life led by the early Christians. This basis is strongly Biblical but it may nevertheless be legitimate to see also the influence of the traditional ideas on friendship with which Basil was familiar and which his experience in Athens, both with Gregory and others, seems to have taught him to approve strongly. Certainly Basil's Christian community does bear resemblances to the kind of life envisaged for true friends by Classical writers, such as the idea that friends should share everything, that they should be closely united by their love, their desire for virtue, and common interests, and the idea that rebuke inspired by love is of benefit among friends. One difference lies in the fact that the monastic relationships are intended to extend beyond a small group of friends to embrace the whole community of ascetics and even beyond its confines into society outside the monastery where the monks are engaged in charitable works. Basil does not adopt a Classical view of friendship unreflectingly but rather adapts certain aspects of it to his thought on the Church and the monastic life, making it serve a strictly Christian purpose and to play an essential role in the pursuit of this purpose. Gregory may have been justifiably disappointed that Basil did not sacrifice everything for the sake of their friendship; but anyone who was not so closely involved with Basil may instead appreciate his ability to extend the applications of some of the traditional characteristics of *philia* to new areas which were to be of great importance to the future of the Christian Church.

CHAPTER 5

John Chrysostom and Olympias

Another Greek-speaking Christian, whose life (347?–407) spans the decisive period which saw the strengthening of Christianity but the gradual dissolution of the Roman Empire, was John Chrysostom. As bishop of Constantinople for about seven years he lived through a period of great political, social and religious turbulence in the eastern capital during the first years of the fifth century, a time of conflict and change witnessed also by Synesius during the two years he spent there. Of all the events and relationships experienced by Chrysostom in his dramatic life, I have chosen to concentrate on just one friendship in order to gain some idea of his view of the possibility and nature of Christian friendship. This was the friendship, based on a shared and whole-hearted devotion to the service of Christ, which developed at Constantinople between him and a woman,[1] the wealthy and high-born lady Olympias, during the last years of his life and which continued until his death. The source of our knowledge of this relationship is largely restricted to the seventeen surviving letters [2] which Chrysostom wrote to Olympias during his exile [3] and enforced travels through what is now eastern Turkey leading to his death in 407. This inevitably provides a partial view of their relationship, dominated as it was at this time by his loneliness, depression and suffering[4] and sheds an unusual light on a man who is primarily remembered as the brillant preacher in the churches of his native Antioch and then as the powerful bishop of Constantinople, the stern proponent of the ascetic life, the critic of luxury and corruption and the prolific writer, for which he is honoured as a Doctor of the Church. And yet the letters which he wrote from

85

exile do in fact provide some of the best evidence for his friendships, his attitudes to his friends and how he faced separation from those to whom he was close. Furthermore, the fact that their friendship continued with such intensity after Chrysostom left Constantinople, is evidence for its strength.

It is unfortunate that none of Olympias' letters to Chrysostom survives but their content can to some extent be deduced from his, and Olympias herself is known also from other sources[5] for she was a well-known figure in her day, admired by many, coming as she did from a family prominent in court circles and distinguishing herself by her refusal to remarry and her passionate commitment to serving Christ. It seems that she was born in the 360s and given a Christian education partly by Theodosia, the sister of Amphilochius, bishop of Iconium, the friend and correspondent of Basil and cousin of Gregory of Nazianzus. Olympias herself was known to Gregory when he was bishop at Constantinople; he mentions her in laudatory terms in the poem, full of moral exhortation, which he dedicated to her[6] while Basil's brother Gregory of Nyssa thought fit to dedicate part of his commentary on the Song of Songs to her. In the life of St Olympias she is described as full of simplicity and humility, untiring in her works of mercy, radiating love, modest, calm and of infinite generosity. When widowed in her mid-twenties after a brief marriage, the emperor Theodosius himself tried to marry her to a Spanish relation of his but she refused and was instead ordained deaconess by Bishop Nectarius, Gregory's successor to the see of Constantinople. In this capacity she devoted herself to the care of the poor and the sick and to hospitality towards clergy and monks, using her great wealth for these purposes, for she owned much property in Thrace, Galatia, Cappadocia and Bithynia, as well as houses in and around Constantinople.

It was during this period, when Chrysostom replaced Nectarius as bishop of Constantinople at the end of 397, that her friendship with him developed for she had reached such a position within the Church that she could act as the bishop's adviser and work as his agent in acts of charity and piety within the diocese. From her behaviour with regard to the prospect of remarriage it is clear that Olympias was a strong and independent character, but she was, it seemed, always ready to listen to her friend and mentor, as when he reprimanded her for wasting her resources in showing greater generosity to clergy and bishops than to the deserving poor, even though her behaviour was probably not as extreme as that of the Roman widows satirised by Jerome in his Ep.22: 'Their houses are full of flatterers, full of guests. The very clergy, whose teaching and authority ought to inspire respect, kiss these ladies on the forehead and then stretch out their hand to receive the fee for their visit. The women, meanwhile, seeing that priests need their help, are filled with pride.' Her obedience to his advice on this matter was to lead to the fatal enmity with Synesius' patron Theophilus of Alexandria[7] who resented Olympias' change of heart and her allegiance to the bishop of Constantinople whom he regarded as guilty of dangerous Origenist beliefs concerning the nature of God.[8] But if Theophilus resented her, others found her wholly admirable; in Sozomen's history she is described as living the perfect philosophical (i.e. spiritual and moral) life in accordance with the laws of the Church. This was the woman who supported Chrysostom as opposition to him grew increasingly strong in Constantinople, largely because of his unpopular attempts at moral reform[9] and who maintained contact with him during his exile from 404 until his death in 407.

The extant letters from Chrysostom to Olympias which reflect these last years of their relationship are of interest from a psychological and historical point of view, as well as from the moral and religious angle: in them Chrysostom offers his friend advice and consolation and provides details of his everyday life and thanks her for her support – it is clear even from these letters that their relationship was not one-sided but that there existed strong bonds of reciprocal feeling and mutual concern. Nicephoras Callistes, the fourteenth-century Byzantine historian, compares their relationship to that between St Paul and Thecla, both in their shared dedication to the Christian life and in their great intimacy which manifested itself in Olympias' care for Chrysostom's everyday welfare and in Chrysostom's detailed spiritual guidance of Olympias.[10]

Although it is true that Chrysostom has not left us in his writings any of his theories about friendship between the sexes, he would probably have regarded a close friendship between a man and woman as possible in so far as the woman was able to repudiate marriage and child-bearing (the latter, particularly, setting her apart from men) and become an independent character.[11] Not only would the rearing of children give women a role clearly distinct from that of men, it would also distract them from the pursuit of ideals which they could hold in common with men and which could form the basis of a Christian friendship. In the early centuries of Christianity the acceptance of martyrdom and virginity were the most radical ways in which women could attain recognition of their equality with men, albeit posthumously in one case. But a more common way was in the rejection of second marriages after being widowed and the adoption of an ascetic life – it seems that the highest accolade for a Christian woman was to be praised by men for attaining as high a degree of virility as their female condition allowed.

It has also been argued by Clark, in her book *Jerome, Chrysostom and Friends*, that equality between the sexes might also be achieved to some extent through the high social status and wealth of these women, and certainly the majority of the friendships between eminent Christian men and women about which we hear did involve aristocratic women of enormous wealth (which they of course renounced or used solely for charitable or ecclesiastical purposes), but no doubt friendships between the sexes could occur at a lower social level, too, although the literary evidence for such relationships is lacking. Furthermore, the attraction of such women may not have been so much that their high social status 'tended to mitigate the lowliness of their female condition' but that their renunciation of such wealth and status was particularly impressive to their fellow Christians. After all, they did renounce it, which would appear to make them just like ordinary women and in fact rich women were generally regarded as more dangerous and to be shunned rather than chosen as ideal friends by dedicated Christians.

Another area in which men and women might be brought together in friendship based on Christian ascetic ideals was that of education and intellectual concerns, as was the case most notably perhaps with Jerome and his friends in Rome. And yet even here, the supposed equality is marred by a certain one-sidedness, for the man is inevitably regarded as the mentor, the source of guidance and inspiration, however willing and capable students the women prove to be. So despite a definite move towards equality between ascetic men and women, their relationships do still complement as well as balance one another, with the women serving and supporting the men in return for guidance. Of course our view of these relationships is blighted by the fact that all our evidence for them is seen through the men's eyes, and perhaps both parties would agree that both service and guidance, both the male and female roles within this friendship, were to be seen above all as means of serving Christ, as when Paulinus writes in Ep.44 to the married couple Aper and Amanda, describing the wife's support for her husband, the bishop:

In the transactions of the world she serves not the world but Christ, for whose sake she endures the world that you may avoid enduring it... No discordant will separates her from your life of commitment... You are her head in Christ and she is your foundation. By her work your foot stands on the Lord's path; and she will share your head because you are one framework of faith united in the body of the Lord.

However, in a letter begging the Roman matron Italica (who also corresponded with Augustine) to continue to work to allay the storms shaking the Church, Chrysostom demonstrates that he can envisage the equality, even superiority of women, not merely in their own sphere but when they are competing on equal terms with men. He writes from exile in Cucusus:

It is true that nature has brought it about that in outward affairs, as in situations involving action and administration, the sexes – by which I mean men and women – are distinct. According to custom women should stay at home while men undertake public and forensic duties. But in divine struggles and those trials undertaken on behalf of the Church, this is not the case. Indeed it is possible, in undertaking these noble struggles, for the woman to outdo the man.[12]

Again, it is the spiritual, ecclesiastical context which is the setting for equality between the sexes; the Church can offer what secular society cannot.

That Chrysostom, who had been brought up as a Christian though he had also had a traditional rhetorical education and studied under the great pagan orator Libanius in Antioch,[13] believed in the value of friendship between Christians is clear not only from his more personal works such as the letters and the *De sacerdotio* (On the Priesthood) which tells of his youthful friendship with a fellow Antiochene called Basil, but also from the numerous homilies, usually concerned with expounding Biblical texts, which he addressed to his congregations. At the beginning of his work on the priesthood, Chrysostom gives a picture of his friendship with Basil which is reminiscent of that between Basil of Caesarea and Gregory of Nazianzus:

I used to have many genuine and true friends, who knew the laws of friendship and observed them strictly. But there was one in the group who outstripped them all in his friendship for me and set his heart on leaving the rest as far behind him as they did the people who regarded me with indifference. He was one of my constant companions. We went in for the same studies and attended the same teachers. We had an equal enthusiasm and eagerness for the studies at which we were working, and the same high ideals produced by common interests.

Furthermore, the two young men came from similar backgrounds and were of roughly equal means which helped to cement their intimacy. Unfortunately this intimacy was broken when Basil made a greater commitment to the ascetic life, while John remained 'fettered with wordly desires'.[14]

Of Chrysostom's homilies the best example is perhaps the second homily on 1 Thess.2 but there are many examples throughout his works of such statements as 'the basis of all good things is nothing other than friendship' or 'nothing is good or worthwhile without friendship'[15] and in the second homily on 1 Timothy he says that nothing is so beneficial as to pursue friendship (*philia*) to the utmost of our power, quoting Jesus' words at Matt. 18:19 and Matt. 24:12 in support of this. It is, he suggests, as a result of undervaluing friendship that heresies arise;[16] on the other hand, where true friendship exists, as in the case of David and Jonathan,[17] all the sins which usually arise through human relations are absent. In the homilies on Acts Chrysosotom puts forward his belief that the man who has many friends is to be envied,[18] though the kind of friendship he admires is clearly one based on knowledge and discernment: in the second homily on the Epistle to the Philippians he warns that those who love without reason form relationships which are weak and even dangerous.

But it is in the second homily on the second chapter of Paul's letter to the Thessalonians that Chrysostom gives his most extensive and eloquent eulogy of *philia*. He first praises true friendship, which he regards as being in a class of its own, obtaining between those who are 'of one soul' (*homopsychoi*),[19] those who would choose to die for each other, so strong is their love. He quotes Sir.6:16, 'A faithful friend is the elixir of life and those who fear the Lord will find one' and 6:14, 'A faithful friend is a sure refuge; whoever finds one has found a rare treasure', and apparently uses *agape* as a synonym for *philia* when he writes that nothing could be more attractive than this kind of love for it is true that a loyal friend is a remedy for life and a strong protection. What is there which a true friend would not do? Does he not provide an enormous amount of pleasure as well as usefulness and security? It is impossible to think of any treasure more valuable than a true friend. We notice here the twin standards of pleasure and usefulness which are familiar from Classical discussions of friendship and Chrysostom speaks here in a characteristically rhetorical style of the pleasures involved: it would be better for us, so he says, if the sun were to be extinguished than that we should be deprived of friends, for 'many who look on the sun live lives of darkness, while those who have many friends never suffer affliction' and he goes so far as to say that a friend is sweeter than this life itself. In the same passage he shows, too, that he knows and accepts as true the saying that a friend is a second self.[20]

As an example of this true friendship which is primarily a spiritual relationship, he rather surprisingly gives the love felt for one another by St Paul and the apostles, rather than the relationship between Jesus and his disciples, on the grounds that Paul was obedient to Jesus' words at John 15:13: this love must of course be our model, too.[21] In this connection he refers also to Acts 4:32 and 4:35 describing the community of the early Church at Jerusalem, to illustrate his ideal of Christian friendship, giving his reasons for this reference: the early Christians provided a perfect example of the *philia* in which all the friends shared everything and were as concerned for the welfare of their friends' souls as for their own. Chrysostom does not merely offer this familiar picture as a model but tries to make it relevant to Christian relationships in his own day, among his own congregation. Is it possible to attain to such perfect friendships now? he asks and his answer is in the affirmative, although he does admit that such relationships are rare, far less common than they were in the apostolic period. The reason for his optimism about the possibility of such friendships is that he believes that it is a matter of will: if Christians really wished to create such friendships, they could do so. Surely otherwise Jesus would not have laid such emphasis on the formation of such relationships among his followers, as he did at John 13:34-5?[22] Chrysostom concludes his homily with an eloquent attempt to convey the rarity and wonder of true friendship according to Christ by developing the image of the rare plant. He writes:

It is as if I were talking of a flower growing in India which no one else had seen: no speech would be sufficient to represent it, even if I used ten thousand words; so also now whatever I say, I say in vain for no one will understand me. This is a plant which is planted in heaven, with branches not of heavy-clustered pearls but of virtue, which is far superior. The pleasure of friendship excels all others, even if you compare it with the sweetness of honey, for that satiates but a friend never does.

and he adds, rather poignantly in the light of future events, 'With a friend even exile would be bearable.'

But the rarity of such relationships is also emphasised in

Hom. 60.3 on the Gospel of Matthew[23] where Chrysostom
expounds Jesus' words at Matt. 18:20, 'Where two or three are
gathered in my name, there I will be in the midst of them', to
apply not to an ordinary congregation of Christians but to
those unusual friendships where the friends love one another
because of Christ rather than for any of the more common
reasons why people love their friends, e.g. because they are
loved or honoured by their friends or because someone is useful
to them – many friends are bound together by similar mun-
dane, secular reasons. But such relationships are neither profound nor permanent, for they have no spiritual basis and are
easily dissolved whenever one of the friends takes offence, feels
jealous or experiences financial difficulties. On the other hand,
the love which exists for Christ's sake stands firm and is
indestructible – here Chrysostom refers to the key texts I Cor.
13:8 and John 15:13 and ends the homily by urging us to
imitate Christ's love. Christ does not love us because we do
good to him; he loves all men whatever they do and however
sinful or unresponsive they are to him.

Chrysostom expands on the idea that there are different
kinds of friendship in the first homily on the Epistle to the
Colossians; of these only one accords with the true Christian
life. This Christian friendship is a spiritual relationship, unlike
the other kinds which he labels the natural ones, i.e. relationships between family members and the relationships of everyday life. To these two inferior kinds Chrysostom applies the
words of the parable (Luke 14:12–14), which ostensibly dis-
courage mutual friendships among Christians, 'When you give
a dinner or a banquet, do not invite your friends or your
brothers or your kinsmen or rich neighbours, lest they also
invite you in return and you be repaid.' Instead he encourages
his listeners to cultivate friendships according to the spirit,
which are not produced by anything earthly but are of
heavenly origin. Such friendship is more than biting time can
sever, and cannot be dissolved either by separation or ill-
feeling, anger or pride, for nothing is stronger than the bond of
the spirit.

Bearing in mind such an exalted attitude to friendship and

Chrysostom's firm conviction that friendship was not only possible but essential in a Christian life, we shall consider his relationship with Olympias as revealed in his letters to her which are full of feeling and direct address in a tone at the same time courteous and intimate, as well as vivid imagery and Biblical examples to reinforce his message. What evidence is there that Chrysostom transferred the theories of Christian friendship into his own relationships with devout Christians? The letters seem to show that at the basis of their relationship was a deep concern for one another's spiritual and physical welfare and it is clear that Olympias worked unceasingly, desperately, on her friend's behalf during his enforced absence from Constantinople.[24] She did all she could to arrange for his return and failing that, to make his exile more bearable, but her lack of success and the harassment which she herself suffered for being his friend often drove her to despair. In his letters Chrysostom is constantly trying to encourage her and to bring her out of her fits of depression by means of spiritual advice and consolation; often his letters to her consist mostly of relevant Biblical quotations and references aimed at inspiring her with hope. For example, in the long Ep. 10 he tries to persuade her to rejoice in her difficulties by reminding her that depression is more to be feared even than death and that the reward for virtue in such trying circumstances will be all the greater,[25] referring to such texts as 1 Cor. 3:8, 'He who plants and he who waters are equal, and each shall receive his wages according to his labour', and such Biblical characters as Joseph and Job, renowned and rewarded for their patience. At other times he uses more personal methods in attempting to cheer her up, assuring her that he is well and that she must not worry about him, for it is this anxiety which is making her ill. He ends the letter by urging her, 'Never cease to pray and to glorify God as you always do, thanking him for your sufferings'; this, he feels, is the best way to shake off her depression. Chrysostom, in his concern for the well-being of his friend, is able to push aside his own problems and make it appear that the only source of his suffering is not the harsh treatment and dangers he is experiencing but Olympias' unhappiness and his disappointment at

not receiving letters from her more frequently to reassure him
that she is making spiritual progress and managing to dispel the
cloud of depression. In Ep.8 he begs her to show her love for
him by listening to his advice and giving evidence in her letters
that it has had the intended effect:[26] this is the only thing which
will console him in his solitude. 'This is one way in which you
can show your affection for me. . .I want you to show the same
cheerfulness as I saw in you when we were together. . .For you
are well aware how much you will restore me if you succeed in
this and can show it openly in your letters to me.' In the same
letter he also encourages her to show strength by praising
highly all her virtues, in particular her patience, charity,
asceticism and humility, but admits that great strength is
indeed needed to bear separation from those one loves.

Finally he urges her to try to value his letters as she would his
presence; the idea that letters can be a more or less adequate
substitute for the friend's presence is of course a popular one
throughout antiquity, but here it is no mere cliché but a
sincerely held belief expressed in the context of strong emotion
and personal suffering. Again and again he urges her that by
maintaining a regular correspondence they can ward off the
pain involved in separation, for letters can almost create the
kind of intimacy experienced when the friends are together. He
also often admits that he is sad at not having heard from her
despite his many letters to her,[27] but more often his letters are
designed to console his friend by reassuring her that they will
meet again,[28] urging her not to give up hope, by expressing his
happiness at her success in bearing her troubles at last[29] or by
assuring her that he is not angry with her for being unable to
get him moved from Cucusus where much of his exile was
spent.[30] All this is in accordance with his belief in the importance in friendship of caring for your friends' salvation by
encouraging and rebuking them so that they may cling to the
spiritual values of their shared faith.[31] Each Christian is responsible for the salvation of all others because of the intimate unity
and mutual dependence which exists between the members of
the body of Christ,[32] which is such an important concept in
Chrysostom's thought, as in the writings of other theologians of

this period of heresy and schism within the Church. This unity must be maintained with love and sin must not be allowed to prevent Christians from becoming 'one soul', as far as possible.[33] One indication of his concern for his friend's salvation is his insistence that the joys of heaven are well worth suffering for here on earth. In caring for a friend's salvation one is also incidentally mindful of one's own, according to Chrysostom, for one will be deserving of far greater heavenly rewards if one leads one's companions on to the right spiritual paths rather than merely caring for others' material welfare.[34]

A further consequence for friendship of the unity of all Christians in Christ is that they thereby share everything, even their joys and sorrows. Spiritual union in Christ can therefore be a source of consolation as well as a responsibility. Chrysostom shows himself to be pained by Olympias' periods of depression (a state of which he himself had some experience) or illness, and overjoyed when she cheers up – as in Ep.12 – because of his great love in Christ and his concern for her which make him experience so directly her feelings, even when far away from her:

I was certainly worried when I heard that you were at death's door. But in my great love for you and my worry and care for what concerns you, I was relieved of my anxiety even before I received your letters, when I received a number of letters from Constantinople reporting your health. So now I am very pleased and happy, not only because of your release from illness but above all because you are bearing so nobly the troubles which befall you.

We have seen that Chrysostom believed strongly in the power of spiritual love [35] which was the source of the true kind of Christian friendship. Nevertheless this did not prevent him from often experiencing longing for his friends and sadness at his extended separation from them. True friendships based on spiritual love in the unity of the body of Christ could indeed be maintained despite separation, as the letters to Olympias and others prove, but Chrysostom admits that the physical presence of the friend is highly desirable and that contact by means of letters is only a second-best. This is a constant theme throughout the correspondence of the exiled and lonely bishop, but it is in a letter to Olympias that he speaks at greatest length of the problems of separation: in Ep.8 he writes that to bear the separation from a loving soul is no small trial and one which requires a philosophical mind. It is not enough for those who love one another to be spiritually united, they also need one another's physical presence[36] for otherwise a large part of their joy is removed. Even St Paul felt anguish when separated from those he loved. It is hard for a soul in solitude to have a conversation with another soul and so, for true consolation, a man needs the friend's presence so that he can speak and listen in turn. Ep.8 was presumably written in one of Chrysostom's blacker moods – often he is less pessimistic about separation, even in exile.[37] However, despite the hardships suffered by both Chrysostom and Olympias during the years of his exile, their close friendship did continue until Chrysostom's death near Comana on 14 September 407. One can imagine Olympias' grief when news reached her of his death and it would seem that she did not outlive him by many years for although she was probably still alive in 408 when Palladius' dialogue was written, in which she is described in the present tense, the same author's *Lausiac History* (chapter 56), written about 419–20, mentions her death and the veneration subsequently accorded to her.

CHAPTER 6

Synesius of Cyrene

Synesius was born some thirty-five years later than Basil and Gregory,[1] contemporary rather with Augustine in the West and John Chrysostom in the East; in fact, his birthplace in what is now Libya lies roughly equidistant between those of Augustine in North Africa and Chrysosotom at Antioch, all of them in areas which were strongly Christian by the end of the fourth century. It is possible that Synesius was born into a Christian family but one which also appears to have claimed descent from Heracles and apparently originated from Sparta; Synesius grew up with strong ties to his Greek past and to Greek culture generally. He did not study at Athens, however, but at Alexandria, a more cosmopolitan city than Athens with powerful Jewish and Christian traditions alongside the pagan. Here he continued his Classical education under the guidance of Hypatia, the teacher of mathematics and Neoplatonist philosophy, and increased his familiarity with the Neoplatonic philosophy according to the theories and principles of which he was to lead the rest of his life. For even though Synesius' familiarity with Christianity also grew, especially during his time at Constantinople, even though he married a Christian and was prevailed upon to become bishop of Ptolemais in the last years of his life, he never relinquished a Neoplatonic worldview and seems to have accepted Christianity only in so far as he could make it accord with Neoplatonism and interpret it in Neoplatonic terms. This is where he differs from Augustine, for example, who also came under the influence of Neoplatonism but who used it as a means of explaining Christianity: for Augustine it was Christianity which came first[2] whereas for

Synesius Christianity was never more than a thin veneer over the philosophical substrate; unlike Augustine, Synesius apparently never relinquished his view that reason was not only prior to faith but superior to it. Apart from an occasional reference to Christian doctrine or exegesis or a Biblical text, his writings are dominated by Neoplatonic terminology, even in his hymns and the homilies on Christian themes, and he does not seem to have felt the need to explore the implications of Christian doctrine or struggle with its paradoxes as so many of his contemporaries did, albeit often using philosophical terms to help them. In the context of theories about friendship in the fourth century, then, Synesius is of great interest as an example of someone who became closely involved with Christianity but maintained in an almost pure form some of the traditional Greek ideas as they were handed down in literature and philosophy.

It seems that it was during his two-year stay at Alexandria, probably between 393 and 395, that Synesius first came into contact with a group of like-minded people outside his family circle; with these young men, and with the formidable Hypatia herself,[3] Synesius came to share a deep commitment to philosophy, a commitment which provided the basis of their friendship which lasted, as is clear from the continuing correspondence,[4] after Synesius had left Alexandria for a life of cultured leisure at home in Cyrene. Gradually, however, he became more involved in public affairs, gaining such a distinguished reputation that he was chosen as the political representative to plead Cyrene's financial cause at the court of the emperor Arcadius in Constantinople. There Synesius spent three years (399–402), mixing in court circles with orthodox Christians, pagans and Arian Goths and forming many new friendships while trying to secure an audience with the emperor to whom he would read his speech offering advice on the current political situation.[5] One of those with whom he came into close contact and whom he much admired was Aurelian, Praetorian Prefect and then consul in 400 and a convert to Christianity.[6]

An earthquake shook the imperial city in 402 and Synesius, his mission at last accomplished, was forced to leave in such a hurry that he had no time to say goodbye to his friends, not

even to Aurelian, his 'dear friend and a consul', as he related in
Ep.61. The next years were spent in Alexandria (where he was
married by Bishop Theophilus, John Chrysostom's great
enemy) and at Cyrene where Synesius resumed a life combin-
ing involvement in politics for the defence of his region[7] against
barbarian invasions with literary endeavour and philosophical
study, though the dangerous political situation often made it
difficult for him to concentrate on his intellectual activities. His
devotion to literary composition and exploration of cosmology
and metaphysics within Neoplatonic bounds suffered another
blow when this same bishop Theophilus chose him to become
bishop of Ptolemais, a post which he probably assumed at the
beginning of 412.

On the face of it, this choice is hard to comprehend and it has
been a source of controversy since late antiquity: to what extent
did Synesius ever become a Christian?[8] Why did Theophilus
choose him? After all, he was renowned as a man deeply
devoted to, and learned in, pagan philosophy and Greek
culture, he had not been baptised (this was not however
unusual even among those chosen for the episcopate) and
furthermore he was convinced that he ought not to accept this
office, both because of his inability, as he freely admitted, to
accept certain Christian doctrines which conflicted with his
Platonist beliefs and because he did not wish to renounce his
commitment to philosophical study. In Ep.105 Synesius writes
to his brother:

I can never persuade myself that the soul is of more recent origin than
the body. Never would I admit that the world and the parts which
make it up must perish. This resurrection, which is an object of
common belief, is to me only a sacred and mysterious allegory ... No,
if I am called to the priesthood, I declare before God and man that I
refuse to preach dogmas in which I do not believe. Truth is an
attribute of God, and I wish in all things to be blameless before him.

It is possible that despite these specific problems Synesius had
become increasingly sympathetic towards Christianity as he
saw how close it came on many points to his own beliefs and
how powerful it was becoming within the Empire, but it
remains true that even after he reluctantly agreed to be made

bishop the evidence points to a continued commitment to Neoplatonic theory in the Porphyrian mould rather than to any dramatic change of direction in favour of Christianity – and however many parellels one may find between Neoplatonism and Christianity, it would not be possible for a committed Christian to ignore the particulars of the Old and New Testaments as much as Synesius appears to have done. Certainly Synesius seems unusual among his contemporaries, but one must beware of dogmatism in analysing his attitudes to philosophy and Christianity; as Kobusch points out, just as there were Platonising Christians at this period, so there might also be Christianising Platonists.⁹ All we know is that he spent the last years of his life fulfilling his duty as spiritual and administrative leader of the Christian church in Ptolemais. These were years of sadness for Synesius for he lost all the members of his family, one by one, and felt that he had lost touch with his friends. One of his last letters (Ep. 10) is addressed to Hypatia, to whom he writes that, if only he could have had letters from her and heard how she was getting on, he should have been relieved of half his own unhappiness, in rejoicing at her happiness; as it is, her silence has merely added to his sorrow and the greatest loss for him is the absence of her divine spirit. It seems that he himself died in about 414, soon after his patron Theophilus, but before Hypatia's murder at the hands of a Christian mob.¹⁰

It is against the background of his dedication to Greek literature and philosophy¹¹ and his obvious familiarity with such writings, as well as his gradual, if only partial, rapprochement with Christianity that Synesius' attitude to friendship must be considered. His views on the subject, as far as they can be grasped, are to be found mainly in his letters, of which there are 156 extant in the edition of Garzya.¹² For although he always longed to devote himself exclusively to a philosophical life so that he could, in unmolested solitude, purify his soul and lead it back to union with the divine, he actually spent most of his life involved with other people, his strong sense of duty leading him to sacrifice much of his leisure for the good of others, both publicly and privately, in person and by letter, before and after his election as bishop.[13]

The scholars who, over the past hundred years, have treated Synesius' life from various aspects have almost all recognised how important friendship was to him, although Crawford and Grützmacher are unusual in devoting a whole chapter to the subject of Synesius' friends.[14] Throughout Synesius' correspondence there is evidence of his concern for the welfare of others: this was clearly a strong principle for him, as is seen from Ep.44(43 G.) when he writes to Joannes that it is impossible for him not to do all he can to help his friends in every way. To his close friend Olympius he writes in Ep.97, 'You may meet many better men than Synesius but you will not come across any more affectionate friend.' That friendship was an aspect of life which he valued is clear from the fact that he calls it an excellent thing (Ep.60) when writing to Auxentius, a friend since childhood and in a letter to Troilus (Ep.73) he even says that the gift of friends is the greatest of God's gifts to man.

However, although most biographers see that Synesius valued friendship, they do tend to treat the subject in a purely biographical manner, concentrating on the problem of identifying Synesius' friends and tracing their careers before and after their encounters with Synesius. Apart from the value of such work as social history, it also helps us to understand what sort of people Synesius drew to him as his friends, but it does not enlighten us to any great extent as to Synesius' personal theories of friendship. What does emerge from such investigations is that Synesius had a few special friends to whom he felt particularly close, as he did to his brother Evoptius: the number of extant letters to him (41 in Garzya's numeration) indicates the sincerity of Synesius' feeling that he could turn to his brother for advice or comfort in any situation, confident of being received with sympathy. In Ep.8 he writes to Evoptius, 'Is there anything we do not share? Everything has combined to unite us in every way to each other.'

While the brothers were studying at Alexandria they were joined by two young men who also became Synesius' close friends, Herculian and Olympius. It is probably these four who formed the 'foursome of sacred friendship' to which Synesius refers in a letter to Herculian (Ep.143), using the language of Pythagorean number-symbolism (presumably under Hypatia's influence) in talking of friendship to a fellow student of philosophy. In the same letter he says that Herculian is his best friend of the triad of men apart from whose friendship he values nothing human.[15] Ten letters survive from Synesius to this friend and it is evident from these that they felt their relationship was based on their shared dedication to philosophy. However, a different aspect of friendship is evident in the eight letters to Olympius (Epp.45,96–9,133,148–9) which contain no philosophical discussion but are concerned rather with people whom Synesius is recommending to his friend or with Synesius' own problems at home in the Cyrenaica. But this does not make the letters impersonal; they are full of tenderness for this friend whom Synesius calls his 'thrice-dear companion' (Ep.97) and to whom, in Ep.149, he addresses the following words, 'Even when you are absent you are always present to me in my thoughts, for even if I really wanted to, I could not forget the sweetness of your soul and your honest disposition. Nothing could be more precious to me than my memory of you, nothing except the prospect of embracing you again.'

Matters of patronage and protection are in fact a dominant theme in many of Synesius' letters, especially those addressed to the influential men he met at Constantinople, such as Aurelian, Troilus, Anastasius, Simplicius, Nicander, Theotimus and Pylaemenes, men who had a strong interest in Greek literature and philosophy but who were also involved in politics. The closest friend among these seems to have been the lawyer Pylaemenes, sixteen of the letters to whom still survive;[16] in them Synesius often expresses his great affection for his friend, as in Ep.129 when he says that of all those he has left behind in the imperial city, Pylaemenes is his dearest friend. These were the men whose company and friendship Synesius enjoyed at different times of his life and with whom he maintained contact by letter when separated from them. He thus built up a correspondence for which he has earned the title of 'the Greek Pliny of the fifth century' and which Photius, the ninth-century

patriarch and humanist, praised for its charm and for the
strength and wisdom of its ideas.[17] In examining these letters
for a knowledge of Synesius' theories of friendship it must be
remembered that his style is often elaborate and rhetorical,
learned and obscure[18] and there is consequently a risk of forcing
too great precision from them.

What idea did Synesius have of the nature of friendship?
How did he accommodate friendship into his philosophical
view of life? It is true that in the *Dion*, a work which contains an
apologia for Synesius' own way of life, he writes that he wishes
that man could always be bent on contemplation and in the
third hymn he expresses a longing to retire from the world,
envying the hermit his opportunities for silent communion and
exalted thought. Synesius would no doubt have found Augustine's early ideal of *deificari in otio*, 'to become a god in leisurely
retirement' attractive.[19] Even in the letters Synesius sometimes
reminds his friends that, for him, philosophy comes before all
else, but if he often feels strongly that he ought to be alone in
order to devote himself to God without distraction, at other
times his attitude to the things of this world, and especially to
friendship, is more tolerant and positive. Philosophy is still the
basis of everything, including true friendships which are joined
by a profound intellectual bond – in Ep.137 to Herculian he
writes, 'And if human affairs join together in mutual sympathy
those who share them in common, divine law demands that we
who are united through the intellect, the best thing within us,
should honour one another' – but among those things lower in
value than philosophy friendship can even be regarded as
something sacred because it is a gift from God. Indeed, in
Ep.96 Synesius seems to place friendship on a par with philosophy when he invokes 'the god who is honoured by friendship
and philosophy alike', in expressing his deep despair at being
chosen bishop. Perhaps he mentions both here because he fears
that they are the two things which he will be forced to abandon
if he is made bishop.

Not only is there a god honoured by friendship: Synesius also
repeatedly speaks of a god who protects friendship or of an
aspect of the divine being which does so. In Ep.49(51

G.),59,103 and 129 he uses the expression, 'By the god of friendship whom you and I share', an expression which is not uncommon in Classical literature, especially in Plato, which may explain Synesius' attraction to it. The phrase originated as an oath sworn on Zeus *Philios*, the latter being one of Zeus' many cognomens, signifying one of his particular attributes. However, it would not be possible to attach much significance to this phrase as it is such a conventional expression, were it not for the fact that in Ep.143 Synesius mentions the same idea expressed in a different formulation: there he calls on 'the god who is the guardian of your friendship' and this variation implies that Synesius did think that God presided over friendships. This idea presumably developed from a belief in Zeus *Philios*, but it is interesting to note that it appears later to undergo a slight change so that it can be applied to the God of the Christians, for in Ep.57 (41 G.), against the prefect Andronicus, definitely written after Synesius' appointment to the episcopate, he writes, 'A table is a sacred thing whereby God who protects friends and guests is honoured' and then immediately refers to Gen.18:8. Here God assumes the attributes of Zeus, and Christian and pagan are mingled.

Usually, however, Synesius' view of friendship remains firmly pagan, inspired by the traditional ideas of Greek writers and devoid of any Christian context. In Ep.123 he refers to Homer when he compares his own friendship with Troilus with that between Achilles and Patroclus, quoting *Iliad* 22.389, 'Even though there shall be complete forgetfulness of the dead in Hades, even there I shall remember my dear friend'.[20] From a more philosophical point of view, not only does the Platonic idea of love[21] and its connection with progress towards wisdom appear frequently in such contexts and clearly influences his view of friendship, but he also refers to both Pythagoras and Aristotle. In Ep.100 to Pylaemenes he mentions the definition of a friend as a second self, attributing it to Pythagoras as had Porphyry in his biography of Pythagoras with which Synesius was no doubt familiar: 'No one will contradict those who approve of Pythagoras' statement that a friend is a second self.' Reference to Aristotle in connection with friendship is made in

Ep.154, a long letter to Hypatia in which he writes on the subject of a book he is proposing to publish, 'If it does not seem to you worthy of Greek ears, and you, like Aristotle, value truth more than friendship', then he will refrain from publishing it. Here he has in mind Aristotle's words in the *Nicomachean Ethics* (1096a 16), 'While both (sc. truth and friendship) are dear, piety requires us to honour truth above our friends.'

These brief references are evidence that, as might be expected, Synesius was well aware of the thoughts of Greek philosophers on friendship: this can be taken to be true even though he does not quote directly from, for example, those sections of Aristotle's *Nicomachean Ethics* which concentrate on friendship. More generally he speaks of such common ideas as that friends are tested in adversity e.g. in Ep.8 to Evoptius. In Ep.44(43 G.) he says that loss of money is preferable to the loss of a friend, a statement which is reminiscent of Classical discussions on the value of friends and in Ep.49(51 G.) he asks, 'Even for a man who possesses power, what possession could be more attractive than a sincere and loyal friend?'

According to Synesius God not only watches over friendships, he also creates them (Ep.137) and keeps friends united by being present to them even during periods of separation. This is true of those friends who share a devotion to philosophy but not in the case of more earthly friendships – in Ep.140 a distinction is drawn between the different kinds of friendship, a distinction inspired by Plato as Synesius himself admits:

Of loves there are some which have earthly and human origins. These are detestable and ephemeral, measured by the presence of the object alone ... but there are others over which a divinity presides and, according to the divine words of Plato, he fuses those who love one another so that from being two they become one.[22]

Certainly he believed in the value of friends having interests in common and this, together with the belief that the best friendships are those between philosophers, explains his determination to encourage Pylaemenes and Herculian in their philosophical studies,[23] with which may be compared Plato's Ep.6 in which the writer exhorts three other men to form a friendship based on philosophy. From this point of view friendship is an exclusive relationship and does not aim to extend beyond a few chosen ones, for philosophy is not available to most people and must in fact be concealed from the masses in order to preserve its sanctity. In Ep.143 he writes, 'If you have approached philosophy sincerely, you ought to avoid the company of those who are not faithful to it.'

God has also granted that friendships should be maintained by correspondence, as Synesius says in Ep.138, in a brief encomium on the value of letters. In Ep.48 he speaks wittily of Pylaemenes' letters as Thrace's most valuable export: no doubt the difficult conditions for sending letters did indeed make it seem wonderful when a letter actually reached its destination and encouraged such hyperbole. Certainly Synesius accepted one of the more commonplace reasons for valuing letters, for he writes in Ep.138 that a letter offers the illusion that a friend is present when he is physically absent, a sentiment he apparently once heard expressed by a sophist speaker. Ep.4(5 G.), for example, is a long letter to his brother, the immoderate length of which he defends by saying that, just as when he is face to face with Evoptius, so in writing to him he cannot have enough of his company and since they cannot be together for the moment, the letter must act as a substitute for their conversation. By making the spirit of the absent friend present, letters can provide a substitute for the ideal of living together which Aristotle had asserted was important for true friendship. Many of his letters also reveal that he regarded them as offering comfort and consolation to absent friends, for although they are in some ways only a second-best, letters can provide the friends with proof of mutual love. Such ideas and expressions are indeed conventional, but the fact that they appear in Synesius' correspondence is of interest in showing that they were still used in a living way at this period. Although Synesius is not startlingly original in his thought on friendship and does not develop the traditional theories to any real extent, this does not nullify the fact that he managed to maintain affectionate friendships for many years in accordance with these theories.

A further function of letters was to provide a means of

helping friends. This is an idea which is essential to Synesius' view of friendship. Many letters contain formal or witty requests for the addressee to help another of Synesius' friends and others themselves contain assistance in the form of advice or consolation. The importance of this principle is illustrated for example in Ep.81 to Hypatia in which he laments the passing of a time when he was able to be a great help to his friends. He writes, 'There was a time when I was of use to my friends and you used to call me the providence of others' and then goes on to urge Hypatia, the only friend he has left, to help two young friends of his by enlisting her friends' support for them. It was generally admitted that friendships could and should benefit those who participated in them and Synesius developed this into a theory whereby he imagined friendship as a chain or an ever-widening circle: two friends did not only assist each other but were also ready to help other friends of their friend, even if they were not yet acquainted, and by helping them they gained new friends and extended the circle. In Ep.16, again addressed to Hypatia, Synesius sends his greetings to her friends Theotecnus and Athanasius and then adds, 'If any one has been added to these, so long as he is dear to you, I must owe him gratitude because he is dear to you, and to that man give my greetings as to my own dearest friend' while in Ep.37(34 G.) the same idea possibly lies behind Synesius' statement that he loves Joannes particularly because of his affection for Anysius.

 The idea of friendship as a chain or circle occurs in a number of letters. In two of them Synesius playfully uses imagery taken from his study of geometry to express this notion; in Ep.131 he explains to Pylaemenes:

There is a certain principle that two things which are equal to a third thing are equal to each other. I am bound to you by the link of association and to the admirable Diogenes by temperament also. Both of you are friends of the one man so you must be united to one another even as you are united to me, the middle link.

Similarly in Ep.93 he reprimands Hesychius for not helping Evoptius – ought he not to treat Synesius' brother as one of his brothers, if it is true that two things equal to the same thing are equal also to each other? In Ep.119 to Trypho we find Diogenes and Evoptius spoken of as connected by their common love for Synesius and in two short letters to Evoptius (Epp.86 and 87) the idea of the circle of friends widening through one another's acquaintances is again hinted at when Synesius writes to introduce two men to his brother. He says that his letter is the cause of the first meeting between Evoptius and Gerontius but that once they have been brought together, Evoptius will love Gerontius for his own sake rather than in order to do his brother a favour and through Gerontius he will make new friends. In Ep.87 he writes to Evoptius that it is for him to welcome Synesius' friends as his own, implying that they will then become Evoptius' friends too.

A variation on this idea is provided by another related image in Ep.100 where Synesius writes to Pylaemenes, 'You (sc. Pylaemenes and Anastasius) are both of you neighbours in my heart ... let your meeting therefore be an act of recognition. Embrace each other and see in this a means of doing me a little good.' We see, then, that despite the restrictions placed on the extension of true friendship by the need for a shared commitment to philosophy, Synesius believed strongly that within such boundaries friendship could and should be extended to an ever-widening circle. For him, friendship as a one-to-one relationship would be meaningless and there is nothing in Synesius' writings to suggest that he thought *polyphilia* undesirable or impracticable.

In certain of his letters Synesius implies that he believed in some kind of law of friendship which men must beware of transgressing, a belief which was supported by the idea that God presides over friendship. In Ep.53 he mentions 'the law of correspondence', which is presumably part of the law of friendship and in Ep.137 he says that if Herculian does not feel as much affection as Synesius, then he wrongs their friendship, but if he does, then he is only repaying 'the debt of friendship'. The implication here seems to be that the law of friendship demands that the love between friends should not only be mutual but also equal. It also demands that the friends give frequent assurances of their love; this is why Synesius is so concerned to write and receive letters and why, in Ep.24, he chastises Simplicius for his long silence: their long-standing and strong affection ought to mean that they correspond frequently for old affection implies present obligation. In Ep.25 and Ep.60 he speaks in stronger terms of transgression of this law of friendship. In Ep.25 he urges Heliodorus, who has not written to him for a long time, to repent if he admits he is guilty of forgetfulness of their friendship, and to restore himself to his friend by writing immediately. In Ep.60 Auxentius, Synesius' addressee, is bitterly accused of having been false to friendship: Synesius says that if he made a formal accusation against Auxentius he would win his case before God's tribunal and that of all godlike men and he urges Auxentius to 'make a cult of friendship'. The language he uses here also suggests the existence of a law of friendship which all friends have a duty to keep but which is likely to be broken by quarrels, insufficient affection or lack of attention, a law over which God presides and which he is thought to have established in his role as Zeus *Philios*.

As for the existence of a Christian tone in what Synesius writes about friendship, we have seen attributes of the god of friendship applied in a Christian context in Ep.57(41 G.), but apart from this the evidence is minimal. On the whole Synesius' attitude to friendship appears unaffected by Christian doctrine and as far as any coherent theory on the subject can be elicited from his writings, it remained a product of his literary, scientific and philosophical education, primarily influenced by the utterances of those Greek philosophers whom Synesius so much admired.

CHAPTER 7

Ambrose of Milan – Ciceronian or Christian friendship?

Among Latin writers of the fourth century Ambrose provides an example of a Christian who retained the influence of Classical literary and philosophical forms and ideas in which he had been educated, particularly in his thought about friendship, even after he had made a definite commitment to Christianity. In the case of Ambrose and, as we shall see, Jerome, this is not to impugn their devotion to the Christian faith but rather to indicate a difference between them and, for example, Basil or Augustine who transformed their knowledge of the Classical views on friendship to a far greater degree in using them to work out an orthodox theological framework for their ideas. Although Ambrose, Jerome and even Synesius often placed what they said about friendship in a recognisably Christian context, this transposition only effected a superficial change and their ideas remained dominated by pagan thought on the subject. Together they offer various kinds of evidence for the extent to which the traditional thought on the subject of friendship was still in use at this period.

Ambrose, as the son of the Praetorian Prefect of Gaul, was given a traditional literary and rhetorical education[1] which led him into a legal career at Rome until he was appointed governor of Aemilia–Liguria, the area of northern Italy of which Milan was the centre. But in 373, only a few years after his appointment to this eminent position, the people of Milan unexpectedly chose this highly educated man, a believing Christian but as yet unbaptised, to be their next bishop. This turned out to have been a wise choice for during the years of his episcopate (373–97) Ambrose proved himself to be a powerful defender of Christianity against paganism, of orthodoxy against Arianism and of the Church against the emperor and the state, as well as an impressive preacher and Church leader.

The question of how far Ambrose was influenced by pagan philosophy in his Christian writings is one which has been much discussed. As he was able to read Greek[2] he was open to the influence of Greek philosophy, whether directly or through the mediation of Philo or Basil and it is clear that he was familiar with the Latin tradition, especially with Cicero's works. The problem of his relation to Cicero is particularly insistent in connection with his work *De officiis ministrorum* which is so obviously based on Cicero's *De officiis* and yet is directed at the Christian clergy and uses Scriptural texts throughout, especially from the Old Testament, to illustrate his ethical advice.[3] Like Cicero Ambrose devotes a section of his work to friendship but it is necessary first to consider the general problem of Ambrose's relation to Cicero before focussing on what he says about friendship in this work as well as in his other writings, notably the letters.

Critics of the *De officiis ministrorum* differ quite dramatically in their conclusions as to Ambrose's use of Cicero, but they seem to fall mainly into two categories, those who believe that Ambrose had a polemical purpose and was above all determined to replace Cicero's authority by that of the Bible, and those who think that it was Ambrose's aim to create a synthesis of Ciceronian ethics with Christian doctrine.[4] The fact that such diverse positions can be held shows how difficult a problem it is to resolve. It does, however, seem that the belief that Ambrose intended to be polemical is less tenable, for a number of reasons which can be illustrated from Ambrose's own words or from the manner in which he uses the Ciceronian material.

Ambrose was clearly familiar with Cicero's *De officiis* but he was not obliged, in writing a work on Christian ethics, to take it as his starting-point. So why did he? If he did so in order to refute pagan ethics, this is not made sufficiently clear in what he says about Cicero and other pagan philosophers. It is true that he does disagree specifically with what they said but far more frequently he tacitly accepts their view on a particular area of ethical teaching, adopting their concepts and their conclusions. For example, he accepts the Stoic distinction between ordinary and perfect duties which he finds in Cicero, though he says he bases this idea on Matt.19:17–21 and Matt. 5:44.[5] He accepts the view that there are two kinds of mental motion, namely reflection and passion (*De off.min.*1.22.98) and that passion must be subordinated to reason if a man is to be virtuous (1.24.105). Although he rejects the philosophers who say that private property is natural, he approved of the Stoic view of property (*De off.min.*1.28.132). He does not agree with the philosophers' view that justice is a matter of not harming anyone except when driven to it by wrongs received, but he does accept, on the question of justice, that more regard should be paid to the person who has conferred some benefit on one. In II.9.49 he adopts the fourfold division of virtue 'in deference to commonly received ideas' and in Book III he demonstrates his agreement with Cicero on the question of conflict between what is expedient and what is virtuous. Ambrose also speaks with approval of the Stoic idea of living in accordance with nature, supporting his attitude by reference to the rather unlikely text of 1 Cor.11:13–14, namely Paul's precept to women to cover their head when praying!

It is also true that the Bible is of central importance in providing examples and support and that Ambrose states that nothing that is not found in the Holy Scriptures can be accepted, but this by no means prevents him from adopting much of what the philosophers, and particularly Cicero, have to offer, for he manages to find Biblical passages which can be said to support most of the pagan ideas. Abraham, Jacob, Joseph, Job and David are taken as illustrious examples, worthy of imitation, to prove that it is virtuous to submit our passions to reason, as Cicero had stated at *De off.*1.39.141. In III.11.74 Ambrose takes the example of Ananias to show that the Bible agrees with the Stoics that fraud ought to be condemned, but he also refers explicitly to the examples Cicero gives in *De off.*III.14.58, 18.73 and 19.75. In Book II he accepts that man's admiration of money has reached such a point that no one is thought worthy of honour unless he is rich: this is what Cicero says at II.20.71 of his work but Ambrose then goes on to show by the example of various Old Testament figures that this vice is one that has been rife for a very long time. These few passages reveal how Ambrose takes the Ciceronian line as his basis and then elaborates on it with illustrations usually drawn from the Old Testament.

This dominant use of the Old Testament is connected with a fundamental attitude which Ambrose holds as to the relation between pagan philosophy and the Bible and which also shows that he was not hostile to the former. His positive attitude to the acceptance of much that he knew to have been written by non-Christian philosophers was aided by his belief, stated on a number of occasions in the *De officiis ministrorum*, that the philosophers derived their good ideas from Jewish Scripture, for 'were Panaetius or even Aristotle putting forward their arguments before David? No, even Pythagoras who was earlier than Socrates, came after David.' (*De off.min.*I.10.31) Ambrose even goes so far as to say that, although Plato and Cicero are rightly praised for their discussion of justice, did not Job, who lived long before them, have the same ideas (I.12.43–4)? In I.28.132 Ambrose expresses his approval of the Stoics' teaching that all things which are produced on the earth are created for the use of men but, he asks, where did they get such ideas if not from Moses' words at Gen.1:26 and David's in Ps.8:7–8?

When it comes to showing that pagan ideas are derivative, the New Testament is more problematic. In discussing the nature of the *vita beata* (life of happiness) Ambrose agrees with the Stoics and Peripatetics that it consists of a virtuous life, as Jesus too implied in what he said at John 17:3, according to Ambrose's interpretation. But if the philosophers and the Gospel are in accordance, 'let no one think that this was only recently said and that it was spoken by the philosophers before it was mentioned in the Gospel. For the philosophers certainly lived before the time of the Gospel but they came after the prophets'(II.2.6). We can see from this passage why the Old Testament was so important to Ambrose in his use of Cicero and his attitude is one which is commonly found in the writings of those Christians, especially in the earlier period, who recognised that the philosophers had come close to the truth in their response to many ethical and metaphysical questions but who needed to explain how this could be before Christ had appeared as the true philosopher.[6]

It has been argued that Ambrose, in his use of the Ciceronian ethical terms, empties them of their original meaning by placing them in a Christian, Scriptural context. It may be true that when he discusses *fides*, for example, he is thinking of religious faith rather than good faith as Cicero would have interpreted it, but this makes no very significant difference to what he is saying, which is very close to Cicero, although Ambrose connects what he is saying with Biblical texts. In the case of *prudentia* Ambrose defines this virtue as fear of God which is not a definition to be found in Cicero, but he does accept from his predecessor that it is the first source of duty. Although justice comes close to being identified with Christian *caritas*, the similarities with Cicero's definition of *iustitia* are still dominant. In short, Ambrose's work remains a mosaic of Scriptural and Ciceronian texts which, though greatly influential in the Middle Ages for the development of Christian ethics, is of interest largely as evidence of how far Cicero could be regarded as compatible with Christian thought. Ambrose may have been successful in presenting the lives of the Old Testament patriarchs as mirrors of virtue to his contemporaries but his debt to Cicero in the structure of the work and the presentation of the material must not be underestimated.

Ambrose's attitude can be illustrated in detail from his discussion of friendship. He follows Cicero in devoting what may seem to us an inordinate amount of space to this area of ethics and for Ambrose, as for Cicero, friendship remains an ethical question rather than being transformed into a theological one, despite a few specifically Christian remarks which Ambrose makes on the subject at the end of the *De officiis ministrorum* where the nature and benefits of friendship are treated at greater length than anywhere else in his writings. Thamin is therefore right to characterise Ambrose as 'un véritable ancien par son culte tenace de l'amitié', in contrast to

Homes Dudden and Hagendahl who assume in their discussion of Ambrose that in the fourth century the Classical concept of *amicitia* was superseded by Christian *caritas*.[7]

In fact, it is not until the final chapter of the last book of this work that Ambrose offers any sustained advice on friendship but he does mention it in connection with other topics earlier in the work, as in the discussion of the importance of *benevolentia*, a correlative of justice which is one of the four cardinal virtues. It is described as an attitude which is reponsible for the formation of friendship (*De off.min.*1.32.167) and although Ambrose immediately gives the example of David's affection for Jonathan, it is clear that he also has Cicero's *Laelius* in mind, the only other Ciceronian work to be referred to by Ambrose in the *De officiis ministrorum*. *Benevolentia* is of course one of the essential elements of friendship according to Cicero. The implicit connection between the works (for here, as so often, Ambrose is not interested in naming his sources) is made more obvious by the fact that Ambrose says that, if *benevolentia* disappears from a relationship, it is as though the sun had vanished from the world: this is undoubtedly inspired by Cicero's statement in the *Laelius* (13.47).

Jonathan and David, the pair of friends which the Old Testament had to offer to stand beside those renowned in Classical antiquity, are mentioned once more in the following chapter of the *De officiis ministrorum*, still in connection with *benevolentia* which Ambrose says expands throughout the Church by fellowship in faith (1.33.170): they are given as examples of friends who strive to imitate one another's virtues, a desire which is said to stem from *benevolentia*. This idea is reminiscent of what Cicero says in the *Laelius* (9.32) where he speaks of the admirable rivalry between friends who are keen to give more than they receive.[8] This association between friendship and *benevolentia* is continued in 1.34 of Ambrose's work where he names one of the many benefits of this aspect of *iustitia* as its ability to make many one, a unity based on shared ideas and feelings. With this may be compared Cicero's similar statements at *De officiis* 1.17.56 where he writes that when two people have the same ideals and the same tastes, it follows naturally that each loves the other as himself; and the result is that many become one, this being one of the criteria of friendship set down by Pythagoras. Furthermore, Ambrose shows here that he approves of Cicero's statement that correction can be something positive in friendship if it is given and received with good-will. It is noteworthy that in this chapter of Ambrose's work (1.34.173) our author sets side by side a statement that goodwill (i.e. *benevolentia*) makes correction bearable and the idea that it is a unifying force; if we turn to the *Laelius* we find that in 25.91–2 Cicero moves from talking about correction in friendship, by way of an attack on flattery as destructive of friendships, to a statement about unity. This close similarity suggests that Ambrose had this passage of Cicero at the back of his mind when he wrote the corresponding chapter of his work, but despite the fact that what he says about *amicitia* and *benevolentia* follows the pattern of what Cicero had written about friendship in the *Laelius* and about degrees of social relationships in the *De officiis*, it appears that Ambrose had no difficulty in adopting these ideas and in setting them in the context of the Christian Church, supporting them, as is his wont, with Biblical quotations, e.g. Prov. 27:6, 'Better are the wounds of a friend than the deceitful kisses of an enemy', one of the texts frequently referred to by Christian writers in connection with friendship.

In Book II Ambrose continues to follow the structure of Cicero's work when he moves on from a discussion of the virtues to a consideration of what is useful. Friendship is not specifically discussed here but we can derive a few hints about Ambrose's view of it from his treatment of love which is of the greatest use to a Christian (*De off.min.*II.7.29). David is given as an example of one whose virtue made him beloved by his friends and from a mention of the friendship between David and Jonathan Ambrose goes on to make the general observation that 'it gives a great impetus to mutual love if one shows love in return to those who love us and proves that one does not love them less than they love us, especially if one shows it by the proofs that a faithful friendship gives' (II.7.37). Here he uses both *caritas* and *amicitia* in a Christian context, as is common in his writings: like Cicero he appears to regard them as synonymous, moving easily between the two without feeling the need to point to any essential difference or incompatibility between them. That Cicero is at the back of Ambrose's mind in this passage seems likely from the fact that he uses the word *redamare* which was coined by Cicero in the *Laelius* (14.49). And in fact it occurs in a passage of the *Laelius* where the importance of virtue as the basis for friendships is stressed, together with the mention of loving those who love us. But Ambrose, instead of referring openly to his pagan predecessor, quotes Sir.29:10, Sir.22:31, Sir.6:16 and 1 Cor.13:7–8 in support of his view of *caritas/amicitia*.

It is in Book III, which is arranged around the question of whether what is useful ought to be preferred to virtue, that Ambrose considers the nature and duties of friendship in greatest detail and gives his most positive recommendation of it to his readers: in III.22.131 he urges powerfully:

Preserve, my sons, that friendship which you have begun with your brother; for nothing in the world is more beautiful than that. It is indeed a comfort in this life to have someone to whom you can open your heart, with whom you can share confidences and to whom you can entrust the secrets of your heart. It is a comfort to have someone trustworthy beside you who will share your happiness, sympathise with your troubles and encourage you in persecution.

His account develops at the end of the book out of the catalogue of virtuous deeds performed by Old Testament figures which is supposed to prove that these models of ethical behaviour combined the virtuous with the beneficial – for Ambrose follows Cicero in believing that only what is virtuous can be truly useful. The story of Esther, Haman and the king of Persia leads Ambrose to conclude that the friendship which maintains virtue, as between Haman and the king, is to be preferred to any external benefits (III.21.123–4); this conclusion in turn develops into a general discussion of friendship, inspired predominantly by the *Laelius* and *De officiis* of Cicero, though Ambrose continues to support what he says by reference to Biblical authority.

This general discussion begins with Ambrose's advice that,

while a virtuous friendship is to be preferred to worldly
advantages, no friendship ought to be put before virtue if there
is any conflict between them: he cites the examples of Jonathan
and Ahimelech as men who rightly put friendship, not before
virtue but before their own safety. Ambrose would of course
have been able to find this elegantly stated in Cicero[9] and he
does indeed admit that various problems concerning our duty
to friends have been discussed by 'the philosophers' (III.22.125),
but he immediately passes on to a consideration of such
problems from the point of view of what the Scriptures say –
though this leads him to the same conclusions as those to be
found in Cicero! Ambrose sees a parallel between Prov.25:18,'A
mace, a sword, a sharp arrow, such is the man who bears false
witness against his neighbour', and what Cicero writes at *De
off.*III.10.43–4 and *Lael.*11.36, for all three texts emphasise that
a man should not bear false witness against his friend.

In the next section of III.22 Ambrose repeats the commonplace that rebuke can be of positive value in friendship, again
referring to Prov.27:6, 'Better are the wounds of a friend'; at the
same time he is in agreement with Cicero's words at *De
off.*I.17.58,'Occasionally rebuke can be of enormous benefit in
friendship', and *Lael.*24.88–90. Such agreement is also evident
in Ambrose's statement here that friendship ought to stand
firm, which can be compared to *Lael.*19.67 and more specifically to *Lael.*18.64–5 where extravagant praise is accorded the
man who proves himself to be a reliable friend.[10] But in
emphasising the importance of fidelity in friendship Ambrose
appeals not to Cicero but to the sayings at Sir.6:16 and
Sir.22:25, and yet these meagre Biblical references do not
prevent the picture of friendship as a whole which Ambrose
builds up from having closer links with pagan thought on the
subject. This is hardly surprising since Cicero had provided
Latin speakers with a more coherent view of friendship than
any which can be derived from the few, enigmatic statements in
the Bible, and furthermore, in the words of Hagendahl, 'It
came naturally to the bishop to embrace the same views (sc. as
Cicero), as he by birth and by his earlier civil service career

belonged to this very class and had had the same conventional upbringing.'¹¹

This is not to deny that Ambrose does occasionally attempt to put friendship in a more explicitly Christian context than is provided by references to Old Testament heroes or popular philosophy. In III.22.128, for example, he refers to Gal.6:2 when he writes, 'Let us therefore carry one another's burdens, as the apostle has taught us, for his words apply to those who are united by love of the same body' (i.e. the body of Christ). But this is not elaborated on or developed; it is merely given as some basis for the conclusion that we should support our friends in prosperity and adversity, in accordance with a sentiment expressed in the *Laelius* in a passage which also speaks of virtue and the pleasure of confidence between friends as does the Ambrosian passage. The question of the proper behaviour between friends in prosperity and adversity is continued in the next section where Ambrose again quotes Sir.22:26, 'If I suffer evil, I shall bear it for my friend's sake', but also seems to be thinking of the *Laelius* passage (17.64) concerning fidelity in which Cicero refers to Ennius' famous and pithy observation, 'amicus certus in re incerta cernitur', for Ambrose writes (III.22.129), 'It is only in adversity that a friend is really tested for in prosperity everyone appears to be a friend.'

The probable reminiscences of the *Laelius* continue in section 131 where Ambrose writes of friendship that it is a comfort in this life to have someone to whom one can reveal one's inmost thoughts, someone who will share your joy and sorrow and give you advice in times of trouble. Is he not influenced here by *Lael.* 6.22 where Cicero writes,'What is more wonderful than to have someone to whom you dare to speak as to yourself?', and then goes on to talk about friendship in prosperity and adversity? This juxtapostion is common to both passages but the difference between them lies in that Ambrose illustrates what he has said with the examples of Shadrach, Meshach and Abednego in Daniel 3:16ff. and of Saul and Jonathan, united even in death (2 Sam. 1:23). It is true that in section 132 Ambrose adds a vaguely Christian flavour to his use of Cicero's discussion of *fides*¹² when he appears to interpret this term as religious faith rather than good faith for he says,'No one can be a friend to a man if he is not faithful to God', a statement absent from the Ciceronian parallel. But once again there is the failure to develop or explain the idea; instead Ambrose returns immediately to a Classical notion when he mentions that friendship makes the superior friend equal to the inferior and says that friendship is impossible between people of divergent character. On the idea of equality it is necessary to look no further than *Laelius* 19.69 or 20.72. As in Ambrose, so in Cicero this topic is followed[13] by the statement that people of different characters have different interests and such differences make the formation of friendships impossible.

The differences between Cicero and Ambrose, however, continue to be negligible for Ambrose echoes Cicero's reference to a friend as a second self, as well as the idea that it is very natural for a person to seek someone else to whose soul his own can cleave, thereby forming one entity.[14] Furthermore, Ambrose's assertion here that friendship is a virtue, not a means of making money, is directly reminiscent of *Lael.*14.51 where Cicero states the same thing in slightly different terms when he writes,'It is far from true that friendship is cultivated out of need; rather it is cultivated by those who are most generous and kind because they are least in need of someone else's wealth and virtue.'

It is only in the final three sections of the discussion of friendship that Ambrose makes a serious attempt to relate the traditional view of friendship to his Christian faith. Section 135 opens with the question,'What is more precious than friendship which is shared by both men and angels?' and a reference to Luke 16:9,'Make friends for yourselves by means of unrighteous Mammon.' But Ambrose does not explain how he believes angels experience friendship (and note that he is using *amicitia* here) nor does he give an interpretation of the Biblical quotation nor show how it relates to the previous sentence: presumably he is thinking of the harmony of the heavenly community and makes a connection with Luke 16:9 which mentions 'eternal habitations'. It appears that he is trying to bring together as many Biblical texts concerning friendship as he can within a short space for he immediately moves on to quote John 15:14, introducing it with the words,'God himself has made us friends instead of servants, as he himself says...' This Johannine text is of course one which is often referred to by Christian writers on friendship, pointing as it does to a correlation between love of God and our duty to love our neighbour; men are joined with others in friendship and are thereby also friends of Christ. This is not something emphasised by Ambrose. Instead he makes the interesting observation that God gave us the pattern of friendship for us to follow so that we might do our friend's will, reveal all our innermost thoughts to our friend and learn his secrets too.[15] He supports this prescription by a reference to John 15:15. It seems, then, that Ambrose did feel a need to justify friendship in Christian terms and he did so by means of the proposition that human friendship, to be genuine, must be modelled on Christ's treatment of his disciples, his friends. 'If he is a true friend he will hide nothing; he will reveal his soul completely just as our Lord Jesus revealed the mysteries of his Father.'

The connection between friendship with God through obedience to his will and human friendships is less clear in the following section, in which Ambrose deduces another characteristic of our relationship with God in Christ: the person who is of one mind with Christ must also be his friend. Here the connection between human and divine seems to be deduced from an accepted characteristic of human friendships rather than the other way round, for Ambrose continues in explanation of his previous statement, 'because among friends there is unity of spirit'. It is consequently unclear whether Ambrose believed that he had deduced a Christian system of human friendship from Biblical references to the intimate, special relationship between man and Christ or that he had based his idea of man's friendship with God on the traditional ideas of *amicitia*, merely adding Biblical references in support of his conclusions.

The interest of Ambrose's account of friendship in the *De officiis ministrorum* lies in the fact that he does adopt so many of the traditional ideas as expressed mainly by Cicero. Although he refers so rarely to Cicero by name it is Cicero who provides the fundamental material and whose ideas or expressions are taken over wholesale. By no means did Ambrose feel he had to restrict his account to what can be deduced on the subject from Scripture; not only was he clearly very familiar with the traditional views – and with Cicero's works in detail – but he was content to accept as many of them as did not overtly contradict Christian doctrine.

There is another passage which seems to be influenced by Ambrose's knowledge of the ancient ideas about friendship. It is a passage not directly concerned with friendship but rather with the love which Ambrose bears his spiritual sons to whom the work is addressed. He compares his feelings with those of Cicero who wrote his *De officiis* for his own son and says that he loves those whom he has begotten in the gospel no less than if they were his own true sons. He explains that grace can produce just as strong a force for love as nature and indeed we ought to love more strongly those who we believe will be with us forever than those who are with us only in this life. Natural sons fail to live up to their parents' expectations but spiritual sons are chosen with a view to loving; the former are loved out of necessity while the latter are loved as a result of an act of judgement which creates a far stronger bond. He succinctly advises his reader to approve of those he loves and to love those whom he has chosen.[16] Here again we are reminded of the fundamental contrast between the pagan and Christian out-look, with the Christian emphasis on the future life and on grace opposed to the pagan attachment to natural, family ties. However, Ambrose moves imperceptibly from this contrast to one more familiar to the pagan philosophers themselves: a contrast between the ties of blood relationships and those of true friendship formed as a result of men's free choice. In subordinating family ties Ambrose finds himself agreeing with the ancients in their belief that choice is a valuable part of friendship for it involves reason and deliberate judgement which should prevent men forming unstable or worthless friendships. So from a distinction between nature and grace we arrive at a parallel contrast between necessity and judgement and Ambrose's elegant concluding advice is reminiscent of many warnings expressed by earlier philosophers about the dangers of creating friendships too hastily. Does not Cicero at *Lael.*17.62 speak of the need to judge and test and choose one's future friends? And at *Lael.*22.85 does he not say tersely, 'One should love after judging, not judge once one loves'? These similarities provide additional evidence that Classical thought about friendship influenced Ambrose's own ethical ideas in a variety of ways although he rarely admits the debt even if he is aware of it.

We find a similar absence of reference to pagan writers, even to Cicero, in the ninety-one letters which survive of those which Ambrose wrote to his contemporaries during the years of his episcopate (373–97). And yet it has been said that Ambrose's epistles deliberately imitate Ciceronian diction and form. In what way do his letters throw light on his relation to the pagan world whether of antiquity or of his contemporaries? Do they provide additional information on Ambrose's attitude to friendship?

Most of his epistles are addressed to Christians, whether bishops, emperors, priests or laymen, but are not primarily personal. Such letters, often very lengthy, are filled with Biblical quotations providing authority and illustration and are usually concerned with decisions to be made in theological and ecclesiastical matters. The letters to Sabinus, however, are of a more personal nature, allowing us to see how Ambrose treated someone he regarded as a close friend rather than as a mere acquaintance or a stranger appealing to his authority as bishop of Milan. He begs Sabinus[17] that they might play together by means of letters[18] so that they might be brought closer together and in Ep.48 (23 B.) he writes, 'May our love for one another in the Lord increase by means of your letters to me and mine to you.' Ambrose feels that in this way he can speak to his friend even when he is alone. Even in these letters of friendship to a fellow Christian a Ciceronian note is occasionally struck, as when he reminds Sabinus that true love is proved by loyalty which is reminiscent of the passage of the *Laelius* where the formation of stable friendships is discussed.[19] To Simplicianus and Theodosius he speaks of the long-standing friendship he has with them both and his statement to Sabinus (Ep.49.1 = 26 B.) that friends' letters can reproduce the conversation of those who are together even between those who are separated seems to echo the words about true friendships at *Lael.*7.23 as well as a traditional idea about the role of letters in friendship.

In fact Ambrose often uses the conventional language of friendship as it is found in numerous Roman letters from Cicero down to Symmachus, whether he is writing to pagans in governmental position or to Christians. To Faltonius Probus Alypius, for example, who was *praefectus urbi* in 391, he talks of the duties of friendship and the payment of friendship's debts by means of letters. Such expressions had developed in Republican Rome when *amicitia* was largely a matter of mutual obligation and support in political circles and they survived into the fourth century in the pagan aristocratic society which prided itself on its continuity with the great days of Rome's past. That Ambrose too maintained some of these links with the past is clear from such letters as Epp.86–91 which are shorter than many of his letters and therefore more similar in form to the letters of his pagan friend – and adversary over the issue of the Altar of Victory – Symmachus, from whom eight letters to Ambrose survive from their correspondence. Indeed, Matthews has written[20] of Ep.87,'The letter is closely analogous, within its own conventions, to the formal notes written by Symmachus for his protégés; and in his correspondence with Symmachus himself, Ambrose appears as a court contact and potential patron, like any other influential figure connected with the government.'

It is true that this judgement could not be applied without reservation to all of Ambrose's letters for their content usually marks them as distinctly un-Symmachean, but in talk about friendship and love Ambrose does combine the ancient concept of friendship with Christian love: this enables him to use expressions associated with pagan society in a Christian context. Although he emphasises the spiritual aspect of friendship as when he says he is of one heart with Felix[21] or that letters can unite men's minds or that love enables one to be spiritually united with a dead friend, this does not mean that he has been able to free himself from an attitude to friendship which is more characteristic of a pagan than a Christian and rather surprising in a man who took such an uncompromising stance against pagan worship. But Ambrose is able to assimilate the pagan view and to see Christian love largely in terms of the traditional idea of friendship.

That this is the case appears to be corroborated by the fact that Ambrose regards human love, even among Christians, as a purely human relationship which, though a support in this life and a source of joy, is not directly connected with man's love for God. Instead of bringing man closer to God, human love is usually seen as potentially destructive of the all-important relationship between man and God. If Ambrose had freed himself from the traditional view of friendship he might have been able to have a more positive attitude to human love, considering the connection between the two parts of Christ's commandment to love (Matt.22:37–9) on which Augustine, for example, lays so much stress. In his letters Ambrose often reminds his addressees, for whose spiritual welfare he is above all concerned, that the duty of a Christian is not primarily to other men but to God.[22] In a letter to his clergy (Ep.81 = 58 B.) Ambrose interprets the words of Eccl.4:9–10, 'Two are better than one, because they have good reward for their hardship. For if they fall, one will lift up his fellow, but woe to him who is alone when he falls', as meaning that it is best to have Christ as one's constant companion rather than relying on the help of mortal friends, in contrast to other writers who use this text in support of a positive view of human friendship. And in his interpretation of Moses' words at Exod.32:37, a passage which he discusses in Ep.66 (87 B.) to Romulus, Ambrose writes that the fact that Moses arranged for friends to be killed by friends, sons by fathers and brothers by brothers shows clearly that religious ties are more important than family ones; true piety is that which prefers the divine to the human, the eternal to the temporal. Of course it would be strange for a Christian to stress human love at the expense of love of God, and warnings against too great an affection for friends are frequent in Christian writers. But Ambrose, though admitting that friendship is to be cultivated by Christians, does not seem able to adapt all that he accepted about friendship from pagan philosophy to Christian doctrine in a positive way. Because he regarded friendship largely in terms of certain duties and obligations to be repaid with interest by friends, he could see all too clearly the danger of these human obligations coming into conflict with man's duty to God.

Other references to friendship in Ambrose's works, though not numerous, confirm our belief that he was very familiar with Classical thought on the subject but that he accepted it only as far as it was loosely compatible with Christian theology.[23] On the occasions when he mentions friendship in his theological works he does not regard it in terms of the human relationship itself but merely as an analogy with the even greater unity of the Trinity. His attitude stresses the gap between human and divine and it is probably legitimate to see this as a reaction against the Arians, who denied the true divinity of Jesus Christ and whom he often attacks specifically; nevertheless, the similarities between human and divine can help us to understand the divine relationship. In his work *De fide* (1.2.18) Ambrose writes, after alluding to Acts 4:32 and 1 Cor.6:27, 'If Scripture says of men that many became as one. . .how much more true is it that the Father and the Son are one in their divinity, between whom there is no distinction either of substance or of will.' Later in the same work (4.7.74) Ambrose applies the well-known definition of friendship given by Sallust in his work on the Catilinarian conspiracy (20.4),'to share the same likes and dislikes' to the unity of will between the Father, Son and Holy Spirit. The traditional language of human friendship is also used in a similar theological passage in the work on the Holy Spirit: here Ambrose writes that there is often agreement of will between men and such agreement has meant that when someone was asked for the definition of a friend, he replied,'A second self'. Ambrose goes on to say that the extreme closeness implied by the expression 'A friend is a second self' is actually exceeded by the intimacy between the three persons of the Trinity, and again he refers to Sallust's definition.

Finally, in the work he wrote about widows[24] Ambrose refers to the saying 'Friends hold all things in common', attributed to Pythagoras, when he writes,'If one of the pagans said that friends ought to hold all things in common, how much more ought those who are related to each other to hold things in common? For we are all related to each other because we are joined in one body.' Here he does seem to be taking a step away from the traditional saying concerning friendship. He accepts the truth of it but then allows his thought to develop from it, moving from the accepted view of friendship to a view of the relation between members of the body of Christ. What is true of friendship is all the more true of relationships within the Christian community. But once again Ambrose is using the traditional ideas to express his view of Christian relationships, making the similarities between them far more obvious than the differences and showing that he found much of pagan thought acceptable to Christians without the need to transform or reject it.

CHAPTER 8

St Jerome

He and I were together right from our tender infancy until we grew up: we were suckled by the same nurses and lovingly carried in the same arms. And when we had completed our studies at Rome, we shared lodgings and ate our food together on the semi-barbarous banks of the Rhine.

Love cannot be bought, affection is priceless and friendship which can cease cannot have been genuine.

These extracts from one of Jerome's early letters[1] show that friendship was something of which he had intense experience and which he valued highly in his youth; yet this is a view of him which is easily obscured by his later experiences and writings, offering a portrait of this brilliant but difficult man as one suspicious, sensitive and closed to the charms of friendship, a man for whom the saying 'Loyalty is rare among men'[2] became as it were a personal motto. Throughout his life, it would seem, Jerome was able to engage in close relationships only with people who were willing to show him due respect and who would not contradict him. Woe betide anyone who criticised Jerome or refused to fit in with his way of thinking! But as a young man, at home in Stridon (in what is probably now Croatia), while studying at Rome, and then at Trier (one of the new cities of imperial residence) and Aquileia, Jerome was surrounded by a number of close friends who apparently shared his interests and his way of life, men such as Bonosus (the friend referred to in the first quotation above), Heliodorus, Rufinus, Chromatius and the aristocratic Pammachius.[3] Already at this time, it appears, they were all Christians, though their dedication to the faith was to increase only gradually. Jerome claims that it was during his stay at Trier in the 360s, while living with Bonosus, that he decided to devote himself to Christ;[4] he and his friend agreed to renounce their wordly ambitions in favour of a life of religious *otium* to be spent in study, discussion and contemplation. On his return to Aquileia Jerome found that several of his friends had also adopted the ascetic life and for a time he joined their circle, until suddenly the group broke up for some reason and scattered – Jerome to Antioch and then into the desert of Chalcis, Bonosus to an inhospitable island off the Dalmatian coast to lead a rigorously ascetic life, Heliodorus to Jerusalem and Rufinus to Egypt, leaving behind Chromatius.[5]

Jerome's friendships with these men did however continue for a while as is demonstrated by the affectionate – if stylistically overblown – letters he wrote to Rufinus (Ep.3), Heliodorus (Ep.14) and Chromatius, Eusebius and Jovinus (Ep.7) during the years 375–7 which he spent at Antioch and in the desert. He calls Rufinus his 'dearest friend', expressing his bitter regret at being unable to join his friend in the Egyptian desert because of recurrent illness, as well as lavishing affection and praise on other members of their circle: Innocentius (to whom he refers in the Horatian phrase, 'part of my soul'),[6] Evagrius of Antioch (who translated Athanasius' influential biography of Antony into Latin and who came into conflict with Basil over the succession of bishops at Antioch),[7] Heliodorus and above all, Bonosus. Jerome exhorts Rufinus to maintain their friendship steadfastly despite their separation – let it not be a case of 'out of sight, out of mind' – and concludes his letter with the famous eulogy of friendship from which the second quotation was taken, with its allusion to Cicero's succinct statement that true friendships are eternal. All this is ironic in view of the way their friendship developed, or rather, turned to implacable enmity some twenty years later.

But although Jerome passionately hoped to be able to share his ascetic life with Rufinus or Heliodorus (who did at least visit him briefly in Antioch), it was alone that he set off for the desert where he stayed for two or three years spent in study and prayer, with occasional visits from Evagrius to temper his solitude and act as postman. His letters at this period show how much he missed his friends and depended on their rare letters; they also reveal, in Kelly's words, 'his prickly readiness to take offence' and 'his rapid switches from bitter self-reproach to self-righteous indignation', characteristics which will be evident again and again in his relations with others. He did presumably keep in contact with Heliodorus who soon became bishop of Altinum, though it is unlikely that they met again: from the mid-390s we have a letter to Heliodorus' nephew, encouraging him in the adoption of the ascetic life, and a letter to Heliodorus consoling him on the nephew's death shortly after.

Although Rufinus settled at Jerusalem, which Jerome visited in 385 before himself settling permanently at nearby Bethlehem, there is no firm indication that Jerome and Rufinus met again[8] even before the serious deterioration in their relations. And yet at this stage their lives had in fact taken a parallel course once again, with both men founding monasteries in the Holy Land in the company of an aristocratic Roman woman, Rufinus with Melania, Jerome with Paula; and it seems unlikely that their paths did not cross, considering the close links between Jerusalem and Bethlehem. It may well be that because they were living so close, they did not need to write letters although these might have provided evidence of the nature of their relations at this time. But as Jerome devoted himself ever more seriously to Biblical translation and exegesis, he was exposed to much criticism. He seems to have felt particularly chagrined by the criticisms of Rufinus who had been such an intimate friend. From the time of his undertaking of a new translation of the Old Testament from the Hebrew rather than from the Greek Septuagint to the height of the complex Origenist controversy in which Jerome and Rufinus became deeply embroiled, the often veiled but always breath-takingly savage attacks on his former friend, with accusations of intellectual simplicity, ignorance, heresy, sensuality and malice, become increasingly frequent in Jerome's writings, and apart from a brief attempt at reconciliation in 397 and the diplomatic efforts of Chromatius, culminate in the second and third books of the Apology Jerome wrote in 401 and 402[9] in reply to the attacks he had heard that Rufinus had made on him in his Apology against Jerome. Any hope of reconciliation was now lost, and yet the break between the friends could perhaps have been avoided if Jerome's friend Pammachius had forwarded to Rufinus the relatively friendly letter Jerome had written; instead, Rufinus was provoked by the public letter (Ep.84) which Pammachius and Oceanus had circulated. Certainly, Augustine in a letter to Jerome probably written in 404, laments the rift between the pair of friends famous throughout Christendom (Jerome Ep.110 = Aug.Ep.73.6). And so the person of whom Jerome had written in 375 (Ep.4) that he was bound to him by the closest bonds of brotherly love was now repeatedly abused as a grunting pig, a scorpion etc., even after Rufinus' death.

And yet, amidst the virulent abuse we find startling denials on Jerome's part of any desire to harm his former friend and occasional nostalgic remarks about perfect friendships.[10] Perhaps Jerome believed himself to be sincere, but it is interesting to note that the same attitude is expressed with regard to other relationships, notably with Augustine: their friendship had developed slowly through their correspondence (for they were never to meet despite both being in Rome in 383, some ten years before their correspondence began) but threatened to miscarry a number of times because of Jerome's sensitivity to criticism. His Ep.102 was written after he had received Augustine's Ep.67 in which the bishop of Hippo again questioned Jerome's interpretation of a passage of Paul's letter to the Galatians which had a bearing on questions of Scriptural authority and expressed his doubts as to the validity of Jerome's new translation of the Old Testament from the Hebrew rather than from the Greek Septuagint: Jerome's anger is thinly veiled by sarcasm and irony and he cunningly encloses the third book of his work against Rufinus with his letter, presumably partly as a warning to Augustine as to what might happen to their friendship if the criticism does not cease! While Augustine regarded Jerome as at fault in his attitude for not being more amenable to friendly rebuke, Jerome attacked Augustine for lack of openness in apparently criticising him behind his back – unfortunately one of Augustine's earlier letters to him (Ep.40) had been diverted to Rome and had been widely read there instead of reaching Jerome privately at Bethlehem; Jerome only came to hear of Augustine's criticisms at second-hand which irritated him enormously. If Jerome portrays himself as an old man, unfairly attacked by the young upstart from North Africa, Augustine in his next letter (Ep.73) shows that he felt that Jerome was jeopardising their friendship by taking offence at Augustine's Ep.40 and by trying to cause offence in his Ep.102.

With one man, however, Jerome did manage to maintain a relatively cloud-free relationship over a number of years and that was with Pammachius, the Christian aristocrat to whom six (two jointly with other friends) of Jerome's extant letters are addressed.[11] They had already become friends during their student days at Rome, possibly in the early 350s but it seems that they then lost contact for many years after Jerome moved away from the centre of the Empire to its northern borders. Their friendship resumed when Jerome received a letter (no longer extant) from his 'fellow student, companion and friend': in Ep.48, written from Bethlehem in 393 Jerome expresses his pleasure at hearing from Pammachius though he had not dared to contact Pammachius for fear of appearing importunate. Pammachius and his friends appealed to Jerome to refute the views on monasticism and marriage held by a certain Jovinian and Jerome complied with their wishes although it meant that he became embroiled in yet another controversy which was to make him the object of much criticism. But Pammachius remained loyal throughout all these controversies, even encouraging Jerome in his attacks on Rufinus during the dispute about Origen.[12] From now on until his death in 410 Pammachius acted as Jerome's literary agent in Rome, publishing his works and attempting to manipulate the public reaction to them or persuading Jerome to make certain alterations. In return Jerome acted as Pammachius' spiritual adviser, foster-

ing his study of the Scriptures, praising him for his asceticism
and the charitable works to which he devoted himself after the
death of his wife Paulina.[13]

In the passionate and satirical attack on Jovinian written at
Pammachius' instigation, Jerome allows himself to indulge in a
certain amount of anti-feminist polemic, largely based on a lost
treatise of Theophrastus, in connection with his characteristically exaggerated depiction of marriage as inferior to chastity.[14]
And yet it would seem that in his own life Jerome was much
happier in his relations with women – as long as they had
devoted themselves to a life of chastity in accordance with
Jerome's views – for it is likely that he regarded them as less of a
threat than men. If the co-operative and supportive Pammachius was to be one of Jerome's few long-term male friends, his
closest relationship, which lasted from the early 380s until her
death in 404, was with Pammachius' mother-in-law Paula of
whom Jerome said that she was the only woman who gave him
pleasure.[15] After leaving the desert Jerome had gone to Constantinople (where he became acquainted with Gregory of
Nazianzus, now bishop of that city, and Basil's brother Gregory
of Nyssa) and thence to Rome where, during his three years in
that city (383–5), his circle of friends widened to include a
number of aristocratic women, mostly widows who had
renounced the idea of remarriage in favour of the ascetic life.
Among his extant letters about one-fifth are addressed to
women, most of them concerned with Scriptural problems and
with exhortations to chastity, either as an alternative to marriage (and it should be remembered that there were strong
family pressures on high-born women to marry and produce
heirs) or after widowhood (which could occur at a very early
age). But since many of these friendships were maintained by
means of personal meetings focussing on shared study and
worship under Jerome's guidance, there was not so much need
for letters and therefore the usual evidence for such relationships is largely lacking. And despite the enormous importance
of these friendships to Jerome for the rest of his life and the great
respect he had for them, he does not theorise about the
possibility of friendship with women. Nevertheless it is clear

that his admiration for them was based on the hard choices
they made in favour of chastity and the renunciation of family
ties,[16] on their devotion to the study of Scripture, their charitable use of their great wealth[17] and their ascetic lives which
were in sharp contrast to the lives of luxury in which most of
them had been brought up:[18] in other words, he loved them for
their dedication to his ideals. In his Ep.24 Jerome presents us
with a picture of the perfect woman in his eyes when he gives a
lengthy eulogy of Asella and in Ep.45, in a letter to Asella, he
describes how his relationships with these women deepened
into friendships: 'Our studies meant that we spent a lot of time
together and this fact meant that we got to know each other
well and this in turn led to mutual trust.'[19]

But it was to Paula and Marcella, both widows of illustrious
birth, and to Paula's daughter Eustochium that Jerome was
closest. Marcella had been attracted to the ascetic life from
childhood after coming under the influence of Athanasius of
Alexandria, briefly exiled in Rome; when her husband died
after seven months of marriage she adopted a life of moderate
asceticism, collecting around her a number of like-minded
women including Ambrose's sister Marcellina and Marcella's
relative Paula, who had also chosen a life of renunciation after
bearing five children and then being widowed. When these
women heard that Jerome had arrived in Rome they were very
keen to be taught by one whose reputation for asceticism and
learning was already high and some of whose letters (e.g. Ep.14
to Heliodorus) they had already read. Soon he became the
focus of their lives as their spiritual and intellectual mentor,
praying with them, commenting on the Bible and teaching
them Hebrew so that they could sing the psalms and read the
Old Testament in the original language. Their admiration for
him was soon reciprocated by his respect for them, a feeling no
doubt accompanied by flattery that these aristocratic women
should admire and support him so strongly. Unfortunately this
pleasure was later vitiated by the rumours of intimacy with
Paula which was one of the things which tarnished Jerome's
name and made him enemies in Rome, rumours which he
bitterly rebuts in his letter to Asella (Ep.45) written when he

left Rome for the Holy Land. But despite these rumours Jerome maintained his friendships with these two women. Paula with great pain left her young son Toxotius[20] and her daughter Paulina and joined Jerome in the Holy Land where she set up a monastery for women in conjunction with Jerome's monastery, and led a life of great fortitude and asceticism. Marcella remained at Rome, keeping the spirit of monasticism alive there, helping to arrange for the condemnation of Origen in the West and continuing to correspond with Jerome until her death as a result of injuries sustained during the sack of Rome in 410.[21]

A number of his letters to Marcella still remain and further evidence for their continuing friendships is provided by the fact that he dedicated many of his Scriptural works to these women, addressing them in the prefaces to these works,[22] mainly commentaries on the Bible which continued to feed their interests even after the group of friends was split up while also being aimed at a wider audience. Although many of the letters take the form of minor treatises on Scriptural problems,[23] some do contain more personal remarks, as when Jerome excuses himself to Marcella in Ep.32 for only writing her a short letter: he imagines her asking indignantly, 'What can be more important than a chat on paper?', to which he replies that he has not time to write as long a letter as he would like because he is so busy comparing Aquila's Greek translation of the Old Testament with the Hebrew original to see whether the Jews have changed anything for anti-Christian reasons. To make up for the brevity of his letter he encloses two letters which he had already written to their mutual friends Paula and Eustochium! Here is an extreme example of how a belief in the unity of the body of Christ affecting the network of close friends worked in practice, allowing the same letter to apply to different friends.[24] In Ep.127 in which he commemorates her life, he tells of how, when they were separated after his departure from Rome, they consoled each other by words of mutual encouragement. Since they were denied the enjoyment of one another's physical presence, they maintained their friendship in the spirit, continually meeting in their letters, vying with each other in doing favours and anticipating each other's greetings. Thus their friendship hardly suffered for they were able to maintain contact by constant correspondence.

His feelings for these two women come out most clearly in the two letters he wrote to console other friends of his for their deaths – to Eustochium on her mother Paula's death in 404 (Ep.108) and to Principia on Marcella's death (Ep.127). He writes to Eustochium:

> I have spent two nights dictating this treatise for you and in so doing I have felt a grief as deep as your own. I say 'in dictating' for I have not been able to write it myself. Whenever I picked up my pen and tried to fulfil my promise, my fingers have stiffened, my hand has fallen and my power over it has vanished,

while to Principia he excuses himself for his long silence after Marcella's death by saying, 'that I have allowed two years to pass without speaking has not been due to any wish to repress my feelings, as you wrongly think, but rather to my incredible grief which has so overwhelmed my mind that I judge it better to remain silent for the moment than produce something unworthy of her fame.' In rejecting marriage and the claims of their immediate family and supporting the cause of Jerome or those causes which he supported, these women were proving – at least to Jerome – the truth of something he wrote in his argument against marriage to Jovinian, namely that friends and relatives whom you can love judiciously are better and safer than those whom you must make your heirs whether you like it or not.[25]

In this connection one of his greatest triumphs was his persuasion of Paula's daughter Eustochium, in her early teens, to devote her life to Christ instead of to an earthly husband; in fact, she seems to have devoted her life to Jerome as well as to Christ, for with her mother she left Rome and joined Jerome at Bethlehem where she lived near him for the remaining thirty-three or so years of her life, leading a life of seclusion, asceticism and Biblical study in accordance with Jerome's ideals for women. It is hardly surprising that Jerome was able to maintain close friendships which survived the strains of daily life with such supportive and obedient companions as Paula and Eustochium, but it is unfortunate that we know nothing of their views of the relationship for this would undoubtedly give us a clearer picture of their own strong characters – and strong they must have been to endure the renunciations and rigours which they voluntarily took upon themselves. But their devotion to Jerome and his harsh ideals (thought by many, even at the time, to be excessively severe) perhaps gives us the key to the problem of reconciling his negative attitude to women, expressed in many of his works, with the love and admiration he felt for these aristocratic ascetics. Although women are created to exist on a lower level than men, they can attain a measure of equality with men by renouncing those aspects of their lives which are particular to their sex, such as the bearing and rearing of children. It is also possible that Jerome was impressed by the high birth and wealth of these women and was flattered by their attentions, so that their lofty social status served to moderate, as it were, the general lowliness of the female sex.

But if Jerome experienced more problems with friendship than most and is known more for his enemies that for his friends, it is nevertheless true that we have in his writings a rich source of Classical sayings about friendship for, as we might expect considering his fascination with Classical literature, he was well acquainted with vast quantities of writings, many of which are no longer extant. His knowledge of pagan philosophy may not have been very profound and his thoughts on friendship based on a pot-pourri of Classical ideas rather than offering anything impressively original, for his interests were not so much philosophical as philological, but the manner in which he refers to traditional thoughts is interesting in that it provides confirmation of Jerome's continued devotion to Classical sources[26] and of his unusually negative attitude to friendship. It is as if Jerome never found in Christianity a wholly satisfactory substitute for the wealth of popular wisdom, elegantly expressed, with which his study of Classical literature had made him familiar and which provided him with a thought-world which suited him.

We have seen how, in the early Ep.3 to Rufinus, Jerome refers to Cicero's words from the *Laelius*, 'True friendships last forever' when he concludes with, 'A friendship which can cease was never genuine' and to Horace's phrase when he refers to Innocentius as 'part of my soul'. In the same letter he quotes from Plautus (*Pseudolus* 179), 'Where are those men to whom you are the apple of their eye?' while in Ep.7, written jointly to Chromatius, Eusebius and Jovinus, Jerome plays with imagery expressing the unity of the friends which was such a common topos in ancient literature. The letter begins:

A written page should not divide those who are united by a mutual love and so I must not divide between you individually the words which I owe to you all together. Two of you, as brothers, are already natural partners, but so strong is the love which you feel for one another that affection unites the three of you as closely as nature unites the two.

In a short letter to Niceas of Aquileia (Ep.8) Jerome quotes with approval the sententious statement of Turpilius (the writer of comedies of whose works only a few fragments remain, but who is referred to by Servius in his commentary on Virgil which may support the view that his work was still available in the fourth century), to the effect that a letter is the only thing which makes friends present to each other even when they are separated ('quae homines absentes praesentes facit'). He jokingly tries to provoke Niceas to write to him, warning that in leaving Jerome he is in danger of tearing apart their friendship, 'something which Laelius, in Cicero's work, sensibly warns against': here Jerome presumably has in mind *Lael.*21.76–7. Another echo of the *Laelius* is found in a letter to Augustine (Ep.105) in which Jerome writes pointedly that one should be able to talk to a friend as to a second self; he does not mention Cicero here but it is likely that his view is influenced by Laelius' rhetorical question (6.22), 'What is more delightful than to have someone with whom you can discuss everything as with yourself?'

Sallust's famous definition of firm friendship is alluded to in a letter to the young girl Demetrias (Ep.130) whom Jerome is predictably urging to remain a virgin dedicated to Christ; he also advises her to submit herself to the wishes of her mother and aunt, in this context reminding her of the 'wordly saying that firm friendship is based on shared likes and dislikes'. In the third book of his work against Rufinus Jerome does mention that this saying comes from Sallust's work on the Catilinarian conspiracy when he pleads with his former friend, 'If we believe in the same thing and wish for the same things and reject the same things (the basis of strong friendships, as is stated in the Catiline)... why do we strive against one another?' In the same work Jerome mentions Pythagorean doctrines, including the two which were fundamental to Classical thought about friendship, namely that friends hold everything in common and that a friend is a second self.

In fact it is clear that Jerome is not only familiar with a wide range of popular ideas about friendships but that he uses mainly those which support his bitter, suspicious attitude towards friendship or those which portray an ideal friendship which, he feels, he is forced to fall short of because of the treachery of his supposed friends. A favourite theme is the bitter observation that criticism and friendship are incompatible. In the dialogue against the Pelagians (1.26) Jerome quotes both St Paul's words at Gal.4:16,'Have I then become your enemy by telling you the truth?' and the line from Terence's *Andria*, also quoted by Cicero in the *Laelius*,'Flattery makes friends, truth engenders hatred.' This same line is also referred to in Jerome's commentary on Galatians where he compares it again with Gal.4:16, this time adding some personal comments of his own:

This is similar to that view expressed by the noble Roman poet who says,'Flattery makes friends, truth engenders hatred'. But consider how much better St Paul expresses it. For the apostle moderates what he says to those whom he has referred to as stupid and little children and makes it specially appropriate to them, and he directs his comments particularly at the Galatians. The Roman poet, on the other hand, is wrong to make a general statement, accusing everyone of this. For flattery which, according to him, makes friends, if it is devoid of any truth is not so much devoted allegiance as cringing and fawning, which clearly ought to be termed hidden enmity rather than friendship.[27]

Such allusions are perhaps most common in his letters to Augustine to whom he was keen to show off his learning (in Ep. 102 he writes, 'If I may say so with respect, I do not wish people to think that you are the only one who can quote from the poets') and whom he felt to be endangering their friendship by being over-sensitive to criticism – and yet the truth was that it was Jerome who could not allow his friends free speech. In the same letter he quotes from Persius when he writes to Augustine, 'I am not so foolish as to be offended if your interpretations differ from mine; neither should you feel offended if I hold a different opinion. What is truly reprehensible behaviour between friends is, as Persius writes, to look carefully at the bag carried by others but to disregard your own.' Jerome chose to use a Classical expression even though he might have referred to Matt. 7:3, 'Why do you see the speck that is in your brother's eye, but do not notice the beam that is in your own eye?' to illustrate this idea.

A similar obsession with the danger to friendship of dissension is found in the works addressed to Rufinus after their friendship had shattered on the rocks of suspected heresy – a constant threat to Christian friendships. In the opening chapter of his work against Rufinus he refers with approbation to Cicero's advice – in a commentary now lost – on how to protect friendships which threaten to break up, advice which he clearly thinks ought to be effective in the case of their own relationship: he addresses Rufinus thus:

It would have been the mark of a sensible man and of a friend, after the reconciliation of differences, to have avoided even the slightest indications of suspicion lest it appear that he had done with deliberation what he had done through accident. Whence also Cicero says in commenting on his reasons for defending Gabinius, 'I have always been of the opinion that all friendships must be guarded very religiously and faithfully, and in particular those friendships that have been restored to good standing after a falling out. For any failure to do one's duty while friendship is intact is excused as being due to folly or, more harshly, to neglect; but if such a mistake is made after the reconciliation, it is interpreted not as neglect but as a violation of that friendship, and put down to treachery rather than folly.'[28]

But even in those writings where he is not concerned with his own problems and with specific relationships, Jerome often offers general moral advice on the value of concord or the question of outspokenness versus flattery, alluding to Classical examples even in Scriptural exegetical discussion, as in the commentary on Galatians referred to above. In his commentary on Matthew, for example, Jerome recalls the story of the Pythagoreans Damon and Phintias in order to illustrate the value of peace and harmony among men, with reference to Christ's words at Matt.18:19,'If two of you agree on earth about anything they ask, it will be done for them by my Father in heaven.' But he does not just mention it but gives the well-known story a spiritual interpretation, applying it to the harmony of will between body and soul: if you can achieve such harmony, God will grant everything you ask.

The story of the Pythagorean friends is mentioned also in the commentary on Micah and in fact the passage discussing the prophet's words,'Do not put your trust in a friend' (Micah 7:5) is the most important text for our knowledge of which Classical ideas and writings concerning friendship Jerome was familiar with, providing us also with a more coherent picture of his own attitudes. First he explains that there will come a time when friendship is impossible: this will be at the Day of Judgement. It is true, he says, that God's warning against friendship does not apply to all friends and to all times, but, his argument goes, even now true friendship is rare for men are devious and untrustworthy. He warns against those types of friendship which occur for the sake of a third thing (i.e. for something other than the friend himself) for in such cases the friend will love this thing more than he loves his friend. It is interesting that for Plato in the *Lysis* a form of friendship based on a third thing was regarded as the best and most stable kind while Jerome takes it as dangerous and vulnerable.

He then digresses from the text in hand and continues by mentioning various ideas of friendship with which he is familiar. For example, he refers to the belief, familiar from Cicero, that the word *amicus* is derived from *amor* and also speaks of the idea of a friend as a second self. Although he does not here refer to Damon and Phintias by name, he mentions their story when he imagines someone objecting to his negative attitude to friendship and giving the example of the positive value attached to friendship in this story. Jerome, however, refuses to renouce his negative view. To reinforce the legitimacy of his attitude he quotes further Biblical warnings against friendship from 2 Tim. 3:1–4 and Matt.10: 35–6 as well as referring to the pagan observation, 'Trust is rare', though he does not mention his source. Another argument used is the familiar one that although a rich man may have many friends, a poor man finds himself deserted: here Jerome appositely quotes Sir.6:7, 'If you want to make a friend, take him on trial.' Again he finds Biblical support for ideas familiar from Classical literature, in the manner of Ambrose.

Jerome's investigation continues with a quotation of the statement which he had cited at the end of Ep.3, 'It takes a long time to find a friend, it is hard to find one and difficult to keep him.' Here he adds the vague information that he found it 'in some rhetorical debate (*controversia*) or other', indicating that it is not his own formulation but leaving it unidentified. He is equally vague when alluding to the Aristotelian idea that two friends form one soul – Jerome says merely that he read it somewhere. But he is more precise when he refers to the work on friendship by Theophrastus[29] for he tells us that this philosopher wrote a work in three books on friendship, putting friendship before love, but arguing that it is rarely found in human society. No wonder Theophrastus found favour with Jerome! It is not clear whether this work was available in Jerome's day or whether he had learned of it from the information provided by Aulus Gellius in his *Attic Nights*.

As in Ep.3 Jerome had referred to the expression of a friend as 'part of my soul', so in the commentary on Micah he quotes directly Horace's phrase from the ode to Virgil[30] where his friend is described as 'half of my soul': Jerome refers to Horace merely as 'lyricus'. Cicero's *Laelius* is however referred to by name when he sets out a few indications of the essential agreement between pagan and Christian or Biblical: he has noticed the similarity between what Cicero says about old

friends at *Lael*.18.67 and a passage in Ecclesiasticus (9.15), 'A
new friend is like a new wine: let it mature and then you can
drink it with pleasure.' But Jerome does venture to move on
from stating the similarities to adding some peculiarly Christian advice on friendship when he says that if a Christian wishes
to partake of that true friendship of which Cicero speaks so
elegantly, it is necessary to be a friend of God as Moses was, as
alluded to in Exodus 33:11, and to emulate the relationship
which Christ had with his disciples. Here, like other Christian
writers discussing friendship, Jerome quotes John 15:15 to show
what Christ's criteria for friendship were. Thus it may be seen
that if Jerome's attitude to the possibility of friendship was on
the whole a negative one, his attitude to the Classical ideas was
positive for he was not afraid to accept them as accurate
observations on this aspect of human behaviour. Although his
interest in them was perhaps primarily academic, he did also
make use of them in his more personal writings and they do
appear to have influenced his own view of friendship (indeed,
as with his attacks on wordly women, his attitude to friendship
was determined more by pagan tradition than by personal
experience), even though he became increasingly sceptical of
the great value attached to friendship in antiquity.

Such wariness is reflected also in his attitude to the related
subject of monasticism for unlike many others and despite his
interest in the subject[31] Jerome shows no marked preference for
the coenobitic over the life of solitude. The ascetic life was a
matter of spiritual warfare which could best be waged in
solitude: to have people around one was just a nuisance.
Admittedly the solitary life is more difficult and dangerous,
allowing the monk to become a prey to pride; it is therefore
sensible for the monk to learn the ascetic life within a community before graduating to the ideal form of monastic life.[32]

Even when Jerome comments on the text of Ps.132(133):1,
he does not take the opportunity to compose a panegyric on the
coenobitic life, although he does mention some of the texts and
ideas which we might expect to find in this context such as the
reference to Acts 4:32 and its connection with 1 Cor.13:5. But
his general interpretation is unusual in that he takes the first

verse of this psalm to refer to the difference, in Jerome's time, between the monasteries and the Church as a whole. In the monasteries one can find complete concord while in the comtemporary Church, unlike in the early Christian community at Jerusalem, people unfortunately have various, and often conflicting, aims.

And so we see that, although Jerome considered community life to have a part to play in the development of the ascetic, he favoured the solitary life as offering greater opportunities for renunciation which was essential to his stark view of monastic life, more so than the ideal of charity. And yet his early experience of solitude and hardship in the desert had not been a very successful or fulfilling experience and when he came to settle in Bethlehem it was in the company of Paula and Eustochium; soon he was surrounded by other devotees of the ascetic life as well as by constant visitors to the Holy Land such as Augustine's close friend Alypius who carried news of Jerome back to Augustine, thus sparking off a friendship by post which lasted for the next twenty-five years. It would appear that Jerome was caught between his theoretical devotion to renunciation and solitude and suspicion of his fellow human beings on the other hand, and a need for the support and company of a few close friends on the other hand. Bethlehem provided him with a satisfying compromise.

CHAPTER 9

Paulinus of Nola

To his contemporaries Paulinus was renowned for his renunciation of his great wealth in favour of a life of poverty and dedication to Christ, as we see from the writings of Ambrose, Augustine and Jerome[1], while to later generations and the Middle Ages the works of Gregory of Tours and Gregory of the Great made him familiar as a man of great holiness and even as a worker of miracles.[2] But if this man made a dramatic break around the year 390, when he was about thirty-five, rejecting the life of the wealthy landowner in France and Spain and high government official in Italy which he had hitherto led, in order to adopt the ascetic life at Nola in Campania,[3] there was one aspect of his life which continued to be important to Paulinus both before and after his 'conversion' to a strictly Christian life and which indeed he regarded as only reaching its fulfilment with his dedication to Christ: this was his unusually strong devotion to friendship.[4] Even in his life of retirement Paulinus managed to maintain a number of his old friendships by means of letters – visits from friends were very rare – and to develop a network of other relationships, mostly among the leading Christians of his day who were pleased to be canvassed for their friendship by someone whom they admired so much but who always treated them with great respect and humility. It would be impossible to chart the course of all Paulinus' friendships within the limits of one chapter, so I shall here concentrate on a few of his most intense relationships with the aim of showing how his view of perfect Christian friendship developed, what its characteristics were and how he attempted to practise it in his relations with others.

Although Paulinus was apparently brought up as a Christian at his family home in Aquitania, it was not until after his conversion to a life devoted exclusively to Christ that his ideas on the role of friendship in the Christian life and the all-important role of Christ in friendship were developed and came to the fore. And yet, from the evidence we have of his close relationship with the poet and professor Ausonius and with Sulpicius Severus, the historian and hagiographer of St Martin (evidence for which dates largely from the time after Paulinus' conversion but which harks back to the former days of their friendship), it is clear that friendship played an important part in his life from an early period. It would seem that Ausonius and Paulinus became friends despite the large age gap between them because of a connection between their families and because of a shared interest in Classical poetry and in writing verse. Ausonius, although not Paulinus' official teacher, influenced him by encouraging his literary talents and by assisting him in his career. Their affectionate relationship continued over many years, even when Ausonius moved to Augusta Trevirorum (Trier) as tutor to the future emperor Gratian and Paulinus was serving in Italy in various administrative capacities. It was only when Paulinus made the decision to reject everything which could not be seen as intimately connected with his Christian aims that problems arose for their friendship.

Of their extant letters to each other which form the only documentation as to the course of their relationship,[5] epistles 17–20 from Ausonius to Paulinus seem to have been written while the addressee was still in Aquitania on his family estates. Any reply which Paulinus may have written to these minor, artificial literary productions is now lost. Full of literary allusions and conceits as they are, they tell us little of the nature of their friendship apart from indicating the friends' shared interest in poetry. In Ep.19.24–5, however, Ausonius does refer to himself as 'your friend and neighbour and supporter' and goes on,'Call me your teacher, your parent and any sacred and flattering name indicative of my affection for you', lines which do give some idea of how they viewed their relations; while in

Ep.20 Ausonius addresses Paulinus as his son which was appropriate considering the wide age difference between them.

Such hints in their earlier letters are supported by what we find in the letters written after Paulinus' move to Spain, after his baptism but before he made the decisive move to Nola with his wife Therasia. The chronology of these letters is not certain but it would seem that Ausonius, worried by his friend's move and his silence, wrote four letters (two of which are lost, the other two being nos.21 and 22 in the collection) before he received a reply. In these Epp.21 and 22 (probably written in 391 and 393 respectively) Ausonius complains that he is being treated with a lack of respect and blames Therasia for the change in the friends' relations. Pleading with Paulinus not to scorn him – for is he not as a father to him – he reminds his friend of his obligations towards the man who educated him and first introduced him to the Muses. These desperate attempts to solicit some form of greeting were finally successful, for Ausonius appears to have received Paulinus' tenth poem in the course of 393. In this verse-letter of 331 lines Paulinus defends himself against Ausonius' charges of neglected friendship and explains the change which has recently come upon him, involving total allegiance to Christ. This is why he can no longer devote himself to what he now regards as the trivialities of the Muses though, he assures Ausonius, he will not cease to use the poetic talents nurtured by his friend for more serious subjects. Furthermore, he tries to explain that his devotion to Christ does not mean that he has no room for love of Ausonius; indeed, the very fact that he is now wholly committed to Christ implies that he loves his friend more strongly than ever, for 'how can a Christian be without love?'[6] and it is God's will that Paulinus feel filial affection towards Ausonius. Paulinus ends the iambic section of this letter by emphasising his gratitude to his friend on so many accounts, thereby attempting to mollify the older man's wounded feelings but also indicating that their friendship was really an unequal one, in which Paulinus owed respect and gratitude in return for Ausonius' guidance and encouragement: that Paulinus regarded Ausonius as his patron, teacher and father, as is clear from this letter, is significant for our comprehension of their relationship which, though very affectionate on both sides, contains more than a hint of the traditional forms of Roman patronage with its formal obligations on either side, alongside the affection and respect (*pietas*) as between father and son which is a constant theme of their letters. This patronage-type of relationship may have been one with which Paulinus was familiar having worked in the conservative circles of government administration with their formality and traditional rules of etiquette and may have suited him particularly for, even after his conversion, when one might suppose that Christianity would rid all friendships of inequality, his relations with such men as Augustine and Jerome are coloured by his sense of these men's superiority to himself.[7]

In the section of his tenth verse-epistle composed in hexameters Paulinus is not afraid to stress again how much he has changed or rather been changed by God who has made him see the truth but he does not regard this as a reason for their friendship to cease: instead, Ausonius should feel pride that his spiritual and intellectual son should have also become the child of Christ. But Paulinus goes on to break the news to his friend that he is in fact about to reject everything that has provided a bond between them, everything that conflicts with Christ's will, not only worldly poetry but also public affairs, so as to devote himself whole-heartedly to contemplation and the service of Christ. One can understand that this came as a shock to Ausonius, especially as Paulinus ends his verse epistle in mildly defiant terms, protesting that he is not lacking in *pietas* but warning that if Ausonius fails to understand his friend's new position, then he must leave Paulinus to win approval from Christ alone.

Ausonius' reaction to the uncompromising stance adopted by his friend is one of incomprehension and sadness. He accuses Paulinus of throwing off the yoke uniting them as equals in friendship, using an image familiar from antiquity, for despite his friend's rejection of his devotion to Classical literature Ausonius continues to allude to pagan myths in this poem, drawing comparisons between their friendship up till now and those of Orestes and Pylades, Nisus and Euryalus, Theseus and Peirithous, Damon and Phintias and Scipio and Laelius! And yet despite his evident disappointment and his frustration at being separated from his friend, Ausonius again and again protests that his love remains firm[8] and even attempts to show that he is in agreement with Paulinus, abandoning all Classical allusions for a moment and saying that he is confident that the Father and Son can bring his friend back in answer to his prayers. He imagines eagerly that Paulinus will arrive at any moment, but the poem ends with a poignant quotation of the penultimate line of Virgil's eighth Eclogue: Ausonius' hope does not last long.

It is likely that Paulinus' eleventh poem was written in reply to Ausonius' Ep.24, both being composed in 394. In it Paulinus again tries to defend himself and provide a convincing statement of his enduring devotion to his old friend, again using the formal language of friendship with mention of the *fides* and *officia* connecting them and the *pietas* he feels for his 'father'. He also employs the image of the yoke to praise Ausonius when he alludes to the importance traditionally attached to equality in friendship but denies that they are equals in merit, only in their love for each other.[9] The letter ends with lines of great respect and affection, lines which are not those of a man determined to break off his friendship, despite his uncompromising dedication to Christ. And yet Fabre,[10] in his desire to see a sharp distinction between Paulinus' attitude to secular and to Christian friendships believes that this long-standing friendship was finally broken off by Paulinus because Ausonius failed to understand his new commitment to Christ. But the course of their relationship after this point is unknown: no more of their correspondence survives and we cannot know what happened between them after Paulinus retired to Nola. It is true that Paulinus did feel strongly the opposition between the temporal and the eternal and that he came to believe that the only genuine friendships are those between dedicated Christians; in a letter to Severus (Ep.1.5) he writes,'Even though he be a brother and a friend and closer to you than your right hand and dearer than life itself, if he is a stranger and an enemy to

Christ, let him be to you as the heathen and the publican.' But
this did not prevent him from attempting to persuade his
mentor to reject his pagan allegiances,[11] treading a careful path
between alienating Ausonius by too dramatic a rejection of all
he had previously valued and failing to put his new point of
view across with sufficient conviction. It may be tempting to
take the simple view that, because of his rigorous attitude to the
Christian life, he would have included his uncommitted friends
in his rejection of everything that was at all tarred by the pagan
brush, but in fact his relationship with Ausonius was saved
because this strict attitude of Paulinus recommended love
above all things. Although Ausonius was apparently never
persuaded to follow his friend in his new commitment, it is
likely that their friendship came to an end not because of their
disagreement but because of Ausonius' death.

But with regard to another long-standing friend whom
Paulinus had known probably since their student days at
Bordeaux,[12] there was no need to persuade him to accept his
friend's new way of life: Ep.5 from Paulinus reveals, amidst the
numerous Biblical quotations which are such a hallmark of his
letters, that Severus made the decision to give up his work as an
advocate, sell his property and live according to the example of
his master, Martin, bishop of Tours,[13] soon after Paulinus
himself – in fact, it was Martin who had urged Severus to follow
Paulinus' example.[14] Unfortunately we know little of their
relationship before their conversions for of the thirteen letters
extant from Paulinus to Severus, all date from after Paulinus'
ordination and all but the first were written from Nola.

The first letter takes the form of a spiritual exhortation
written from Barcelona, in which Paulinus congratulates his
'most dearly beloved brother' on his positive attitude to the
spiritual life, urging him, 'Let not our feet be diverted from the
ways of the Lord or from treading the narrow path, should the
wicked or foolish voices of worldly men from time to time bark
around us' and begs him to make the journey to visit him for he
longs to see Severus and hopes that the longing is mutual. But
Severus was to visit him neither at Barcelona nor at Nola, to
Paulinus' constant disappointment, as we see from the follow-

ing letters, written to Severus in Gaul over the next few years,[15] in which Paulinus' sadness and even anger are often evident amid the repeated invitations:

I grow tired of inviting and awaiting you. I have now no prayers or words to say to add to the entreaties and letters so often and so vainly showered on you. Now that the hope of a meeting with each other is dashed, you have left but one avenue to our friendship; your words I repay with words, desiring to refresh my heart with these fruitless consolations if with no other.

And not only was Severus unable to visit his friend but his letters were also irregular and on occasion Paulinus had to wait two years[16] to receive a letter from the man who, despite the vicissitudes of their relationship, remained for many years his closest male friend.

That Paulinus did love Severus deeply is clear from many of his letters. He often addresses him as 'my dearest brother who shares one soul with me and is the better part of myself in Christ' or 'my dearest friend whom I respect and long for and who shares one soul with me', and in Ep.11 he writes to Severus,'Through you above all I experience . . .through the gift and word of God, that nothing can be compared to a faithful friend', alluding to the passage on friendship in the sixth chapter of Ecclesiasticus. Furthermore there are extant more letters from Paulinus to Severus than to any other friend: it may be that fewer of them were lost over the years but it remains true that Paulinus tried to write to his friend at every opportunity to maintain the intimacy of their previous relationship, despite his constant disappointment that Severus usually wrote to him only once a year.[17]

Severus, like Paulinus, was an aristocrat with literary interests and unlike Ausonius he was of the same generation as Paulinus and came to be a sharer of those Christian ascetic ideals upon which they believed their firm friendship to be founded. In Paulinus' letters to Severus we find the same concern with devotion to Christ above all else as in the letters to Ausonius, but here the picture which emerges is a more detailed one of the perfect friendship in Christ, based entirely on Christian doctrines with hardly a hint of Classical influence. In fact, as will be seen, his theories of Christian friendship actually overturn many of the accepted pagan theories of friendship, although Paulinus does not draw explicit attention to this. It is as if Paulinus was the most successful of all those of his contemporaries who broke with their worldly past in ridding his subsequent writings of allusions to his Classical heritage and in interpreting all aspects of his new life in terms of his relation to Christ.[18] In this he stands in contrast to Jerome who, with a similar background and education, never really freed himself from the influence of Classical literature, despite his avowals to the contrary. Although Paulinus' theories of Christian friendship are evident also in letters to other friends, it is mainly from his affectionate letters to Severus that our knowledge of these theories derives and indeed his relationship with Severus offers one of the best examples of a Christian friendship at this period. It is however a pity that Severus' letters have not survived.

Firstly, so far from feeling there to be a conflict between friendship and devotion to Christ, Paulinus believed that the love of Christian friends for each other derives from the love of Christ. Love of Christ and love of friends can therefore co-exist happily as long as the friends place Christ above all else, as Paulinus frequently urges Severus – and all his other correspondents! – to do. In fact, the friendship is strengthened by the shared devotion to Christ and it is indeed only once both friends have decided to commit themselves wholly to Christ and withdraw from the world (a necessary consequence of total commitment, so they believed) that their friendship can be truly fulfilled. This idea can be illustrated by Paulinus' words to Crispinianus urging him to renounce his worldly commitments, 'I have begun to love you as a future comrade in Christ' and by the passage in Ep.40 in which Paulinus speaks of his pre-conversion friendship with Sanctus, contrasting secular friendship with that founded in Christ's love:

For it is a long time. . .since I began to love you and I have loved you continually, though not with the love of Christ but with the friendship of human intimacy which has flattery on the lips but no roots in the heart. For the friendship not built on Christ is not founded on a rock. So from time to time it is troubled by a slight breeze and is loosened; it bears a short-lived bloom produced by some transient attraction but then it quickly withers away like grass and like the flower of the field quickly falls. But the Lord's love abides for ever. It binds us to each other both for life and death because the love of Christ is as strong as death.[19]

Related to this belief is the startling idea that Christian friendships, in such circumstances, are perfect from the start and do not need time to mature and conversely, that those Christians who have devoted themselves to a life of imitation of Christ are close friends whether they have yet come into contact or not. These ideas are in the background of what Paulinus writes to Severus and are also evident in the second letter he wrote to Augustine (Ep.6.2) where he says that since he has known Augustine through his writings and through the kindness of Augustine's friends Aurelius and Alypius,'my love for you has become so rooted in me that I seem not to be embarking on a new friendship but rather to be resuming a long standing intimacy', as well as in his first letter to Florentius, bishop of Cahors, in which he writes:

I rejoice in the Lord that the letter written by your holy person has visited me and first established the liaison between us, for previously I had not the favour of your acquaintance, and now by God's sudden kindness I have gained full assurance in your friendship as if it were of long standing. As Scripture says,'A new friend is like new wine; it shall grow old and you shall drink it with pleasure.' In fact you bettered that statement of the prophet for you have begun to love me with such perfect attention at the very outset of this friendship that you have given me the sweetness of long established love.[20]

The reasons for these striking characteristics of Christian friendship are that, according to Paulinus, they are created by God's grace and all such friends are members of one body, sharing one head, living off one bread and sharing the same house.[21] This is what distinguishes such friendships from purely secular relationships as Paulinus makes clear in his letter to Pammachius (Ep.13), describing their friendship in the following terms:

Please do not measure our friendship in terms of time. For ours is not that worldly kind of friendship which is born more often from hope than of faith, but the spiritual friendship sprung from the fatherhood of God and joined through the hidden kinship of the spirit. So it is not the experience of years by which it grows in love and it does not depend on or expect proof. Rather it should be strong and mature at its very birth like a true daughter of truth, for since it arises from Christ, it overflows at the very start.

To Eucher and Galla Paulinus writes in Ep.51:

We have become known to each other not by human friendship but by divine grace and it is by the inner depths of Christ's love that we are joined. Therefore between our hearts there must inevitably abide that perennial harmony which was joined at Christ's instigation, for what force or forgetfulness can separate what God has joined together?

In Ep.11 to Severus which has been called 'le chant de l'amitié'[22] – a description which certainly applies to the first half of the letter – Paulinus writes,'How can we pay the Lord back for this grace in addition to all that he has given me? For through his grace he has united me to you not only as a most beloved friend in our earliest life in the world but also as an inseparable companion and partner in the spiritual brotherhood of his affairs'.

For Paulinus the conviction that God creates friendship is connected with the idea that God has predestined certain men to be friends from the beginning of time. In 395 he wrote to Alypius at Thagaste that the love which united them had come from him who predestined them to be his from the beginning of the world (Ep.3). God in his prescience has formed the two of them in such a way that they share one faith, one will, and united by the love of God they are able to know each other through the revelation of the spirit without ever having met. This is the case, too, with his special friendship: in Ep.11 Paulinus says that the Lord chose Severus to give to Paulinus as his inseparable and dearest friend and that as a result Paulinus loves his friend as himself 'because together we have one heart and one soul in Christ'. Paulinus explains, 'That intimate friendship of an earlier life, when we still loved the things which we now reject in Christ, marked us out for each other in the love of Christ. Yet it was through that earlier close intimacy that we progressed towards the connection by which through God's intervention we are now tied.'

Friendship as a purely spiritual relationship is also regarded as an important means of spiritual progress, as is clear from all Paulinus' letters which are concerned not with contemporary secular events but with his own inner development and that of his friends.[23] Letters are most useful in this respect as they can express encouragement and exhortation and serve to remind the reader of helpful Scriptural passages. But sometimes Paulinus succumbs to the feeling that the friend's presence would be even better: his letters are full of longing for Severus and in Ep. 1 he make one reason for this desire evident when he urges, 'Come and see me so that we can help each other and strengthen each other's faith.' Realising from Alypius' account and from his reading of some of Augustine's writings that he and Augustine share the same ideals, he ventures to address him, although they have never met, because he feels that the love of Christ has already bound them together and because he wishes to gain spiritual guidance and strength from his illustrious contemporary (though it would seem that when Paulinus wrote his first letter to Augustine, the North African was not yet a bishop). Prayer is another means whereby friends can help each other on the path to salvation: Paulinus often asks his friends to pray for him that God may forgive his sins of which he is so deeply aware and in Ep. 13, for example, he in turn includes a prayer for Pammachius who is in need of comfort and spiritual strength after the death of his wife Paulina, the daughter of Jerome's companion Paula.

Of course, as soon as two committed Christians realise that they are bound together in friendship, a great leap in spiritual progress can be regarded as being made for from that moment they can feel Christ between them[24] and by loving each other they prove that they are truly disciples of the one who laid down his life for his friends.[25] And even before they know each other they can be said to be friends for are they not joined as one soul and one body as members of the body of Christ? Here is one instance of how Paulinus' radical and often paradoxical[26] theory of friendship goes beyond the traditional theories, using similar images and expressions but intensifying them or turning them on their head, as when he writes to Pammachius that, since Christian friendships do not need time to mature, they do not depend on or expect proof – unlike in the pagan view of friendship which was heavily dependent on proof.

A more practical consequence of friends being members of one spiritual body was apparently that they would share one another's feelings and illnesses, something which, as we have seen, was strongly experienced by John Chrysostom, too. Paulinus writes cheerfully to Severus that he has suffered the same malady as his friend and 'to me this was most welcome testimony to our harmony in all things', with reference to St Paul's words at 1 Cor.12:26. He explains this in the same letter when he tells Severus that their friend Vigilantius also experienced the same illness 'because the Lord who makes us one and who joins all his people in indivisible spirit refused to allow even the states of our bodies to differ from each other'.[27]

The emphasis on the intimate relationship between Severus and Paulinus might mislead us into forgetting that for Paulinus Christian friendship certainly could and should spread further, beyond the pair of friends, in so far as all Christians are members of the body of Christ. Indeed each friend has a duty to introduce his friend to others, thus spreading his love, or rather that of Christ, further afield, just as Alypius helped Paulinus and Augustine to get to know each other[28] – and Paulinus felt that the intimacy between Alypius and himself was particularly fostered by the fact that they had both been close to Ambrose at Milan, for that bishop had baptised Alypius and had nurtured Paulinus in the faith.[29]

On the other hand, it was apparently not counter to the Christian perspective for a friendship to focus so strongly on two people, as is the case with Severus and Paulinus. How did Paulinus justify such a special relationship? Presumably since it is a matter of grace, the reasons for God's actions are hard to fathom and in fact Paulinus does not appear to question why God chose Severus to give to Paulinus as his friend, even while they were still involved in secular pursuits. No doubt God foresaw that the end result of this relationship would be that

Paulinus loved his friend as himself 'because we have one heart and one soul together in the Lord', alluding to Acts 4:32, and that their friendship would be eternal now that they have both been 'converted':[30]

> That intimate friendship of our earlier life, when we still loved the things which we now reject in Christ, marked us out for each other in the love of Christ. Yet it was through that earlier close intimacy that we advanced towards the connexion by which through God's intervention we are now tied. For we always loved each other so scrupulously that no affection could be added to our mutual love except the charity of Christ,

writes Paulinus to Severus in Ep.11.5. His confidence in their unity in Christ is so strong that in this same letter he even interprets the text of Matt. 24:40,'Then shall two be in the field; the one shall be taken and the other left', as meaning that God has made the two friends and taken them to himself – an unusual interpretation of a text which is normally taken to imply division and destruction in an eschatological context rather than unity.[31]

Fabre in his book *Saint Paulin de Nole et l'amitié chrétienne* tries to convince his readers that Paulinus, in accordance with his view of the gulf dividing the secular from the divine and eternal, made a sharp distinction in his use of the words *amicitia* and *caritas*, applying the former only to non-Christian friendships and the latter to those perfect relationships created by God. But Fabre has difficulty explaining away Paulinus' use of *amicitia* in contexts where he is apparently talking of Christian friendships, especially in his letters to Severus. It is true that *caritas* is used much more frequently for, in Christian friendships, the friends are bound together by the *caritas* of Christ, but Fabre goes too far in his determination to prove his theory which leads him to misinterpret or neglect certain passages. It should also be remembered that *caritas* is not merely a Christian synonym for *amicitia* but that it can refer to the love felt by the friends as well as the relationships between them. Similarly, although Paulinus most often uses 'brother' (*frater*) in addressing his Christian friends, he does occasionally use *amicus* without implying that he is talking to a non-Christian: he calls

Severus his 'friend (*amicus*) in the love (*caritas*) of Christ' and in
Ep.11.5 writes of the special divine grace in his *amicitia* with
Severus.[32] Such instances show that Paulinus did not feel that
the use of the word *amicitia* was anathema in Christian circles:
while *caritas* is applied exclusively to the love in Christian
relationships, *amicitia* can be used of either secular or Christian
friendships.

It is not clear what the course of the friendship between
Paulinus at Nola and Severus at Primuliacum was after about
404 when it seems that the latest extant letters from Paulinus to
his friend were written (Ep.28 and 32). Although there are no
more letters this may not mean that their relationship came to
an abrupt end for they are still evidently on affectionate
terms;[33] it is more probable that the correspondence from this
later period has been lost, as is unfortunately the case with the
letters between Paulinus and Ambrose and those of Paulinus to
Jerome.

If some of the documentary evidence for these friendships is
lacking, this is even more true of one of Paulinus' closest and
most long-lasting relationships but one which is not usually
included among his friendships. This is his relationship with his
wife Therasia whom he married around 385. As in the case of
Jerome's relationship with Paula, the lack of documentary
evidence makes it hard to derive a clear or detailed picture of
their relations for, ironically, the more inseparable they were,
the less need there was for letters and therefore the less evidence
there is for the strength of their relationship. However, the fact
that both men shared their lives with these women for many
years surely proves that they were on terms of such intimacy
and harmony that their relationships could be said to be based
on ideals of friendship.[34] One indication of their unity of
purpose in the case of Paulinus and Therasia is perhaps the fact
that most of Paulinus' letters are sent from Therasia and
himself jointly and as far as we can see, Therasia was also often
mentioned by their correspondents, whether in abusive terms,
as by Ausonius, or in laudatory terms, as by Augustine,[35]
showing that she was regarded both as an important part of
Paulinus' life and a strong character in her own right. Like

close friends they lived together and shared the same ideals
(though Gregory of Tours outlines one occasion when they
clashed on a point of principle and Paulinus was subsequently
proved right to have opposed Therasia's lack of generosity),[36]
united by their love in Christ as well as their marriage bond,
and indeed there are many aspects of their relationship,
especially after they had agreed to live as brother and sister
rather than husband and wife (following the early death of
their baby son) which are recognisable as characteristics of true
Christian friendship. The fact that they determined together to
renounce their sexuality while remaining within the unity of
marriage freed them, as far as possible from the differences
separating them, making them more equal and therefore
qualified for Christian friendship.[37] Such relationships of
shared dedication to chastity and an ascetic life in Christ within
marriage were apparently becoming more common at this
period,[38] as in the case of Paulinus' friends Aper and Amanda
to whom he writes in Ep.44, 'She (Amanda) is restored and
reinstated into unity with you, for Christ's love joins you with
spiritual bonds which are all the stronger for being more chaste.
You have passed from your bodies into Christ's.' Here the
familiar idea of unity in the body of Christ is combined with
language appropriate to the adoption of chastity. Paulinus and
Therasia were themselves praised for their exemplary way of
life by Augustine in a letter addressed to them both as his
'brothers' (*fratres*)[39] in which he speaks highly of them as
disciples of Christ; their continence has allowed Therasia to
become like a man and her husband's equal in their all-
important devotion to Christ as well as liberating them to enjoy
the bond of friendship more purely.

In Carm.21 Paulinus gives an account of his early life before
he settled at Nola, including mention of his marriage to
Therasia in Spain. Here he uses the metaphor of the yoke
which had been used in Classical literature to refer not only to
marriage[40] but also to friendship. Perhaps both areas of application are relevant when Paulinus (addressing St Felix) writes,
'You allowed me to be yoked in marriage by human dispen-
sation so that you might gain instead the lives of two of us and

through the yoke of the flesh the double salvation of our souls could compensate for the delay in the salvation of myself alone.' Here the unity of the body is seen as a way of achieving spiritual unity in a Christian context, thereby putting ths relationship on a par with Paulinus' other Christian friendships.

But even if we may be persuaded that the relationship between Paulinus and Therasia can be included among the ideal Christian friendships in which Paulinus believed so strongly, when faced with his relationship with the martyred saint Felix[41] we may find it harder to be convinced. How can one speak of friendship with someone whom one has not only never met but who has been dead for a century? And yet Paulinus himself, in the Natalicia poems[42] he addressed to Felix, portrays their relationship not as one-sided devotion to the memory of the dead but as the Christian friendship *par excellence*. This is perhaps more understandable if one views the relationship within the context of Paulinus' emphasis on friendship as a spiritual bond with Christ firmly at its centre and on salvation and the after-life which influences all his ideas about the aims and possibilities of Christian friendships: with Felix Paulinus discovered a relationship which was all the more spiritual, and therefore more perfect, because Felix had triumphed over death and passed into the world of the eternal and truly spiritual. Furthermore, what we know of Paulinus' unusually strong enthusiasm for close personal relationships makes it less surprising, perhaps, that he should have developed a personal relationship with the saint with whom he could feel on more intimate and affectionate terms than with Christ. In the martyr the human element could be recognised and identified with more strongly than in the God made man.

It is true that Paulinus never refers to their relationship as an *amicitia*,[43] though he speaks in terms familiar from traditional expressions of friendship, as when he says in *Carm.*21.474, that Felix shares his house with Paulinus since he allows Paulinus to treat Felix's possessions as his own. He may not use the word *amicus* to refer to Felix's relation to himself but he does call him the friend of Christ; this alerts us to the fact that despite the feeling of intimacy with Felix, Paulinus believed that Christ was the focus of everything, though the idea of Christ as the mediator between man and God is often replaced by the idea of Felix as the mediator between Paulinus and Christ. And yet there are many similarities between this relationship and those of Paulinus with other friends, both that with Ausonius, as his use of the terms *dominus* and *patronus* in addressing Felix indicate, and with those people who shared his commitment to Christ. As with such friends it is Christ who has brought them together in an intimate bond; 'Christ has handed me over to you, his dear friend, to be your own from my first years on earth', Paulinus writes in addressing Felix in *Carm.*21.

Felix, he believes, assists him in his spiritual progress by bringing him closer to Christ, his privileged position as martyr allowing him to mediate between the human and divine and to help Paulinus to carry out Christ's commandments. Paulinus addresses Felix as 'medicina mihi' which is reminiscent of the passage on the benefits of friends from Ecclesiasticus (6:16) which Paulinus quotes in a letter to his friend Victricius; indeed the context of this quotation might have applied as well to Felix as to Victricius,'For a good friend is a cure for the heart and when two are happily joined together, Christ stands between them.' In *Carm.*21 Paulinus expresses his belief that it was Felix who brought him to Christ when, as a boy, he first visited Felix's shrine in Campania and after Paulinus' commitment to Christ it is Felix who, because he has been born to eternal life, is able to undo the bonds of sin and mortality which fetter Paulinus, thus bringing him to salvation. The belief that Felix can assist Paulinus' spiritual progress[44] in this radical way is connected with the conviction running through the Natalicia poems as well as many of his letters, that Christ's sacrifice in laying down his life for his friends and his resurrection mean that death can be overcome and man is saved from mortality and sin. The miracles associated with Felix show that by means of Christ's sacrifice he has triumphed over death, thereby proving the efficacy of Christ's sacrifice for mankind. This is why Felix is so important to Paulinus, this is what lies at the heart of their relationship and what ultimately distinguishes it from his friendships with Ausonius, Severus, Amandus or

Delfinus. To Paulinus Felix is not merely a kind of friend: instead he is the most perfect friend because he alone of all his friends is truly alive since he lives in heaven;[45] such a view is characteristic of the topsy-turvy attitudes consequent on a total commitment to the Christian message.

Felix may be of great spiritual benefit to Paulinus, but are there any elements in their relationship which allow it to be mutual and therefore to qualify as a friendship? Certainly Paulinus feels enormous gratitude to Felix and respect, as well as deep affection, believing as he does that he has had this special relationship with the saint since his childhood. This affection is well illustrated by Paulinus' longing to be at Nola by Felix's shrine, which he expresses in the first Natalicium, composed in early 395 before he left Spain for Nola (*Carm.*12.15–17): such an intense longing is reminiscent of how he longed for many years to see Severus and welcome him to Felix's shrine.[46] Furthermore, Paulinus regards himself as Felix's servant, preserving his shrine at Nola and fostering his cult: so much, at least, he can do in return.

Although, therefore, it must be remembered that Christ remains at the centre of the Natalicia and that Paulinus recognises that Felix is primarily the saint of Nola rather than of Paulinus personally, it is nevertheless true that Paulinus did see his relationship with Felix as a form of friendship. By describing this unusual and intense relationship both in terms of traditional Roman forms of patronage, with Felix offering protection in return for Paulinus' service and devotion, and in terms of perfect spiritual relationships, Paulinus was extending the concept of Christian friendship to apply to a startlingly new situation. The paradox of this relationship is that although in some ways it offers an example of the perfect Christian relationship, it remains a relationship based on inequality (generally agreed to be unacceptable in Christian friendships since all are made equal in Christ), as in the traditional relations between *patronus* and *cliens* or *amicus*.[47]

CHAPTER 10

Monasticism and friendship

It was during the fourth century, as the threat of religious persecution came to an end and the supreme self-sacrifice, martyrdom, ceased to be a reality of everyday life, that Christian monasticism developed into an organised movement in both the eastern and western parts of the Roman Empire.[1] This century, when monasticism in its various forms was spreading so rapidly, is of great importance for it was at this time that so many of the theories upon which later monasticism was to be based were first worked out. Furthermore, in these early stages of its development the monastic life was still regarded as the life of the true Christian, the Christian who was most intent on the pursuit of perfection, and was not yet seen as something very separate from the life of those Christians who did not completely renounce the things of this world: those who opted for the monastic life were merely regarded, on the whole, as preferring a more radical approach to the question of Christian perfection.[2] As a result of this proximity between the way of the monk and the life of clergy and laity, it is possible to see how the language of the legislators and theorists of monasticism overlaps at many points with the language used by Christian writers of this period in their discussions of friendship: in several aspects the ideals of friendship in Christian terms and the ideals of monasticism appear to coincide.[3]

The immediate origins of monasticism are not to be found in the centres of civilisation but are to be traced to the desert regions of Syria and Egypt.[4] In this account we shall concentrate on developments in Egypt which were more directly influential on contemporaries, particularly in the West. Here, in the early part of the fourth century, two distinctive but not completely dissimilar trends of ascetic life were established under the influence of two dominant personalities destined to catch the imaginations of many people. These two were Antony and Pachomius, the former apparently providing the inspiration behind the growth of interest in the eremitic and semi-eremitic forms of life, the latter being the first organiser of the coenobitic or communal life.[5] It is here that the influence of Classical culture is least evident for it must be remembered that those who adopted the monastic life were often largely un-educated members of the rural population who had had no contact with the learned culture which left its mark on most Christian writers of the period; this means that in certain ways friendship in a monastic setting shows marked differences, not only from Classical theories of friendship but even from con-temporary Christian ideas about friendship. And yet, despite its radically altered perspective, monastic friendship is worked out according to many of the same rules affecting close relationships in society as had formed the basis for pagan ethical theories.

According to Athanasius's *Life of Antony* which, together with Antony's letters,[6] is the primary source for our knowledge of Antony and his attitude to the ascetic life, he gave away all his possessions at an early stage, following the example of the apostles as recorded at Acts 4:35 and the strict advice of Christ at Matt. 19:21.[7] Subsequently he lived in a hut in his village, doing manual work to support himself and the poor until he withdrew into the desert where he lived for twenty years on his own, relying on his friends to deliver bread twice a year and leading a life of prayer and renunciation. But this dramatically ascetic way of life did not long remain unknown or unemulated though it never became as common as the semi-eremitic and coenobitic forms of monasticism. As Antony's fame spread in Egypt, groups of admirers gathered round him, eager to imitate his way of life. Although Antony felt driven as a result to retire even further into the desert, to the solitude of the so-called Inner Mountain, he did occasionally return to the Outer mountain to give spiritual advice and he visited Alexandria twice to give the Christians support and to help his friend Athanasius against the Arians.

Antony's withdrawal into the desert has been termed 'a flight in order to return' and from this point of view may be compared to the experience of the Platonic philosopher who has a duty, when once he has made the difficult ascent into the upper world of light and truth, to return to help those who have not yet fully faced the light.[8] Indeed, despite the fact that he persistently refused to preside over an ascetic community and his belief that it was in solitude that he could most properly strive for spiritual perfection, it would not be true to say that Antony did not consider it important to care for his fellow human beings or to deny that he believed that monks ought not to separate themselves off from the body of the Church. With the rapid development of eremitic monasticism during this critical period of the Church's history, there was a danger that it might become a schismatic movement but, largely through the influence of Antony's views and his alliance with Athanasius who played such an important part in Church politics and the struggle against heresy, it remained orthodox, though at a remove from normal Church life.

In his seventh letter, for example, Antony reminds his readers that they are members of the Catholic Church and urges them to recognise the spiritual love he bears them, distinguishing it from physical friendship which is unstable, a prey to external circumstances. In Ep.2.9 he writes that because he and his friends are all members of the body of Christ and of one another their love for one another should be very strong; whoever loves his neighbour loves his own soul. This sentiment is reminiscent of the traditional view of a close friend as a second self or as the same soul living in a separate body, though in the Christian view the friends are in fact regarded as part of the same (spiritual) body. Another difference within a similar framework of ideas occasioned by Christian belief is the thought that an important part of the duties of friendship consists in prayer for one's friends, especially when separated from them.[9] The efficacy of such prayer is dependent on the community of friends in the body of Christ.

Another Biblical text referred to by Antony in his letters is John 15:15 when he exhorts his followers to devote themselves to Christ and the fulfilment of Christ's commandments.[10] This is of course a text which occurs frequently in discussions of Christian friendship as being the only instance where Jesus speaks of his disciples as friends, thereby apparently giving a positive value to friendship.

The attitude to his fellow Christians expressed in his letters is supported by a number of things which Athanasius says in his biography of Antony. He shows how the young Antony was impressed by the mutual love displayed by certain local ascetics; inspired by them he came to feel strongly not only the desirability of an ascetic life but also of harmony and love in the Christian community, with all the members of Christ's body being filled with the same enthusiasm for the ascetic way of life.[11] Indeed, it seems that Antony later managed to realise such a community among his followers in the desert[12] where, according to the specific information provided by such writings as the *Apophthegmata Patrum*, the *Historia Monachorum* and the *Vitae Patrum*, friendships based on a common spiritual purpose often developed between master and disciple or between two or more of the brothers. Even among those who lived in solitude the duties of hospitality, of providing spiritual advice and support, and the need to meet for the celebration of the Eucharist provided opportunities for the development of stable and intimate relationships. If a younger monk visited an elder who was renowned for his spiritual attainments, admiration for the elder's great virtue might provide the initial incentive to start a friendship: the young man would love the elder for his virtue and stay by him to profit from him spiritually and to serve him, while the elder would love his disciple for his devotion and his obedience.

In all such relationships, certain rules of conduct seem to have obtained by common consent. Although it was considered wrong to seek out the company of one's fellow men for the sake of human companionship (for this was a sign of spiritual immaturity), the formation of close relationships for the sake of progress in the ascetic life was clearly valued. Such relationships offered the opportunity to lay down one's life for one's friend in accordance with Christ's commandment at John 15:13 – the monks appear to have interpreted this as implying the necessity for humility, obedience, renunciation of one's own will and even, in some cases, strangely enough, the submitting of one's soul to sin for the sake of a friend. When the Abba Pimenius is asked the meaning of Christ's words he replies, 'If someone hears an ill word from his neighbour and could retort in similar fashion but struggles within himself to endure it, forcing himself not to speak evil in return out of a desire to hurt his friend – such a man is laying down his life for his friend.' Many different examples of obedience to this commandment are given in the *Verba Seniorum* (being the Latin version of the Systematic Collection of *Apophthegmata Patrum*), as in the story of the two monks who went to town to sell what they had made. In the town they became separated for a time during which one of them happened to commit fornication. When his friend met up with him again and suggested they return to their desert cell, the other said, 'I am not coming, because when you left me I fell into temptation.' His friend was keen not to let him fall by the wayside, so he said, 'Exactly the same thing happened to me. Come on, let us go and do penance together so that God will forgive us both.' The older monks told them how they must do their penance and the one who was not really guilty secretly did penance for his friend rather than for himself.[13]

Kindness and tact were also expected from the monks in all their dealings with others as part of their duty to love, as is illustrated by a story in the section headed 'On Love'.[14] Related to this is the belief, often emphasised, that a monk should under no circumstances rebuke his fellows or make any judgement on their conduct, however nefarious it may seem to be. This is a reaction which is not found recommended in traditional discussions of friendship or even normally among Christians, where advice and rebuke, if gently administered, were regarded as beneficial to the friend's moral and spiritual development. One might expect this to be all the more true in the monastic life in which spiritual progress was all-important, and indeed it is true in the coenobitic life where the monks lived in continual and close proximity. However, because of the extreme emphasis laid on humility by the anachoretic ascetics, especially through the constant awareness of one's own faults and sins, judgement and condemnation of others' faults were strongly discouraged. To achieve this, a monk should always be rebuking himself, carrying before him his own sins so as not to see his friend's sins.[15] In fact, the importance attached to renunciation and self-sacrifice actually helped friendship to flourish for these virtues were thought to promote the harmony of wills essential to friendship. The striking simplicity, even naivety, of their attitudes is demonstrated by the story of the two monks who shared the same cell and the few belongings they had and lived in complete harmony: one day one of them said, 'Let's have an argument like other men do', but the other said that he did not know how to have an argument. So the first one said, 'Look, I'll put this brick in the middle and say, "It's mine" and you say, "No, it's not yours, it's mine", and in that way we'll start an argument.' But when they had put the brick in the middle and the one said, 'It's mine', the other responded, 'No, it's mine', the first one said, 'Well, if it's yours, take it', and that was the end of their quarrel.[16]

There were, however, occasions when a monk had a duty to break off a friendship, if his friend fell into errors of faith and refused to return to the paths of orthodoxy. In such cases there was the danger that the friend might seduce him into error, separate him from God and thereby drag him down to hell, which would of course benefit no one except the devil.[17]

It is true that friendship is not a virtue which is particularly focussed upon in the *Vitae Patrum*, as are patience, obedience, humility or continence, but it is nevertheless constantly referred to as existing among the anchorites of the desert and as benefiting them in their search for spiritual perfection. The love to be found in a stable and loyal friendship was considered to have the power to raise the friends to heaven,[18] offering inspiration, support and opportunities for the practice of those Christian virtues highly valued in the monastic life, whether coenobitic or solitary (for their view of friendship did not involve the friends necessarily living together and friendships could be maintained even in a life of solitude).

If we now look in greater detail at the characteristics of the monastic system developed by Pachomius, we shall indeed find certain similarities to the solitary way of life: the basic aim of the ascetic is the same in both systems, namely a striving for perfection by means of continual devotion to God, through prayer, ascetic practices, obedience and manual work. But it is clear that human relationships do play a more obvious part in the system of Pachomius, the man whom Palladius describes as very fond of his fellow men and devoted to his brothers.[19] Pachomius' decision to dedicate his life to the service of God led him to establish communities of disciples on the margins of the cultivated land bordering the Nile, less geographically remote than Antony's ascetic practices. In these communities of a shared life of prayer and work, obedience was the watchword for the disciples, compassion for the superiors responsible for discipline.

Unfortunately there is doubt about the genuineness of the more direct evidence for the nature of the Pachomian way of life but it would seem that the so-called Rule of Pachomius is reliable,[20] a work which is said to have been translated from the Greek by Jerome, through whose version it would soon have become known in the West around the beginning of the fifth century. This is a collection of 142 precepts which reveals that, despite the fact that Pachomius' communities were founded on the idea of serving and loving one's fellow human beings, certain problems were thought likely to arise as a result of the fact that the monks lived in such close proximity to one another. For example, it was not always easy to maintain correct and balanced feelings of love for all the other members of the community. Although the Rule is not always specific about what the problems were, certain of the orders given provide us with a sketchy picture of everyday life in the community. Precept 47 tells us that the superior had to give permission to a monk who wished to tend a sick monk or relative and in precept 93 it is said that no one is allowed to wash or anoint another monk unless told to do so; no one is permitted to talk to anyone in the dark (94), no one may remove a thorn from a friend's foot without permission (96) and no monk may hold another's hand nor sleep beside another monk on his little rush mat – indeed each monk, whether sitting, standing or walking, had to keep a span's distance from anyone else (95).

More specific warnings as to the dangers involved in close relationships between the monks are given by Pachomius in the work which Lefort, in his edition, calls the *Catéchèse à propos d'un moine rancunier*.[21] In this work, which survives only in Coptic, Pachomius stipulates that a monk must not be the friend of any young man, in the sense that he must avoid all physical satisfactions because friendships of this kind are as destructive as fire. He advises the monk to seek peace and purity to enable him to see God. Later, however, he adds, 'Let us love men for then we shall be the friends of Jesus who is a friend to men',[22] so clearly it is only certain kinds of attachments which are to be resisted at all costs. It is only when love ceases to be purely spiritual, when it ceases to have virtue as its basis and its aim, that it becomes dangerous. When pure, love for other men brings the monk into a more intimate relationship with God; when non-spiritual, it separates man from God.

It was in the following generation of Pachomian monks that the problems involved in friendships of a partly physical nature appear to have been recognised very clearly. Pachomius' disciple and successor as leader of the community, Horsiesius, who died in about 380, left substantial fragments of a work (again surviving only in Coptic) referred to by Lefort as *Catéchèse (b)*, which treats of the terrible wickedness of particular friendships within the monastery.[23] In this work the Abba, presumably in his role as spiritual father, appears to be giving a sermon to a specific person. He begins by announcing that he will speak of the excellence of monasticism which has fallen into decadence as a result of the beauty of young men by which the monks have been seduced, and he exclaims, 'Keep away from those who are younger than you and you will escape all tribulation, all affliction, all temptation, all sickness, in this place and the other.' Then he actually names the object of his invective – unhealthy friendships which are detested by God and angels alike. Horsiesius imagines that the monk may answer his attack by saying, 'So you are trying to teach me enmity?', but the Abba replies that on the contrary he believes that monks should live in peace with their neighbours because of the divine precept to love one's neighbour as oneself which is so fundamental to all Christian life. But the trouble is that according to Horsiesius, the monk who is a prey to a particular friendship becomes dangerously secretive, 'anxiously looks this way and that and is on the watch for the right moment to give his friends what he had hidden in the folds of his cloak'. The discussion closes with a pointed question to the monk, 'If then, you madman, you have nothing to be ashamed of in your friendship, why do you then blush and fear to talk to your friend openly?' and Horsiesius reminds him that the beauty by which he has been seduced will fade, leaving only the terrible punishment for the sin, which he describes as bitter-tasting honey.[24]

In contrast to the description of unhealthy friendships, Horsiesius goes on to describe what he calls the friendships of the people of heaven. This is the love of those people who become attached to men who are in control of their physical appetites, who are filled with wisdom, who have learned prudence, who are perfect, friendly and diligent listeners and who are firm in the faith of the community: such men seek after peace and purity, they do not accuse others, they do not attempt to alienate the feelings of one man for his companions and they persevere in all actions pleasing to God. Clearly the monk who becomes obsessed by the physical characteristics of his fellow monks and is overfriendly to some to the exclusion of others, is regarded as a traitor to God's commandments and to the ideals of the monastic life: like the heretic he separates himself from God. Horsiesius' description of the ideal monastic relationship, which he is not afraid to designate as friendship, is in strong contrast to the characterisation of the wicked kind of friendship which even Christian monks are unfortunately prone to. This 'friendship of the people of heaven' reminds one of the common asseveration that true friendships can only exist among virtuous people and, in Christian contexts, among those whose yearnings are all directed towards God. Horsiesius' work also shows that he felt that friendships which were not truly Christian and not in the true monastic spirit were a real threat in the Pachomian communities already in his time, so soon after their initial establishment and the explosion of enthusiasm for Pachomius, communities which had been organised partly to guard against the dangers of the solitary life. The problems inherent in intimate community life had been hinted at by Pachomius in his Rule, but Horsiesius saw clearly the need to denounce them in specific terms so as to protect the community from that negative side to human relations, the positive side being that divine friendship which was pleasing to God. In the words of Theodore, another of Pachomius' close disciples, 'The law on which the community rests cannot be realised until the bonds of a purely natural love, a love which is according to the flesh, have been broken and all the brothers have been enveloped by spiritual love.'[25]

The Pachomian community was also designed to combat the innate human tendency to selfishness, by laying down the rule for all monks that there was to be no personal property: all goods were held in common and all the monks worked for the benefit of the whole community. This ideal was often said to be inspired by the life of the apostles at Jerusalem.[26] It has, to be sure, been pointed out that the relevant text of Acts 4:32 is not mentioned by Pachomius, but Bacht and Lefort have drawn attention to the fact that, although the text is not referred to in the Rule, it is mentioned in the Sahidic *Life of Pachomius*.[27] And certainly Pachomius' immediate disciples often refer to the life of the apostles at Jerusalem in the first century – Horsiesius in combination with Hebr.13:16, Theodore when he says that it is God's favour that the holy community appeared on earth by which God has made known to men the apostolic life so that they might be reflections of the apostles. In the following generation Cassian, in Book 18 of his *Conferences*, puts into the mouth of the Abba Piamun whom he had visited at Diolcus an interesting account of the development of monasticism, an account which may not be considered historically accurate[28] but which does indicate how widespread was the belief at this period that monasticism could be traced back to the first Christian community at Jerusalem.

Another aspect of the life according to Pachomius' Rule which is also recognisable as one of the traditional ideals of friendship is that of equality. Horsiesius writes that all members of the community should be equal if they all have perfect humility and he warns the heads of the houses in the monastery not to show favouritism to any of the monks in their charge: 'You must act with equality to all lest you should perhaps love someone whom God hates or hate someone whom God loves. Do not allow someone, for the sake of friendship, to do wrong and do not be hard on one man and indulge another or your work will be in vain.'[29] This equality was the result of the obedience and humility before God and before the superiors of the community which were enjoined on all the monks and which manifested itself most obviously in the uniformity of life within the monastery: all the monks were treated in the same way except in the case of illness or similar special circumstances, according to the discretion of the superiors.

Thus we see that not only was the love of God and neighbour set at the heart of monastic theology but in certain respects this theology, though developing from a different basis, bore a similarity to the pagan ideal of friendship. This is true in a more obvious manner in the works of John Cassian (350/360-440/450?) who was writing in the century after the deaths of Antony and Pachomius; here it is more likely that a direct influence of pagan theories will be evident than in the case of Cassian's predecessors, for Cassian was more widely learned, more cosmopolitan than either Antony or Pachomius. As a devotee of the ascetic life he had visited the monks of Egypt and Palestine before settling in Gaul where he organised two monasteries and wrote on monasticism. During his travels he may well have met Jerome at Bethlehem and he certainly met John Chrysostom at Constantinople when he accompanied the group of persecuted monks during the Origenist controversy;[30] indeed, after Chrysostom's downfall Cassian, it seems, was sent to Rome to intercede on his behalf with Innocent I. Although Cassian spent his early life in the East, it was to the West that he transmitted his knowledge of Eastern monasticism and it was here that his influence was strongest.

Leaving aside the precise part played by Cassian in the development of Western monasticism, we shall turn our attention to that section of Cassian's writings which is of particular interest to this study, namely the investigation into the nature of friendship in the monastic life which provides the subject of *Conference* 16, subtitled 'On Friendship'.[31] In this book the Abba Joseph propounds his theories of monastic friendship to his eager listeners, the young men Cassian and Germanus, in an exposition which is both rigorous and practical and which is throughout deeply concerned with the problems of close friendships with specific regard to the monastic virtues. It is perhaps surprising to find one whole book of the *Conferences* devoted to friendship, especially since the advice on friendship is apparently given by a hermit. However it must be borne in mind that, when Joseph speaks of his own experience of friendship in his youth, he may be referring to a period before he became a strict anchorite and be thinking of friendship developing within the semi-eremitic form of life and possibly also in the coenobitic, though no specific reference is made to this. Joseph focusses on the intimate relationship between any two monks not necessarily living together. A further consideration is that it is likely that Joseph's advice contains much of Cassian's views: after all, Cassian did not write the *Conferences* until some thirty or forty years after he had visited the Egyptian desert and it is highly improbable that he could then remember everything that the desert fathers had told him. If we are right to perceive traces of Cassian's own attitudes and learning overlaying the advice of the fathers, then this may help to explain the apparent references to the theories of friendship formulated by, for example, Cicero and Sallust, whose works Cassian may have studied when he moved to the West and became familiar with Latin. A further possibility is that the theories of friendship put forward in such unusual detail in the sixteenth *Conference* were influenced by traditional Greek thought with which the Abba Joseph may have been familiar, seeing that he is described by Cassian as 'carefully trained in Greek eloquence'.

Joseph's discourse arises out of the interest he shows in the relationship between Cassian and Germanus and develops as a reaction to their explanation that they are brothers according to the spirit rather than by blood and that since they renounced the world and chose the monastic life – first the coenobitic and then the eremitic – they have been united in a constant and inseparable union.[32] Joseph, who has had a similar experience in his youth, expresses his approval of their relationship since it promises to conform to the category of true monastic friendships. He begins by pointing out that there are in fact many different types of friendship, only one of which is truly spiritual and has the ability to last through all the vicissitudes of mortal life. Those which are based on passion, desire for gain or consanguinity and which can obtain equally well between wicked men, are liable to be broken off after a short time if the friends are separated for a period or if there is no longer any mutual benefit to be gained. Such a view is closely allied to the Classical theories about inferior forms of friendship, as expressed for example by Cicero at *Lael*.9.32.

The only friendship which cannot be terminated is that which is not based on gratitude for favours received nor on a contract nor on the force of nature, but on shared virtues alone. Joseph describes it as a relationship which cannot be dissolved by any event nor by any interval of distance or time, indeed not even by death itself.[33] One might suppose that such a friendship would be the prerogative of all Christians but Joseph is more realistic than to say this. Indeed, he admits that he has known Christians who have become very good friends, united in the love of Christ, but whose friendship had not remained firm because, although they had a good basis for their relationship, they were unable to maintain an equal fervour for the purpose they had undertaken. The reason for the instability of their friendship lies in the imbalance of virtue in the friends, an imbalance which is necessarily destructive in the long run, according to Joseph. Those who hope to have a permanent

friendship must both share one purpose and one will, both
desiring and rejecting the same things: the phrase Joseph uses
here, 'unum velle ac nolle', is strikingly similar to Sallust's
famous definition of friendship.[34] In order to attain to this state
the friends must both strive to progress in virtue, mortifying
their own wills and so cleansing themselves of egotism and
passion. Here the Ciceronian belief in the importance of the
harmonious agreement of wills in friendship seems to be
combined with the Evagrian ideal of spiritual purification.[35] It
is as a result of the attainment of the spiritual state of *apatheia*, a
state of selflessness and renunciation of passions and worldly
ties, that this true friendship, like love, can flow into the soul
and then spread to others. The startling conclusion is thereby
reached that it is only the soul which has been purified by
ascetic training in the monastic life that can experience genuine
friendships.

Such a conclusion shows that Cassian did not regard friendships merely as a 'spiritual exercise' in the words of Owen
Chadwick;[36] it is important to remember that according to
Cassian friendship is itself a state to be attained with difficulty
and much effort and that the existence of a true friendship is
evidence that the two friends involved have reached a high
degree of virtue and purity. Cassian's view is well summed up
thus by Fiske, 'By the total renunciation it demands, friendship
is the means to attain perfect love and also is itself the highest
form of *caritas*'.[37] When friends do reach this point they are able
to experience the joy of friendship which the prophet expresses
in the opening words of Ps.132(133), 'Behold, how good and
how pleasant it is for brethren to dwell together in unity!' Here
Cassian is not necessarily applying this verse to the coenobitic
life as do other monastic writers of the period; in fact, Joseph
says specifically that the first verse of the psalm ought not to be
interpreted from the point of view of physical place but
spiritually for, he explains, there is no point in living together
with others if one differs from them in one's habits and
purpose.[38] It is rather the case that, for those whose friendship is
based on equality of virtue, separation is no obstacle to a stable
friendship. The Classical ideal of a shared life is here pointedly

abandoned as unnecessary for those of similar aims and beliefs whose friendship is based on the *caritas Christi*.[39]

The discussion develops from this point as a result of a crucial question which Cassian modestly attributes to his companion Germanus: what happens if there is a conflict between what one friend believes to be in accordance with God's will and what his friend wants to do?[40] Even the essential virtues of humility and obedience will not solve this problem. Should he give up what he believes to be right or defy his friend? Joseph's uncompromising answer is that in such a case one unfortunately cannot hope that the friendship will last for it does not live up to the ideals which he set forth earlier. If the two friends truly shared one will and one purpose, no conflict would have arisen.

But if Joseph is uncompromising he does recognise that such a friendship is only for the perfect and that no friends can hope to attain to such perfection immediately or without great effort. He therefore proceeds to lay down six rules for those on the road to perfection and the perfect friendship, which is reached when the friends both possess the virtues of peace and patience.

The first step on this road is to reject all the things of this world and to prize nothing belonging to us higher than the most precious love for our brother. This is in accordance with Cassian's belief that renunciation is a fundamental characteristic of the monastic life, whether eremitic or coenobitic; it also indicates that friendship is highly valued and not regarded as part of worldly life. The next step is for the friends to curb their own wills lest either of them should think that he is wiser than the other and consequently wish to follow his own desires rather than those of his friend who might have a clearer perception of God's will: this advice is connected with the necessity for obedience and humility.[41] Thirdly the friends must be persuaded of the fact that nothing, even what seems most useful and necessary, is as valuable as love and peace. Fourthly Joseph advises that on no account, either for just or unjust causes, should the friends allow themselves to get angry – this is a point which will be developed at some length later because of its importance for the preservation of friendship. Here it goes closely with the fifth point which is that we ought also to try to cure our friend of any resentment he feels against us. The final piece of advice, which is to help in the fulfilment of all the previous ones, is that the monk should live each day as if it were his last: such an attitude puts all transitory feelings into perspective. Joseph sees clearly that anger and disputes usually arise out of trivial matters which, for a moment, are regarded as of importance.

But how will obedience to these rules promote harmony between the friends? If a monk, for example, does not cling to anything as his own – a human tendency which is the source of many disputes – then he will be able to preserve the unity which existed also among the early Christians at Jerusalem. Here Joseph cites Acts 4:32 where the idea of spiritual unity and the sharing of property are also set side by side. In fact, he goes further, not only emphasising the apostles' renunciation of property but also applying this text to the renunciation of man's own will. If a man can reach such a degree of renunciation in loving his friend then he will also, according to Joseph, be imitating Christ who said (Matt.26:39), when he was about to lay down his life for his friends, 'Nevertheless, not as I wish but as you wish it', as well as fulfilling Christ's words at John 13:35, 'If you love one another, then everyone will know that you are my disciples.'

Thus, according to the Abba Joseph, in the preservation of friendship nothing is to be preferred to love[42] and nothing is so persistently to be rejected as the destructive force of anger. This passion is substituted, as it were, for flattery which was regarded by the ancients as so detrimental to friendship. Here the influence of Evagrius is evident although he is not named. If one is to extirpate anger, one must cut away both its 'worldly' cause and that which causes anger between spiritual brothers: the former is identified with an attachment to worthless, worldly things while the latter is defined as diversity of opinions. This can be overcome by cultivating a spirit of humility and a harmony of wills in all things by means of calm discussion leading to truth, thereby showing obedience to St Paul's words at Phil.2:1–4.

Having stressed the importance of friendship for the spiritual life in terms reminiscent of pagan praise of ideal friendship, Joseph continues in a way which is also strongly reminiscent of pagan theory when he distinguishes different degrees of love. The first he calls by the Greek word *agape*: this love is owed to all men, even to our enemies, in accordance with Christ's precept at Matt.5:44. The second, *diathesis* or *adfectio*, is apparently legitimately given only to a few special friends who are joined to you by the similarity of their way of life and equality of virtue. This distinction drawn between what is usually regarded as the characteristically Christian love and what one might consider to be the type of love connected with the traditional view of friendship seems to justify the existence of special friendships among Christians, as long as the friends also feel *agape* in the correct way, extending their love beyond the bounds of their friendship. Not only is such a close relationship legitimate, it is in fact considered superior as long as it is not an exclusive relationship. Abba Joseph here gives the examples of Jacob's love for Joseph and, from the New Testament, Christ's love for his disciple John, to illustrate and justify *diathesis*. In the case of John he explains that this deep affection for one particular disciple did not imply that Jesus' love for the other disciples was lukewarm but that he felt superabundant love for John because of John's chastity and purity. Far from condemning such special, partial feelings, Joseph regards them as more sublime, for to him they imply the perfection of virtue and great love.

In conclusion, Joseph takes the text of Song of Songs 2:4, 'Order the love within me' and applies them to his hierarchical view of love which embraces friendship in a form recognisable to us. Love which is truly ordered is that which feels hatred for no man but loves some particularly on account of their merits. Joseph – or Cassian – shows that he has rather a different, more positive, attitude to special friendships from that of Basil, for example, although it is true that Cassian, like Basil, is aware of the dangers of such relationships in cases where *agape* is presumably not strong enough or where the monks have not yet reached a sufficient degree of virtue and renunciation from the physical and worldly. In a small community it must indeed have been difficult to achieve the correct balance between *diathesis* and *agape* – one may remember that even Jacob's love for Joseph was hardly a source of harmony within the family.[43] Certainly Cassian does not approve of friendships which are in any way tainted by homosexuality because they would be inspired, at least in part, by physical characteristics and feelings.

This digression on the different kinds of love is followed by a return to the discussion of the more negative aspects of friendship, with Joseph condemning feelings of pride, false humility, obstinacy and again anger. All these feelings are realistically characterised and the point is emphasised that it is not only the behaviour resulting from these passions but the feelings themselves which have to be guarded against; the intention is as dangerous as the act. True humility must be reflected in the inner man as well as in the way he behaves and such humility will give a man strength to bear what others may inflict on him and even to appease the anger of others, while the man who speaks words of patience but in his heart is keen to win praise for his humility, at his friend's expense, is certainly not fulfilling the love recommended by Paul, the love which seeks not its own, never wishing to profit from another's loss. This firm recommendation of complete humility in friendship brings us to a statement by Joseph of the difficult Christian paradox that the man who submits and does not strive to defend his own ideas and wishes is the one who shows strength and superiority, obedient as he is to the apostle's precepts at Rom.15:1 and Gal. 6:2. However, if the weaker of the two friends is unable to bear any injury and cannot learn humility, there is no hope of the friendship lasting: Joseph states that equality of purpose and virtue are absolutely essential to a permanent friendship.

With reference to earlier ideas about friendship it is interesting to note that Cassian here refers to this view as 'seniorum sententia', i.e. the view either of 'men of old' or of the 'desert fathers', depending on one's interpretation of 'seniores'. The idea of the permanence of friendship being dependent on equality of virtue and purpose had already been expressed in a

slightly different form in chapters 3 and 5, which is why
Cassian refers to it here as 'the above-mentioned view'. If we
compare the versions in the three chapters, it is noticeable that
the same concepts appear, though expressed in a variety of
ways. In the third chapter there are three variants: (1)
'Genuine and lasting love (*dilectio*) is that which grows with the
perfection and virtue of both friends equally'; (2) 'As we have
said, the only reliable and indissoluble bond of friendship
(*amicitia*) is that which is based on equality of virtue'; and (3)
'Love (*dilectio*) can only last without any disruption in relationships where there is a shared purpose and a shared will and
shared likes and dislikes' (*unum velle ac nolle*); in chapter 5 we
find the following version, 'We have said that the full and
perfect grace of friendship (*amicitia*) only exists between men
who can persist in perfect virtue and who have the same wishes,
the same aims and who never, or very rarely, disagree', while in
the twenty-fourth chapter Cassian writes, 'According to the
above-mentioned saying of the men of old, love (*caritas*) can
only be stable and lasting between men of equal virtue and
identical purpose.'

   Commenting on the version in chapter 5 the seventeenth-
century commentator of Cassian's works, Alardus of Gaza,[44]
explicitly links this with Cicero's definition of true friendship in
the *Laelius*. It is true that Fiske points out that although 'the
virtues that Cassian describes as necessary for friendship are all
directed to maintain union of mind and will, *consensio* . . . they
are not Ciceronian fidelity and constancy but rather Evagrian
purifying virtues, aimed at removing obstacles to peace',[45] but
it is possible that what Cassian refers to as 'seniorum sententia'
may be derived from Cicero's *Laelius*. Cassian's variations on
this theme show that he is not quoting directly but seems rather
to be paraphrasing something he remembers. Could his statements about the need for equality and sympathy be a summary
and reworking of *Lael.*18.65? Many of the words used are
similar and it is possible that Cassian, as a Christian, was
particularly attracted by a section which dealt with the importance of *fides* (faith, loyalty) as the basis of friendship. The fact
that Cassian does not mention Cicero is hardly surprising since

his mouthpiece is an Egyptian monk, not an academic and we have anyway seen that Christian writers often fail to refer specifically to their sources if those sources are pagan or, as in the case of Evagrius, doctrinally suspect. It is of course possible that Cassian knew only vaguely of such a statement as something that had been handed down from the men of old and did not in fact himself know the ancient authors, though this seems less probable in view of the number of possible reminiscences of Cicero in the sixteenth *Conference* and the similarity of his phrase, in chapter 3, 'unum velle ac nolle' to that of Sallust. The question of the relation between Cassian and the Abba Joseph is also relevant at this point but difficult to answer. It certainly seems likely that the words placed in the mouth of Joseph are a mixture of Cassian's memories and his own thoughts and if this is the case it is not easy to distinguish them. The other possibility is that the phrase 'seniorum sententia' refers to the sayings of the desert fathers themselves, but it may be that Cassian is here creating a deliberate ambiguity, playing on the two meanings of 'seniores'.

In the final chapter of the sixteenth *Conference* Cassian again refers to the same idea, here attributing it to 'prudentissimi viri' ('very wise men', a phrase as tantalisingly vague as the reference to the 'seniores'). This occurs at the end of a chapter which returns to the distinction made in chapter 2 between two kinds of friendship, the one of a contractual nature and maintained by an earthly love, the other based upon a shared desire for perfection and obedience to St Paul's words about love. The former is interpreted by Alardus of Gaza as referring to a physical friendship, with the contract mentioned by Cassian indicating a sort of lovers' oath between two friends which excludes other members of the community. In this context Alardus compares what Cassian advises in his *Institutes* (ii.15), namely that one must ensure that no monk, especially among the younger ones, spends any time alone with another or is found holding hands with another, with Basil's condemnation of such relationships in *Const. Mon.* 29.

As a coda to Cassian's portrayal of friendship in the ascetic life it is worth considering another section of the *Conferences* which may have a bearing on his view of friendship in a Christian context. In *Conference* 1.10 he is writing about the inequalities inherent in life in this world and the consequent need for fraternal charity to redress the balance. In the next world, however, the duties of fraternal charity will no longer obtain because there will be no inequality there. Instead, everyone will pass from the multifarious practice of charity in this world to an everlasting love of God, experienced equally by all, and contemplation of the divine. Cassian is not here explicitly concerned with friendship but it may be legitimate to say that these ideas imply that friendship can be regarded as a very special relationship for Christians because it exists, already in this world, between equals. Indeed, it may even be regarded as a divine relationship, not only because it is modelled on the relationship which Christ had with his Father and with his disciples, but also because it provides a foretaste of the equality which is to exist among men in the world to come.

St Augustine

Throughout Augustine's long life (354–430) friendship was to play an important part, both in his everyday relations with others and in his thought.[1] He valued his close friends highly and many of them remained his friends from youth to old age, men such as Alypius and Severus who, like Augustine himself, became bishops in North Africa. Other friendships developed in later life, as in the case of the government official Marcellinus whom Augustine became acquainted with at the time of the council of Carthage in 411 and with whom he maintained a correspondence when they were separated until Marcellinus' execution in 413. Augustine could also maintain affectionate relations over a number of years with men whom he had never met, as with Paulinus at Nola, with whom a friendship developed through their correspondence because they could recognise the friendly feelings each had for the other and they both adhered to the same Christian ideals. Although Augustine's thought was not static and he was led by a variety of factors to adapt his early ideas on many subjects in the course of his life, it is nevertheless accurate to say that he remained true to the ideal of friendship, in one way or another constantly giving it a central place in his way of life and in his theology, relating it closely to his idea of the supreme good (*summum bonum*) in terms of which his theological ideas were frequently expressed.

Examples showing how Augustine valued friendship from his youth onwards may be taken from the *Confessions*, written in the period 397–401, in which he looks back with a critical eye on his early life in North Africa, Rome and Milan from the viewpoint of a committed Christian and in which friendship is one of the main themes, as well as from the letters written throughout his life to friends all over the Roman Empire, expressing his affection and giving all kinds of advice and spiritual guidance. In the *Confessions* Augustine refers to the 'bright path of friendship'[2] and writes that friendship is a delightful bond, uniting many souls into one (II.5.10). In Book IV he describes his close friendship (referred to as 'sweeter to me then than all the pleasures of life') with an unnamed young man while he was teaching at Thagaste[3] and explains how grief-stricken he was when the friend died prematurely, because the young Augustine had put so much energy into loving his friend and missed his companionship deeply. But although he valued this relationship so much at the time – and it made him appreciate the truth of Horace's reference to a close friend as half of one's soul – when he looks back on this period with greater maturity and with strong Christian convictions he sees that this grief was reprehensible for it meant that he was loving his friend more than he loved God. After his friend's death he found precious consolation in other friendships when he moved to Carthage and some of these friends were to stay with Augustine in Rome and Milan, men such as Alypius and Nebridius who shared with him the crucial period of his conversion, providing him with valuable support. It is clear from the *Soliloquies*,[4] written at Cassiciacum shortly after his conversion, that Augustine would have found it very difficult to be without his friends at this time, feeling as he did that, if they shared the same aims, then friends could help one another in the attainment of those aims, leading one another on in the search for God.

Many of Augustine's letters also reveal him as greatly appreciating the pleasures and duties of friendship in later life, too. To Anicia Faltonia Proba, who had fled to North Africa when the Visigoths attacked Rome, he writes in Ep.130 that in all human affairs people find nothing if they do not have a friend, here echoing Laelius' words, 'How can life be worth living without the mutual affection of friends?'[5] This moving letter of Augustine's to the rich widow, the grandmother of the young Demetrias whom Jerome was to persuade to take a vow of lifelong chastity, was probably written in 412 when he was in his mid-fifties. We are reminded of Peter Brown's comment that, 'In middle age he remains delightfully and tragically exposed to that most unfathomable involvement of the soul – friendship'[6] and that in this Augustine had not changed much from the young man portrayed in the *Confessions*. This is confirmed by such statements as that found in the work *On the Trinity*, written during the first decade of the fifth century, where Augustine is arguing that we naturally love what is good, as for example 'the soul of a friend with the sweetness of agreement and the fidelity of love' (8.3.4), or in Book 19 of the *City of God* which Augustine wrote during the last years of his life where he asks rhetorically, 'What gives us consolation in this human society filled as it is with errors and troubles, if not the sincere loyalty and mutual love of true and good friends?' Even in old age when he was witnessing the break-up of the Roman Empire under the pressure of barbarian invasions, he could still afford to value friendship highly and to draw comfort from it.

But how exactly did Augustine define friendship and what did he consider to be its essential characteristics?[7] It seems that he was influenced in his youth by the traditional, Classical ideas on the subject, especially as transmitted by Cicero's *Laelius*. His description of his early friendships in the *Confessions* certainly has much in common with the traditional descriptions of friendship and often contains echoes of the expressions used in these accounts. Although he wrote the *Confessions* several years after the events of his childhood and youth portrayed in this work and despite the fact that these events are viewed from the radically altered perspective of the bishop of Hippo, the accounts of his early relationships do appear to present an accurate picture of the feelings and beliefs, later regarded so critically, of the young Augustine. The use of so many Classical allusions in talking about his early, sinful friendships is significant; it appears to reflect the author's attempt to express the imbalance, the lack of perspective in his view of human friendship at that time, and to indicate how far he was still entangled in an anthropocentric view of the world, so characteristic of pagan thought. As we have seen, he refers to Horace's phrase, 'half of my soul' with reference to the friend who dies young. In the same chapter of the *Confessions* (iv.6) Augustine mentions the friendship of the legendary characters Orestes and Pylades which was traditionally taken to represent the ideal friendship and which had been referred to amongst others by Cicero in the *Laelius* (7.24): Augustine, however, says that unlike these two friends he was not even willing to sacrifice his life for his friend whose death had made Augustine afraid to die and yet, unable as he was to come to terms with mortality and to rid himself of a deep attachment to mortal things, he felt that life was not worth living without his friend.

When he describes what it was that he valued in his early friendships, the list of shared activities and common interests among these friends differs little from the kind of interests of which Cicero would have approved. Of the friends at Carthage Augustine says that their shared interests and mutual love produced a unity of souls, thus making a single being out of many (*ex pluribus unum facere*): this phrase is very similar to that used by Cicero in the *Laelius* (25.92) when he writes 'so that many should, as it were, become one soul' (*ut unus quasi fiat ex pluribus*) and in the *De officiis* (1.17.56) where we read that nothing is more conducive to unity in friendship than the sharing of good habits, for in those friends who share the same interests and the same wishes it happens that each one loves his friend as much as he loves himself, thus realising Pythagoras' ideal that many should become one (*ut unus fiat ex pluribus*). This emphasis on complete unity among friends is taken very seriously by Augustine and is one of the elements of his early view which will have an important part to play not only with regard to friendship but also in the development of his theological and ecclesiological ideas.

The death of his young friend upset Augustine deeply. In analysing his grief and shock in the *Confessions*, he resorts to another Classical expression when he writes, 'I was amazed that other men should live when he was dead for I had loved him as if he would never die and I was even more amazed that I should live when he was dead, for I was his second self' and further on in the same chapter:

I felt that his soul and mine had formed one soul in two bodies and so life became hateful to me for I did not want to live with only half a soul but it was perhaps the same feeling which made me frightened to die, in case he whom I loved so much should die completely.[8]

Such is the way Augustine describes his earliest experiences of friendship before he left for Italy in 382. There was much which he later considered to have been wrong with these close relationships but there were also elements in them which continued to have a place in his view of friendship. For although his view of the world did change radically after his conversion, some continuity did remain in his attitudes. It is true that he became dissatisfied with a fundamentally humanistic form of friendship, adapting his view of the subject after his conversion in accordance with his new ideals and with a view of love derived from what St Paul and St John had said on the subject, as well as from the teachings and example of the incarnate Christ. His dissatisfaction is evident from the tone of the *Confessions* in which he criticises his early relationships, not because friendships ought to be avoided by the dedicated Christian but because he can see that these were not genuine friendships. Like the poet Gérard de Nerval, Augustine could look back and see that his error had lain in the fact that 'J'ai préféré la créature au créateur'.[9] But the fact that there was a certain continuity between his attitudes before and after his conversion in 386 is shown both by his continued attachment to such ideas as unity and shared interests, and by his persistence in using the traditional, Classical language relating to friendship. Indeed, the very fact that he regarded friendship in terms of a 'true' friendship, superior to various other forms of relationship which commonly passed as friendship, indicates that he was still using pagan theories as the framework for his ideas.

Most fundamentally, perhaps, Augustine did not cease to use the word *amicitia* in discussing friendships among Christians. To Jerome he writes quite happily of 'Christiana amicitia' which, it is clear from a number of contexts, is what he regards as true friendship.[10] He does not attempt to replace *amicitia* completely by *caritas*, although the latter is never used in a negative context unlike the related words *amor*, *amicitia* and *dilectio*. But the fact that *amicitia* can be used of a sinful, worldly attachment, as it is at James 4:4, does not mean that it invariably refers to an inferior kind of human relationship. Even after his whole-hearted dedication to Christianity Augustine continued to refer with approval to Cicero's definition of friendship as 'agreement about matters human and divine together with benevolence and affection', as in the *Contra Academicos* 3.6.13 and in Ep.258 to Martianus. As we shall see, his belief that there existed different types of friendship, only one of which could be called true friendship in Christian terms, allowed Augustine to continue to speak of *amicitia* without feeling that he was compromising his beliefs, for at its best, he believed, *amicitia* could be inspired by *caritas*, instead of being in opposition to Christian love.

But apart from such lexical continuity, what evidence is there for the fact that Augustine's view of friendship after 386 contained a number of recognisably 'Classical' characteristics while nevertheless being transformed into a distinctively Christian concept? It must be understood that to separate out the Classical from the Christian elements in this way is an artificial exercise but one which may help us to appreciate the different strands in Augustine's impressive view of friendship; it should however be remembered that these are very satisfactorily combined in Augustine's thought and that the presence of the Classical does not mean that his view of friendship is not wholly in harmony with his Christian beliefs.

The references to Cicero's definition of friendship made by Augustine in the *Contra Academicos* and Ep.258 have already been mentioned. In the *Soliloquies* which, like the *Contra Academicos*, was written during his stay at Cassiciacum, Augustine appears to have another passage of Cicero in mind, this time from the *Laelius*, when he says in his discussion with Reason about the possibility of knowing a friend intimately, 'For I consider that to be a very fair law of friendship which states that no one should love his friend either more or less than himself.'[11] Here he shows approval of an idea which Cicero apparently finds repugnant, for at *Lael.*16.56 the suggestion that we should have the same feelings towards our friend as we do towards ourselves is rejected. It may be that at this point of the *Soliloquies* Augustine also has in mind the second part of the twofold commandment which, as we shall see, became central to his view of Christian friendship – it is not impossible that the influence both of Cicero's discussion and of Matt.22:39 can be detected here. Certainly it is striking, if he does have Christ's commandment in mind, that he speaks of the 'law of friendship' (*lex amicitiae*).

On other questions regarding the nature of friendship Augustine, it appears, would have agreed with the standard views put forward by Classical writers. In his work *De diversis quaestionibus 83*, which was written before Augustine became bishop, he accepts Cicero's definition of friendship as 'a desire for good things for someone for his own sake, together with a reciprocal desire on his part' and in answer to the question of whether all things have been created for man's use, he refers to the traditional idea that friendship can be sought either for the sake of some usefulness which it brings with it or for its own sake or for both these reasons.[12] The former definition, reminiscent as it is of the Aristotelian one given at *Rhet.*1380b 35–1381a 1, will recur in Augustine's later writings where he gives more precise details of the 'good things' from a Christian point of view.

The traditional connection between friendship and benevolence is also adopted by Augustine without further discussion. We have already seen that he quotes Cicero's definition of friendship, involving benevolence, on a couple of occasions and the two nouns are often linked in his writings, as when he writes 'Where there is benevolence, there is friendship' in the work on Christ's sermon on the mount.[13]

At the end of his unfinished work of exegesis on the literal meaning of Genesis,[14] written in 393 during the controversy with the Manichees, Augustine mentions the idea of friendship being based on similarity of character, an idea which may

remind the reader of the view expressed in the *Laelius* (20.74)
and which seems to have found favour in antiquity, namely
that people of different characters have different interests and
these differences are an obstruction to the formation of friendships. But here Augustine has included the idea in a discussion
of the concepts of image and likeness in connection with
Gen.1:26 and the problem of man's precise relation to God.

In Ep.155.1 to Macedonius Augustine expresses the belief
that in the case of true (i.e. Christian) friendship, the relationship ought not to be valued according to the number of
temporal advantages which it provides but should rather be the
result of purely gratuitous, uncalculating love. The fact that he
here has in mind a human relationship derived from and
focussed on Christ does not invalidate the point that he is in
agreement, with regard to the first part of this statement, with
Cicero who rejects those friendships formed in the hope of some
profit (*Lael*.9.31): Cicero, however, would not have been
impressed by a gratuitous love but rather with one inspired by
the prospective friend's virtue. A further echo of Cicero in a
Christian context, with an underlying polemical note, can be
detected in the work *Contra duas epistolas Pelagianorum*,[15] dated to
the years 420–1 and addressed to Pope Boniface at Rome, in
which Augustine writes, 'For what else is friendship (*amicitia*), a
word which is derived from love (*amor*) and which can only be
loyal in Christ, in whom alone it can be everlasting and
happy?' Here we have a reference not only to everlasting
friendship, as at *Lael*.9.32, (though the basis for this is very
different in the two works) but also to the idea that there is an
etymological connection between *amor* and *amicitia*, an idea
expressed at *Lael*.8.26 where Cicero speaks of 'love, from which
the word friendship is derived'.[16]

With regard to another idea about friendship often mentioned in the writings of pagan antiquity Augustine feels no
need to adapt it or point to any change dependent on the
transposition to a Christian setting. This is the belief that it is
better to be a nettle in the side of your friend than his echo.[17] It
is no coincidence that this idea is most prominent in Augustine's letters to Jerome for mention of it comes in response to

Jerome's hypersensitivity to criticism of his exegetical and translation work and is indicative of one of the problems Augustine came up against in his relations with Jerome. In the first letter of their correspondence (Ep.28) he attempts to smooth over the fact that he has been critical of Jerome's interpretation of Gal.2:11–14 when he writes, adopting Biblical, proverbial language, 'Stronger is the love of the salutary rebuker than that of the flatterer pouring oil on the head.' The theme of the friendly rebuker occurs again in Ep.73.2.4 when Augustine, in reaction to Jerome's indignation, writes, 'Acute was the observation made by the man who said, "Often the criticisms of those who are hostile to us are more useful than friends who fear to rebuke." ' It is not clear whether Augustine is here quoting verbatim or paraphrasing, but it is possible that he has *Lael*.24–5 in mind. That this is the case is even more likely in Ep.82.4.31 to Jerome in which he quotes Terence's proverbial line from the *Andria*, 'Flattery produces friends while truth engenders hatred' which Cicero had quoted at *Lael*.24.89. In Ep.82 Augustine compares it with Prov.27:6, 'The wounds inflicted by a friend are a better sign of loyalty than the kisses freely offered by an enemy.' He does not refer either to Terence or Cicero by name but calls the line quoted a common proverb, dismissing it as unworthy of Christian friendships. In fact at the end of this letter to Jerome Augustine reverts to the same theme when he mentions that their relationship should contain not only affection (*caritas*) but also freedom of speech (*libertas amicitiae*) which would allow for criticism without offence. As it is, Augustine feels that their friendship is not as perfect as it might be.[18]

The ideal of openness and intimacy which Augustine sought in his friendship with Jerome had been expressed by Cicero in the question, 'What could be more pleasant than to have someone with whom you can discuss everything as with yourself?' (*Lael*.6.22) and Augustine does indeed frequently refer to this idea in his letters. Aurelius, bishop of Carthage, for example, received a letter from Augustine in which the bishop of Hippo writes that Aurelius' letters afford proof of the love between them which allows Augustine to converse with Aure-

lius – by letter – as if with himself,[19] and in Ep.38 to Profuturus
two Ciceronian phrases appear to be combined when Augustine writes tenderly, 'You know all this, but since you are a
second self to me, how could I wish to say anything to you apart
from what I say to myself?' The Ciceronian passage at *Lael*.6.22
crops up also in Ep.187 when Augustine writes that Dardanus,
the addressee, is so very close to his heart that Augustine can
talk to him as to a true friend.

It is not only in the letter to Profuturus referred to above that
the phrase 'a second self' occurs; indeed, it is a phrase which is
common in Augustine's writings as it is in Cicero's, applied to
close friends such as the young man whose death is recorded at
Conf.iv.6.11 or Severus whom Augustine addresses as his second
soul. Related to this idea is the one that intimate friends form
one soul in two bodies, an idea which Augustine seems to be
alluding to in his first letter to Jerome[20] in which he writes of
Alypius (who had recently visited Jerome in the Holy Land)
and himself, 'Anyone who knew us both would say that we
were two separate people only as to our bodies, not our minds,
for we are in complete agreement and on terms of perfect
intimacy although we differ in merit in which he surpasses me.'
And in Ep.110.4, in a letter to Severus in which Augustine
complains that his friend is too lavish in his praise, he writes
that Severus is his second soul, indeed, their souls are one: here
there seem to be allusions both to the phrase 'a second self' and
to the idea of one soul in two bodies. While reprimanding
Severus for his unrealistic encomium (though Augustine realises
that this stems only from Severus' great and admirable love for
him), the writer of the letter subtly manages to indicate the
strength of their friendship and their intimacy, thereby paying
a compliment while gently rebuking.

The letters may provide the richest source of expressions of
friendship but one should not overlook the less obvious sources,
as for example a passage from the *City of God* where Augustine is
condemning the idea that souls in heaven experience cyclical
returns to mortal misery.[21] Here he alludes to the Classical
notion, attributed by Cicero to Bias, that one should love one's
friend as if he might some day become an enemy.[22] Like Cicero

Augustine rejects this view – for how can you love a friend
properly if you suspect he will one day be your enemy? – and
uses this as a parallel to support his idea that souls in heaven
would be unable to love God truly if they knew that they would
have to leave him to return to earth. We have already seen that
Augustine shared with his Classical predecessors a belief in the
importance of reciprocity in one's relations with others: this is
stated firmly in the *De fide rerum invisibilium*[23] and it is clear from
his letters to Jerome that Augustine's personal experience
endorsed this belief when he encountered difficulties in striving
to prevent his relationship with Jerome from running aground
in one-sidedness, as he saw it.

But if there were many expressions connected with the
traditional views of friendship which Augustine felt happy
about using even after his conversion, how did his view as a
dedicated Christian differ from that of a pagan intellectual? It
will be seen that the differences are in fact dramatic and radical
despite the fact that some of the traditional ideas were regarded
as compatible, sometimes in an adapted form and always in the
context of a different world-view, with Augustine's Christian
beliefs and the matters which he, as a Christian, considered to
be of importance. In the words of O'Connell, Augustine
believed that 'what is best in the world of culture, when
examined in depth and purified, coheres with the Christian
message, properly understood'.[24] For example, the Classical
definition of a friend as *alter idem* or *alter ego* could be regarded
as relevant to the second part of the divine commandment to
love God with all your heart and with all your mind and with
all your soul and to love your neighbour as yourself; but the
motivation for this was not merely an attempt to salvage as
much of the pagan cultural heritage as possible – rather, in the
case of Augustine, the traditional picture of friendship actually
helped him in his understanding of this commandment which
he set at the centre of his thought. It was therefore inevitable
that his interpretation of it should affect his view of Christian
friendship as well as being influenced itself by his personal
experience of friendship. When we look at the writings where
he discussed this essential text (Matt. 22:37–40) it is clear that it

is often connected in his thought with other Biblical texts such as St John's first Epistle, Christ's commandment to his disciples at John 13:34 and at John 15:12–15 and St Paul's praise of love in 1 Cor.13 and Rom.13:10.[25]

Another text which is important to Augustine's view of man's love of God and man is Rom.5:5, 'The love of God, poured forth in our hearts by the Holy Spirit which is granted to us', as is 1 Cor.4:7 where Paul asks pointedly, 'For what do you have which you did not receive?', both of which influenced his belief that love and friendship are given by God's grace rather than being instigated by man himself, a belief which is of course in harmony with the particular emphasis he placed on the need for grace in human affairs in general. According to a passage in the *Confessions* (IV.4.7), for example, 'There can be no true friendship unless God cements the bond between two people by means of the love poured forth in our hearts by the Holy Spirit which is granted to us.'

Before considering in detail Augustine's view of friendship with regard to its Christian characteristics, some indication of his interpretation of the twofold commandment should be given. It appears that after his conversion he began by being concerned primarily with the first part of this commandment, namely the nature of man's relation to God, possibly under the influence of Neoplatonist philosophy with its interest in the ascent of the soul to the divine. At the time of his stay at Cassiciacum his love still focusses on such intellectual concepts as Truth and Wisdom and his God is still the god of the philosophers, as is evident from the works he wrote there and shortly afterwards, such as the *De quantitate animae* and the *De immortalitate animae*. Friends (and Augustine had surrounded himself with several) are regarded as fellow seekers along the path to wisdom but any broader view of relations with one's fellow men seems to be lacking in his thought at this period.

Although the development to a more balanced Christian view was a gradual one, it is nevertheless legitimate to point to the time of Augustine's ordination at Hippo in 391 as an important stage in this development, for it was then that he was forced to confront the Scriptures more rigorously in order to be able to preach as Bishop Valerius ordered him to do. Yet even before this we note a change in the focus of his thought: in the work *De moribus Ecclesiae Catholicae* written in the years 388–90 he had already placed *caritas*, based on truth, at the centre of Christian life and this shift is supported by the references to Rom.5:5 in sections 23 and 29 of this work, to Rom.13:10 in section 50 and to the twofold commandment in sections 13,47,49,57 and 62. Here, too, we find the statement that God is our highest good and the following interpretation of the second part of the commandment:

You are loving yourself in the proper way if you love God more than yourself. You should behave towards your fellow men as you do to yourself, in other words, you must make him love God with perfect love; for you do not love him as yourself if you do not manage to lead him to the good which is your goal, too.[26]

This view of the relation between man's love of God, his love of himself and that of his fellow men lies in fact at the heart of Augustine's view of friendship. The vague prescription derived from Cicero, that a friend should wish for good things for his friend, is given a dramatically new direction in the work *De diversis quaestionibus 83* (31.3). If God is seen as the highest good towards which everything must be directed and if all love must focus on God before all else for it to be truly Christian, friendship among Christians gains a new perspective.

But if the twofold commandment was now finding its rightful place in Augustine's thought,[27] there were still problems to be solved concerning the correct relation between the Christian's love of God and his love of man. It was not easy for Augustine to reconcile the strongly monist, Neoplatonic programme of desire exclusively for the supreme good with the twofold commandment which involved loving something temporal, belonging to this lower world of sense and imperfection. Would not love for one's fellow men inevitably detract from love of God? And how could love of others be given sufficient value if the highest good was to give oneself up to God? Augustine's answer to this dilemma seems to have come partly from his belief in the highest good as a good which can only be possessed by being shared, and partly through his exploration of the terms 'use' (*usus*) and 'enjoyment' (*fruitio*) and the phrase 'for the sake of God' which proved very useful for the accurate formulation of his mature view.

As O'Donovan has shown, Augustine ceased to use these terms in connection with love of God and love of man at about the time he commenced writing the *De doctrina Christiana*, in the late 390s. In the earliest works after his conversion he had placed God alone as the object of 'enjoyment': all else including man was to be the object of 'use'. This was one of the dangers inherent in emphasising God as the highest good to the neglect of the second part of the twofold commandment. Augustine's distinction can be explained in terms of Stoic doctrines set forth in Cicero's *De finibus* in which the author speaks of enjoying the highest good, drawing a distinction between what is to be sought for its own sake and what is sought for the sake of something else, a distinction which is often found in Augustine's thought. But in the first book of the *De doctrina Christiana* he moves away from his original application of 'use' to the Christian's love of his fellow men. At first he explains that there are some things which are to be enjoyed, others which are for use, and only those which are for enjoyment make us happy (the search for happiness being the motivating force for all human action). To enjoy is to love something for its own sake while other things are to be used to attain what we love; and so in this mortal life we must use this world to reach God, for it is only in the enjoyment of the eternal and the spiritual that we can obtain true happiness.[28]

It is noteworthy that Augustine here makes use of two ideas found in Cicero's discussions of friendship. Firstly we see a resemblance to the Ciceronian distinction between what is useful and what is pleasurable, whereby friendship can be classed as both because it is founded on virtue: Augustine draws a distinction between what is to be used and what is to be enjoyed and says that some things fall into both categories. That he knew of Cicero's distinction is evident from *De div.quaest.83* (31.3) where he quotes the relevant passage from Cicero's *De inventione* (II.55.166). Secondly Augustine uses the phrase 'for its own sake' which appears to be taken over from Cicero's statement that a friend is to be loved for his own sake[29] but Augustine here uses it in connection with love of God alone, rather than love of friend or neighbour. This phrase was to prove useful when he faced the question of whether people ought to 'enjoy' or 'use' each other, in answer to which he concludes that men are to be loved for the sake of God, for all things apart from God are to be loved for the sake of something else rather than for their own sake. Man must not even love himself for his own sake – even man's self-love must be focussed on God. Love of man is certainly legitimate for Christians but this love must be referred to God as the true standard and source of stability in human relations, as well as being the very source of that love. This view developed in the *De doctrina Christiana* is reflected in the *Confessions*[30] where Augustine addresses God, 'Happy is the man who loves you and his friend in you and his enemy for your sake' and in Ep.155 in which Augustine writes to Macedonius that the only truly blessed life is to be found in Christ:

This is the source from which true friendship flows, not to be valued by temporal advantages but to be drunk in through freely given love. No one can be a true friend of man unless he is first a friend of Truth; if friendship does not come into being spontaneously, it cannot exist at all. The philosophers have much to say on this subject, but one does not find among them true affection, that is, true worship of the true God.

In *De div.quaest.83* (71.6–7) certain more practical precepts on friendship are given in connection with the belief that only a true love of Christ will provide a sound basis for friendship. Alluding to Gal.6:2 Augustine writes that it is the law of Christ that we should bear one another's burdens and continues, 'For by loving Christ we are able easily to bear another's weakness, even that of someone we do not yet love because of his own virtues', summing up his advice in the previous chapter on the value of openness and willingness to love in forming friendships. This work seems to have been written shortly before the *De doctrina Christiana* which might explain why Augustine uses the phrase 'because of his own virtues' (*propter bona sua*) here: the usefulness of the phrase 'for the sake of God' to describe human friendships and the danger of using such phrases as 'for his own sake' of human love has not yet been recognised by Augustine but will become clear in the course of the writing of the *De doctrina Christiana*.

The phrases 'for the sake of something else' and 'for the sake of God' enabled Augustine to dispense with the unsatisfactory distinction between 'use' and 'enjoyment', unsatisfactory because it did not really accord enough value to love of our neighbour: the second part of Christ's commandment appeared to be set too far below the first part. By the end of the first book of the *De doctrina Christiana* we find Augustine describing the twofold commandment in these terms, 'Love of a thing which can be enjoyed and of something which can enjoy that thing with us' and even using the term 'enjoyment' of the love of our fellow men in a positive sense because of the essential addition of the phrase 'in God'.

It can thus be seen how in Augustine's thought human love came to be more highly valued and more closely linked to man's love for God rather than being in conflict with it. Gradually his thought had changed to the point when it could be said to harmonise with and to be inspired by 1 John 4: he had moved from his originally humanist view of friendship through an attitude which stressed love of God at the expense of love of man to a view which valued love of man within a theological perspective. Independent evidence for the value Augustine placed on the second part of the commandment is provided by what his close friend Severus writes to him in Ep.109.2, 'You are so good because you inspire us to a love of our fellow men, a love which is both the first and the final step to love of God.'

With regard to another problem concerning the commandment to love your neighbour as yourself, namely the question of what the phrase 'as yourself' means, we have already noted that Augustine could attach a positive meaning to the idea of self-love latent in this phrase, in that the love of self is directed primarily to love of God. In Ep.177, for example, Augustine explains succinctly that no one loves himself unless he loves

God and so when we love a friend as ourself we must wish him, too, to love God above all else. Such an idea is hinted at in Ep.23 when Augustine writes to Maximius, 'God knows that not only do I love you but I love you as myself for I am well aware that I wish the same good things for you as I do for myself.' It is referred to more specifically, again in the context of close personal relations, in Ep.130.7.14 in which he writes to Proba, 'Inasmuch as we love ourselves in God, if we really love Him, so also, according to the other commandment, we truly love our neighbours as ourselves if, as far as we are able, we lead them to a similar love of God. And so we love God for his own sake and ourselves and our neighbours for His sake.' Indeed, in Ep.155.4.15 Augustine argues that love of self is nothing other than love of God, otherwise Christ would not have said that there were two commandments, but three – love of self, love of neighbour and love of God.

The connection between Augustine's interpretation of this part of the commandment and his view of Christian friendship may be illustrated by a number of passages from his writings. Ep.258 affords a Christian reinterpretation of the Ciceronian definition, maintaining the form but changing the context. It is in explanation of this change that Augustine writes to Martianus:

And so I thank God because he has allowed you to become my friend at last, for now there is between us that agreement on matters human and divine together with kindness and love in our Lord Jesus Christ who concluded all his divine precepts with the twofold command-ment, 'You should love the Lord your God with all your heart and with all your mind and with all your soul' and 'You should love your neighbour as yourself' . . . In the first of these there is agreement on things divine, in the second on human matters, together with kindness and love. If you hold firmly to these two things our friendship will be true and everlasting and it will not only unite us with each other but also with the Lord himself.

The idea that the Christian should love God in his friend if he is to love his friend properly is an essential one for Augustine's theory of Christian friendship. It is expressed in Sermon 336.2.2, 'He truly loves his friend if he loves God in his friend, either because God is in him or so that God may be in him' and in the work *Contra Faustum* (22.78) where he writes, 'A man loves his friend for God's sake if he loves God's love in his friend.' Such, according to Augustine's belief, is the correct relationship between love of God and love of man: friendship is by no means rejected but is intimately connected with man's love of God, lest man should be seduced into loving the creature more than the Creator, a danger of which Augustine is very conscious. But how exactly is friendship (*amicitia*) related to love of neighbour (*amor proximi*)? Are the two regarded as identical[31] or is friendship just part of the wider concept of love of neighbour? Somehow Augustine's view of friendship had to come to terms with Christ's command that the Christian should love even his enemies, for he had no intention of neglecting this difficult addition to the fundamental commandment.

As to the question, 'Who is my neighbour?' it is clear that Augustine believed that the word referred to every man by virtue of his humanity, whether he was a Christian or not, for he very frequently reminds his readers that a person's neighbour is every other person. In Ep.155.4.14 he writes with reference to the second part of the twofold commandment, 'The question of one's neighbour has nothing to do with the closeness of blood relations but with the fellowship of reason in which all men are partners' and in the second commentary on Ps.25 he writes more explicitly, 'Your neighbour is anyone who like you is descended from Adam and Eve. We are all neighbours according to the condition of our earthly birth . . .'[32]

But if the Christian was to love all men, including his enemies, what room was there for the particular, mutual love of friendship? In fact, although Augustine strongly believed that all men must be loved in virtue of their common descent from Adam, he does not seem to have considered such love to be the complete fulfilment of the Christian duty to love. There are other important elements in his view of love and friendship which must also be taken into consideration, such as the idea that there are different kinds of love, different degrees as it were in a hierarchy of love – the *ordo caritatis* which is such a central concept in Augustine's thought. The different loves were distinguished by their objects, the only correct kind being that where God was the ultimate object, with other loves subordinate to this in the proper order. Such a view enabled Augustine to safeguard the belief that all objects of love in this world are good because they are created by God and yet to maintain that some objects are more proper to love, as he explains in Ep.140.2.4, 'Everything which God has created is good, everything from the rational being to the lowest body; and so the rational soul does well if it maintains the order and by distinguishing, choosing and evaluating, subordinates the lesser to the greater, the physical to the spiritual, the lower to the higher, the temporal to the eternal.' While *caritas* is an upright love which can include love of man as well as of God as long as the human love is focussed on God, *cupiditas* is the love which values more highly things which ought to be accorded less value. The most forceful statement of the radical distinction between love of God and love of all else is to be found in the early work *De moribus Ecclesiae Catholicae* but this view was later moderated to allow for a greater integration of the two loves in accordance with the twofold commandment.[33]

In fact, the idea of the *ordo caritatis* was closely related to Augustine's interpretation of the twofold commandment. It also allowed him to distinguish between different degrees of human love and thus to find an important place for friendship within the range of love of neighbour. It is essential to see that Augustine believed that ideally all men would love one another in God, with an intense, mutual and ordered love. However, such a state is impossible in this life.[34] All that can be hoped for now is that a Christian should love a few men reciprocally, in an intense friendship founded on love of God, and extend his love as far as possible to others, including enemies, non-Christians, etc. This he explains in his letter to Proba, surprisingly, perhaps, using *amicitia* of an unrestricted love:

Friendship must not be restricted within narrow limits. It should embrace all people to whom love and affection are owed, although it will be stronger towards some, less so to others and it should extend as far as our enemies for whom we are commanded to pray. And so there

is no one to whom we do not owe affection on account of the
fellowship of our shared nature, even if our love is not mutual. But it is
right that we should particularly love those who love us in return with
a holy and chaste love.[35]

While maintaining the aim of extending love to all men,
Augustine still shows that he values reciprocal love most highly,
as he demonstrates wittily in Ep.192, using images of payment
and debt when he writes:

But I always owe love which is the only thing that makes someone still
a debtor even once it has been paid back ... It is not lost when it is
given back but rather it grows by being given back ... How can you
deny your friends love when love is owed even to your enemies? But
while love is paid with caution to one's enemies, it is paid back to
one's friends with security.

Although love may start as a one-sided feeling of benevolence,
this is not enough: the true aim of Christian love is to encourage
a constant and mutual relationship in Christ, whereby the
friends will make one another fit to reign with Christ in the next
life. Did not Christ command his disciples to love one another
as he loved them, i.e. humbly and gratuitously?

Augustine's belief that the ideal love is mutual, thereby
conforming to the ideal friendship as described by ancient
writers, is in fact based on the idea that it is the Holy Spirit, sent
by God, which inspires true love in man and which forms the
bond between men as it does between the Father and Son
within the Trinity. The idea of reciprocity is also implicit in St
Paul's exhortation at Gal.6:2 which Augustine often refers to
with regard to the truly Christian human relationship, as in the
De div.quaest.83 (71.1) where he writes, in discussing this text,
'There is no better proof of a friend than the carrying of his
friend's burden.'

But if this was an essential characteristic of Augustinian love
which made it resemble the Classical ideal, it differed dramatically from this ideal in another important respect. Augustine
believed that only in heaven can human relationships be
perfect, when God will truly be all in all. He thus adds an
eschatological perspective which not only alters his view of
human relationships radically but also enables him to make full

use of the necessary but regrettable distinction between mutual
love and benevolence which exists in this life. His ideal was no
earthly society but a heavenly community of mutually loving
members of the City of God (described as 'a perfectly ordered
and perfectly harmonious fellowship in the enjoyment of God
and a mutual fellowship in God')[36] and only here would men be
able to know one another completely and to form a perfect
intimacy, as friends aimed to do. It is noteworthy that Augustine often uses language harking back to Classical discussions of
friendship in his description of the heavenly community, as in
the work *On the Trinity* (3.4.9) where he speaks of the spirits
joined together in 'perfect peace and friendship' (using the
word *amicitia*) and 'united in one desire by means of some kind
of spiritual fire of love'. In a similar description in Sermon 16
Augustine warns his listeners not to please their friends if it
means offending God and advises them in such circumstances
to reject their human friend so as to have God as their friend.
'But', he goes on, 'in that place where you will have God as
your friend, you will not be without your closest friend', in
other words, if you are united to your friend with a truly
Christian love, focussed on God, then that friendship will not
only survive death but actually reach fulfilment in heaven
where there are no more enemies, only friends, and where you
will have God, the saints and angels as your friends as well as
the close friends you managed to make in this mortal life.

Already in the *Soliloquies* Augustine had expressed some
doubt as to the possibility of knowing one's friend intimately in
this life and as his hopes of attaining a life of perfect wisdom this
side of the grave receded, so did his hope of reaching perfect
understanding of his friends, although in certain early writings
he was still willing to venture the belief that 'no one is known
except through friendship'.[37] It is perhaps in his letter to Proba
[Ep.130] that he speaks most movingly of his disappointment
with human friendship, while retaining the belief that without
a friend to share them a man will find many things in life hard
to bear. But how can anyone find a friend of whom he can be
completely sure? For just as man remains a mystery to himself,
so one man can never know the inmost recesses of his friend's

heart. How can we be certain that our dearest friend will remain loyal? Such feelings are expressed in a letter in which he encourages the widow Proba to turn her attention from the darkness of this life to the future life when the Lord will come and reveal the thoughts of our heart. Here Augustine alludes to St Paul's words at 1 Cor.4:5, as he does also in Ep.92, addressed to the widow Italica, who like Proba had moved from Rome to North Africa and whom he consoles by reminding her of the Christian's hope that when those we love die, we do not lose them but send them ahead to the place for which we ourselves are heading; there our love for them will be stronger and our understanding of them deeper, for nothing will remain hidden from our closest friends in that place where everyone is our most intimate friend. Again in the *Enchiridion* Augustine refers to 1 Cor.4:5 when he writes that we mortals cannot know the hearts of our fellow mortals but in the next life our love for one another will blossom fully when God reveals the secrets of our hearts: if even in this life there can be such great love that a man will lay down his life for his friend, just imagine how strong the love in heaven will be.[38]

From such writings it becomes clear that Augustine's pessimism concerning the possibility of perfect friendships in this life is tempered in an important manner by the eschatological perspective: not only does the Christian have the hope of perfect relationships in the life to come but he can even regard the formation of friendships in this life, imperfect and uncertain though they be, as a foreshadowing of the true unity and intimacy to come, in so far as they are spiritual relationships in which the friends are united as to their minds which is the best part of them and in so far as the friendships are founded on a shared love of God. Only friendships which have these characteristics will qualify for eternity.

However, a further characteristic of Augustinian friendship must not be forgotten: in order to be eternal, friendships must be extended as far as possible throughout mankind already in this life. As Augustine points out to Laetus in Ep.243,[39] only to the extent that the things of this life are shared in a spirit of love will they be eternal and this applies to human relationships as well. The sharing of goods was of course one of the fundamental characteristics of friendship in antiquity but Augustine gives the idea a new meaning, again affected by his eschatological perspective, just as the Ciceronian statement, 'True friendships are everlasting' receives a new interpretation in Augustine's view of friendship. Certainly Augustine recognises that the extension of friendship will necessarily be limited and yet he insists that the attempt must be made. Indeed, it is in the nature of the true love which inspires friendship and is a gift from God, to contain a creative element of such power that it can turn an enemy into a friend.[40] By loving another human being *qua* human, the Christian can bring his fellow man to a knowledge and love of God so that the human love becomes transformed and they find themselves bound by a common love of God which makes their relationship as much like a true friendship as it can be in this life. The neighbour becomes a brother, a friend in Christ.[41] This is how Christian friendship, regarded as part of the theological context, can be extended and maintained, not in spite of the commandment to love your neighbour but rather because of it. The goal of all true love of neighbour is to bring one's fellow men, even one's enemies, to salvation and to do this one must strive to create a unity of love focussed on God, based on Christ and inspired by the Holy Spirit, in other words a network of Christian friendships including as many people as possible. It is only when we have managed to bring our neighbour to the same understanding of the true faith as we ourselves hold that we shall be able to share everything truly with him, only when we have, in Cicero's words, 'agreement on all things human and divine together with good will and love'.

In adding a creative element to his view of friendship, Augustine makes it a more dynamic relationship than in the traditional picture. This element is of course paralleled by the creative force of God's love for man for we love him because he first loved us despite our sins. Although we may love someone because he is virtuous, as in the Ciceronian view of friendship, we may also love him in order that he might become just, i.e. in order that the love of God may be kindled in his heart and he may respond to our love with mutual feelings. In this way men may attain that love which is the true fulfilment of Christ's commandment whereby they love one another because they all belong to God, so that they may be brothers to His only Son, as Augustine writes in his commentary on the Gospel of John. 'They love one another with the same love with which He loved them when he intended to lead them to that final place where all their needs and desires would be satisfied and where God would be all in all.'[42]

Dependent on the creation and extension of such friendships was the unity of the body of Christ which became the focus of Augustine's ideas on the importance of a unified community. A belief in the importance of unity had naturally figured in his thoughts on friendship even before his conversion. Afterwards it continues to occur in connection with friendship, as in the early work *De ordine* where Augustine writes, 'Is not the main aim of friends to become one? And the more united they are, the closer friends they become,'[43] but is used increasingly in the context of the idea of the Church as the body of Christ, formed by Christians loving one another and God: once again an idea traditionally connected with friendship has been extended to apply to a question of a theological or ecclesiological nature.[44] As Augustine explained to Felicia in Ep.208, it is common membership in the body of Christ which brings Christian friends so close together. By being members of the true Church and by loving one another in Christ, Christians are able to create that unity which is so hard to achieve in this life but which will attain perfection in heaven. This unity is essential in Augustine's eyes as the root of peace, that peace which was continually shattered in his lifetime by heresy and schism – which Augustine no doubt regarded as tragic[45] but necessary, for peace could not be had at the expense of theological truth: it was for the heretics to abandon error and return to the Church, where unity, love and peace alone could be found. Only within the Church could man form those relationships which would attain perfection in the next life and conversely only by forming such mutual loving relationships could the unity of Christ's body be maintained: such was the aim of true love of neighbour.

However, despite the emphasis on unity Augustine apparently did not think it necessary for friends to live together or to experience one another's physical presence for this unity to be created. This resulted from his conviction that Christian friendships were spiritual relationships in which the intimacy of the friends derived from the bond created by Christ's love rather than from the sharing of everyday experience. The friend's absence could not, in theory, harm the relationship. This belief is evident not only in the case of the relationship between two individuals but on a wider scale, as when Augustine writes to members of the clergy who had abandoned the Donatist for the Catholic Church:

> It is not your absence which saddens me, for we are part of that Church which, however far it extends throughout the world, through God's favour forms the one great body of the great head which is the Saviour. As a result, however far apart we are even in the furthest corners of the world, yet we are together in Him in the unity of whose body we remain. How much closer together we are when we are in the same body than we would be even if we lived in the same house![46]

In fact we find here the idea, commonly expressed in Augustine's writings, that friendship maintained *in absentia*, when based on the body of Christ, is no second-best but actually more stable, more intimate than the traditional friendship in which friends are supposed to live in close proximity and see one another often.

The conviction that it is not necessary for friends to live together for them to be intimate is also based on the belief that friends are present to one another in their minds, so that they can be closer to one another in their thoughts than they would be if sitting side by side without communication.[47] A more obviously Christian context is given to this popular idea in Ep.194 in which Augustine writes to the future Pope Sixtus that, although he cannot see him with the eyes of the body, yet he can embrace and kiss him in his thoughts by means of Christ's faith, grace and the members of His body. Remarkable in this context is the allusion, in Ep.218, to Rom.5:5, a text which we have seen figuring frequently in discussions of Christian friendship: here Augustine writes, 'Whether absent or present in body, we wish to have you in the one spirit by means of which love is poured forth in our hearts, so that wherever we may be in the flesh, our souls will be inseparable in every way.'[48]

But it is not only our friends to whom we can become closer and more intimately known by means of Christ's love. Love of our friends can also afford us some knowledge of God – a fact which obviously makes Christian friendships even more valuable. Sage has observed that the *anima una* 'est pour S.Augustin, à partir de 407, l'énigme et le miroir par excellence où il nous est donné dès ici-bas à comprendre, comme nous le pouvons, le mystère de Dieu'[49] and Augustine himself makes this clear in commenting on St John's Gospel and first Epistle.[50] Although we cannot see God in this life, we not only deserve to see him by loving our friend, but by loving in a reciprocal relationship we shall also love Love itself which is the bond between the two friends: this love is God the Holy Spirit. In connection with his belief in the relation between human friendship and knowledge of God we may note that in exploring the nature of God Augustine even uses the language of friendship in his attempts to explain how the Holy Spirit relates to the two other members of the Trinity: he describes the third member of the Trinity as something consubstantial and co-eternal shared by the Father and the Son and considers using the term *amicitia* to explain its nature most satisfactorily but rejects this word in favour of *caritas*, presumably because of the text of 1 John 4:8 where God is said to be *caritas*. The analogy between human friendships and the Trinity goes further for in the *De Trin.*7.6.12 and elsewhere Augustine speaks of the essential characteristics of the Trinity as unity, likeness and equality, all of which were traditionally regarded as characteristic of ideal friendship. And if friendships could lead to some knowledge of God, an awareness of the unity of the Trinity could conversely lead to the formation of intimate human relationships, for by imitating the Trinity and clinging to God we are granted unity with one

another and with God in the Holy Spirit.[51] Human friendship
is thus absorbed into, and profoundly enriched by, its association with Augustine's theocentric world-view firmly based on
the Christian Scriptures but making use of theories of friendship for its clarification.

Augustine was unusual in laying such emphasis on the belief
that true love of neighbour, alongside love of God, plays an
essential part in man's progress towards a knowledge of God.
This was an idea which developed out of his early views and
experience of friendship and which found fulfilment in his
thoughts on the monastic life, for he came to regard this form of
life, based on the unity created by Christ's love and by the Holy
Spirit, as the most perfect means possible of gaining some
knowledge of God because God himself, as love, is present in
the community of Christians loving one another intimately in
God and spreading the love which God has granted them.
Although such monastic communities are strictly part of the
Church and have the same aims as the ordinary Christian, they
do offer a way of life which is a more accurate foretaste of the
life in heaven than does the Church at large, with all its
inevitable distractions and imperfections. As will be seen, many
of his ideas on the monastic life overlap with his views on
Christian friendship and love of neighbour.

Augustine's personal attraction towards the coenobitic life is
generally acknowledged to have been influenced by his lifelong
devotion to friendship and his need to be surrounded by close
friends who shared his interests and aims.[52] The scattered
allusions to his early friendships in the *Confessions* show how
influential his friends were, both for good and for bad – as in
the case of the pear-stealing episode described in Book II.
Although he regarded all his pre-conversion friendships as to
some extent sinful because they led him away from God or put
the friends before God, Augustine's experiences did provide
some kind of model for the later forms of communal life which
he organised. At Carthage, where he fled to try and forget his
lost friend, he shared his life with a group of friends whose
common interests (based on a commitment to Manichaeism)
and mutual love offered him comfort. He describes vividly the

attractions of these relationships at *Conf.*iv.8.13; he may have come to regard them as wrong, but it is also clear that he looked back on them with nostalgia:

> We could talk and laugh together and exchange small acts of kindness. Together we could read delightful books and we could both be serious and joke together. Sometimes we would disagree but without any ill-feeling, just as a man differs with himself and even these rare instances of disagreement added spice to our usual agreement. We could all teach each other something and learn from one another. When we were apart we missed our friends sorely but welcomed each other joyfully on our return.

The similarities as well as the differences between this experience and that of the monastic life developed by Augustine are evident if we compare this passage with the laudatory description of the ascetic community within the Catholic Church which he gives in the *De moribus Ecclesiae Catholicae* (31.67): he speaks of those who have scorned and abandoned the seductions of this world and joined together in a most chaste and holy way of life, spending their lives in prayer, reading and discussion. They own nothing of their own and lead a life of complete harmony, directed wholly towards God.

An intermediate stage between these two forms of community life is provided by Augustine's experience at Milan, shortly before his conversion.[53] In the *Confessions* he relates how his old friends Nebridius and Alypius who had accompanied him from Africa gave him support during this period of emotional problems and metaphysical anxieties. The three of them, whom Augustine describes as united in their fervent search for truth and wisdom, continued to pursue their worldly aims while becoming increasingly dissatisfied with their way of life, to the point where they planned to make a break with the troubles and distractions of this life and withdraw, together with six or seven other friends, to lead a communal and organised life of peace and study. One of the characteristics of this community was to be the sharing of property with the intention of making their relationships more open and frank and the group of individuals more of a unity. This was a principle which was to dominate the Augustinian form of communal life, but whereas later Augustine will emphasise that the principle of communal property is derived from Acts 4:32, here it arises out of the spirit of friendship.

However, their plans for a community of friends came to nothing as yet for some of them were married and others, including Augustine, were hoping to marry and marriage, they felt, was not compatible with their view of an intellectual community. In this, too, there is a hint of an element which will of course be fundamental to Augustine's monastic theories, namely that of chastity and segregation from the opposite sex. Although Augustine uses the word *mulierculae* (VI.14.24), with its possibly slightly patronising undertones, of the women who were preventing these men from realising their ideal, it is perhaps not so much the intellectual inferiority of women which posed a problem but rather the responsibilities and exclusivity of marriage which would obstruct the ideals of complete communality. But the influence of the traditional ideas about friendship as being primarily a relationship between members of the same sex, and the male sex at that, is no doubt to be detected, too.[54]

It is true that another influence on Augustine in his development towards the adoption of a form of monastic life was his encounter with the life of Antony as told by Athanasius. Although the principle of an intimate, mutually loving community was already too strong in his thought to make him consider the eremitic life, Augustine was deeply impressed by Antony's asceticism and also by the story, related by Ponticianus, of how Antony's example had inspired two friends in Milan to make a decisive break with the world, giving up their government posts and breaking off their engagements so as to be able to withdraw into a nearby monastery and become *amici Dei* (friends of God).[55] It was not long before Augustine finally reached the point where he truly believed it right to resign his post as professor of rhetoric and to abandon the idea of marriage. The conversion of Alypius and Nebridius occurred at much the same time and at last the friends were able to realise their plans to live together away from worldly concerns, at

Verecundus' country house at Cassiciacum, where they spent
the time in study, prayer and philosophical discussion.

In the years following Cassiciacum, however, the element of
philosophical friendship grew to have a more strongly Christian character. And yet Verheijen has drawn attention to the
similarities between the ideal life described in the *De ordine*,
written at Cassiciacum, and the monastic precepts formulated
by Augustine in the influential *Regula*,[56] written some ten years
later: he sees the influence of the Pythagorean importance
attached to friendship in the *De ordine*, an influence which
reveals itself also in the *Regula* with its emphasis on communal
property, community life and the extension of mutual love
throughout the community and beyond, although this later
work is firmly based on Scriptural texts. But it certainly seems
possible that Augustine derived such ideas from contact with
Iamblichus' *Life of Pythagoras*, produced earlier in the fourth
century, finding them compatible even with his specifically
Christian vision.

It appears from the *De moribus Ecclesiae Catholicae* that when
Augustine returned to Milan to be baptised by Ambrose, he did
visit the monastery which Ponticianus had told him about and
that he also studied the monastic life at first hand in the year
that he spent at Rome before returning to Africa for good. But
even before they left Milan he and his friends had decided to
live together a life of devotion in Africa where they could most
usefully serve God and this plan was put into practice when
they reached Augustine's home town of Thagaste in 388. Here
they set up a community based on the renunciation of all that is
personal and private (Augustine having sold his family property), within which their friendship was strengthened by the
fact that the aims they held in common focussed not on the
unstable things of this world but on God. In this community of
Christian ascetics which was at the same time a group of well-
educated friends, including Evodius, Severus and Alypius,
Augustine was to spend three years, reading, studying, praying
and writing letters. As yet its members had few responsibilities
outside the community but Augustine still apparently felt
himself prevented by his commitments from visiting Nebridius

who had stayed in Carthage to look after his mother: the
tension between their desire to meet and their responsibilities to
others which is evident in their letters to each other is reminiscent of that experienced by Basil and Gregory when separated
after their student days at Athens.[57]

In 391 Augustine made his fateful visit to Hippo where he
was ordained against his will. It is ironic that the reason for his
visit was a desire to persuade a friend to renounce his worldly
concerns and to enter the community at Thagaste but the
result was instead that Augustine had to leave Thagaste,
though he was allowed to transfer his community to Hippo,
thereby avoiding the necessity of abandoning the quasi-monas-
tic life because of the demands of the priesthood.[58] In fact, the
move to Hippo may be regarded as beneficial for it enabled the
community to expand both in practical and theoretical terms,
acquiring new members as well as a broader vision of the role of
the community within the Church.[59] As ecclesiastical responsibilities drew many of the members away from Hippo, Augustine undoubtedly felt the loss of his friends keenly, but from a
more positive perspective he could witness the spread of the
network of Christian friends which had developed around him.
Such expansion would have been in accordance with his
growing belief that mutual Christian love must gradually
spread to embrace more and more people.

If Augustine from an early stage regarded his community as
emulating the life of the first apostles at Jerusalem, the development of his thought saw certain changes of emphasis within this
idea as he moved from an attitude stressing the importance of
the renunciation of property and the sharing of all things to a
view which lays more emphasis on spiritual unity. The text
from Acts which inspired this idea is referred to by Augustine
many times in those works which are concerned with the theory
and practice of the monastic life[60] and is placed at the head of
the *Regula*, 'For you are all gathered together into one body so
that you may live in a spirit of unanimity and may have one
soul and one heart.'

Firstly Augustine stressed that the renunciation of personal
property was what distinguished the *monachus* from the ordin-

ary Christian and so it can be seen that the monastic communities which had developed from the group of friends who shared everything in accordance with the Pythagorean ideal of *koina ta ton philon* were now founded on the similar idea expressed in Acts 4:32.

Renunciation of personal property was for Augustine the *sine qua non* of another characteristic of the monastic life, that of spiritual unity. This, too, was based on Acts 4:32 but was also common to the Classical ideal of friendship: to a Christian educated in Classical thought and literature the Scriptural 'one soul and one heart', implying a unity through grace which is a reflection of the unity of the Trinity, would be reminiscent of the phrase 'one soul in two bodies' so often used of close friends by many writers, including Augustine.[61] The connection between renunciation of property and spiritual unity is made explicit in the commentary on Ps.132(133) in which Augustine addresses his congregation rather than a group of monks; he explains that the sharing of property among the members of the community creates suitable conditions for spiritual unity and mutual love, free from jealousy or selfishness.

Another Pythagorean ideal, that of 'friendship of all towards everyone' can also be detected in the Augustinian ideal of the community as 'one soul': this is the belief that love must not only be mutual but should extend beyond a few friends, for ultimately it must embrace all the members of the City of God. It was a belief which, like the emphasis on unity, was developed especially in order to combat the Donatists with their schismatic tendencies.

But if unity, community and extension of love were common both to the traditional ideals of friendship and to Augustine's monastic theories, there were also important differences. First and foremost there was the eschatological aspect which came more and more to dominate Augustine's thought as we have already noted in connection with his view of friendship. This manifests itself in the monastic writings particularly in the addition of *in Deum* or *in Deo* (in God) to his quotation of 'cor unum et anima una', reminding us that the unity of souls joined by the Holy Spirit will only be perfect in the next world when it can rest in God;[62] until then the single soul of Christ (*anima unica Christi*) is ceaselessly engaged in a striving towards God which is aided by the fact that the many souls are one in Christ although it cannot reach its goal in this world.

Another aspect of Augustine's theories which transforms the ideals of friendship is the idea, already referred to in connection with his writings on St John's Gospel, that man's contemplation of God, imperfect though it may be in this life, is assisted by the form of life in the Christian ascetic community within the Church by means of the love between the members of the community: God is present in this love because he is love.[63] Although this idea is foreign to the traditional theories of the benefits of friendship, it should be remembered that for Aristotle *syntheorein* (shared contemplation) is the highest good provided by virtuous friendships.[64]

Augustine's view of friends forming one soul is enriched by his belief, evident in his mature thought, that a unity of souls necessarily involves profound intimacy with Christ as well as with one's fellow men. Christ and Christians bound together through baptism form the *anima unica Christi*, a concept relating both to the body of Christ and to the phrase 'cor unum et anima una' from Acts 4:32. As we have seen, Augustine believed that this unity, though never to be perfectly realised in this life, comes closest to perfection in the monastic life which offers an original and profound form of the ideal of friendship as worked out in the theories of Classical writers discussing the problems of human relationships. Augustine's attraction to friendship and his early ideas on the subject seem to have attained a deeper significance in the context of the Christian's imitation of the apostolic community at Jerusalem and of Christ's love for man, for whom he laid down his life, the greatest thing one friend can do for another according to John 15:13 – a text frequently cited by Augustine. Christian friendship does not mean just human companionship and support in this life, but involves true discipleship of Christ and brings with it a foretaste of the knowledge and love of God and of our fellow men, which can only be perfected in the extended community of mutual love which will be the fulfilment of the City of God.

Conclusion

With Augustine we reach the culmination of fourth-century Christian theories of friendship, for it is he who arguably provides the most profound views, touching on many areas of Christian life and doctrine and according a crucial role to friendship in each Christian's progress towards salvation. And yet Augustine, as much as any of the late antique personalities discussed in this book, accepted the legitimacy of many of the theories developed by philosophers and other observers of human nature in Greek and Roman antiquity. Was this because the Classical formulations on the subject of *philia/ amicitia* were merely elegantly expressed clichés, common and acceptable to most cultures? No, although often expressed in memorable and oft repeated form, the ideas on friendship developed in Greece and Rome stand out in the history of ideas because of their sophistication and because of the importance attached to them, as is clear from a wide variety of literary genres. But even these facts would not explain why friendship suddenly became once again a crucial concept among so many of the Christian writers in the fourth century, for Christians were under no obligation to accept everything from their pagan heritage and in fact would only accept such ideas after close scrutiny. Why did these leading Christians decide to adopt or adapt so many of the theories familiar to them from their traditional Classical education, clearly finding them relevant to their own circumstances and even helpful in exploring the implications of their total commitment to Christ? It is perhaps important here to distinguish between two groups among these patristic writers who, despite the fact that they shared a common culture and a standard of education unusually high in antiquity,[1] reacted in rather different ways to the traditional thought on friendship familiar to them. Whereas Synesius, Ambrose and Jerome reveal themselves as very interested in, and positive towards, the Classical theories, whether predominantly Greek or Latin, others felt the need to create more of a synthesis, working the Classical theories more subtly into the texture of their Christian beliefs. They regard true friendship as a divine gift enabling Christians to come closer to one another and to God, but also involving certain more practical duties such as mutual support and encouragement and rebuke in all-important spiritual matters. As we have seen, the Classical theories as to the best basis for friendship, usually agreed to be virtue, and ideas of spiritual unity between friends, are transposed into areas of Christian theology and doctrine where the requisite spiritual unity is based on the mystical body of Christ. The ideal of virtue uniting friends, particularly emphasised by the Stoics, was not rejected, but it was not regarded in Classical terms, rather as a combination of love of neighbour and love of, or spiritual closeness to, God. Christ's love inspires and forms the basis for friendship, while union with the divine provides its aim. From the Platonic philosophy the Christians might be said to have adopted the idea of friends united by a higher good in a search for truth. The main legacy of the Aristotelian theories was the belief in the different kinds of friendship, though most Christians came to divide up the true kind of friendship, superior to the common relationships based on utility or pleasure, into a two-tier system which included both a general love towards all of mankind and a more specific love, uniting a few friends in a reciprocal bond. It is perhaps surprising, considering the common view of the relationship between friendship and Christian love, how often these fourth-century writers reveal their belief that the exclusive, mutual love is superior to the general love.

As to the reasons why both these groups reacted so positively to the concept of friendship, we can but speculate. One may suggest that it was indirectly due to the fact that in the post-312 world of toleration for Christianity, the hitherto largely local-

ised and inward-looking Christian communities were able to
open out and become more aware of other communities
throughout the Roman world: Christian ideals of brotherly
love, as well as the practical demands of the expanding Church
would encourage contacts between Christians working for the
faith in different places. Furthermore, the fact that Christianity
was now tolerated did not mean that it was safe, for paganism
still offered a certain threat to its continued growth and the
multiplicity of heresies within or on the fringes of Christianity,
demanding to be dealt with by argument or suppression,
meant that those Christians who believed themselves to represent the orthodox faith felt the need to band together, to join
forces against a common threat. Such circumstances are likely
to have made them feel that friendship, with its ideals and
obligations, was useful in emphasising the spiritual but practical links uniting them in whatever part of the Empire they
happened to be.

Another consequence of the increasing involvement of the
Church in secular affairs which resulted from Constantine's
edict, was the growth of the monastic movement which
expressed a dissatisfaction on the part of many Christians
with the way the Church was moving towards compromise
with the secular. The enormous popularity of ascetic ideals,
which rejected such compromise as far as was possible
but which nevertheless affected and penetrated the Church
itself, had an important effect on the ideals of friendship adopted by so many Christians and may help to explain
why the Classical theories of friendship could gain such
currency in a new context, even among those who held
important positions within the Church but who shared
a commitment to celibacy. We have seen that friendship
was definitely countenanced and, within certain guidelines,
encouraged in the monastic life developing particularly in
Egypt in the fourth century, and that there are a number of
similarities between the formulations on friendship of, for
example, Pachomius and those which survive from antiquity.
This is true even though the Pachomian monasteries were
primarily Coptic-speaking – Keith Hopkins reminds us that the

monks were taught to read Coptic which 'represents a cultural resistance of native Egyptian against the dominance of Greek speakers and writers; by proxy it was, presumably, also aimed against the dominance of Roman rule'.[2] But even if we do not wish to explain such similarities as exist as the result of the direct influence of Classical culture – and it is possible that the monastic ideas developed in more or less isolation, dependent only on the Bible,[3] it is nevertheless true that in the fourth century – and consequently through the Middle Ages – the Christian ideal of friendship is intimately bound up with the ascetic ideal. In this it goes further than the Classical ideal which saw itself as usually distinct from kinship ties, if not incompatible with them, although the Epicureans and Neoplatonists were perhaps the only groups who seem to have been attracted by the formation of a circle of friends which set itself apart from ordinary society and its duties. For the Christian, asceticism and friendship can set the person apart from the conventional ties of kinship and family without allowing him to reject the bonds of human affection and ties of obligation altogether. In both Classical and Christian views of perfect friendship, this relationship is seen as superior to 'natural' kinship relations as well as to relationships based on utility or pleasure, either because it is based on virtue and free choice or because it is a spiritual, non-physical relationship, the creation of divine grace and firmly based on shared doctrinal allegiances. 'Love's tie is stronger than the ties of blood'.[4] For the ascetic, friendship offered a position halfway between the rejection of secular life which fidelity to the original ideals of early Christianity seemed to demand, and complete renunciation of society and human fellowship which did not seem permissible if Jesus' exhortation to love one's neighbour was taken seriously. As a result, for the fourth-century Christian, a devotion to the ideals of friendship went hand in hand with a devotion to celibacy. Synesius is the only example of one whose 'conversion' did not involve a renunciation of a desire for marriage, or, in the case of Paulinus, a renunciation of the physical obligations of marriage. Friendship within marriage was

consequently hardly countenanced, even less so than in traditional Roman society.[5]

But despite this dominance of the ascetic ideal in the most
interesting of the Christian theories of friendship which we have
seen developed by such men as Basil and Augustine, the
detachment from the 'real' and the secular which this involved
did not prevent these new theories – or old theories in a new
context – from being very realistic and psychologically subtle
and perceptive as well as theologically coherent and faithful to
the Bible. Nor did the prominence of friendship imply the kind
of sentimentality which seems to dominate modern views of
friendship: strong friendships involved a large amount of
mutual obligation and loyalty. Only heresy on the part of one
of the friends was regarded as legitimate grounds for 'divorce',
but at this period this was a very real threat to friendships, as
we see in the case of the suspicions between Jerome and
Rufinus. The suspicion of heresy could not only break friendship but create strong enmities, too. The very importance
attached to friendship was closely linked to the ever-present
threat of schism and hatred, a threat which became very
painful reality for John Chrysostom, for example, in his
persecution by Bishop Theophilus of Alexandria. Many friendships inevitably became 'political', as allegiance and loyalty to
one person might involve enmity with another, whether one
liked it or not, as when Paulinus' perhaps naive approval of
Pelagius came under attack from Jerome and Augustine. This
was the obverse side of the strong and far-reaching alliances
formed in friendship. These writers were not men of leisure, idly
composing conventional literary pieces to impress their
acquaintances: although their letters do contain conventional
expressions, such as the idea that letters can make absent
friends seem present to one, this is largely due to the fact that
literary composition in antiquity was very much based on
imitation of previous models and formed by certain rules,
worked out in detail by rhetorical theorists, but this does not
mean that these formulations did not express sincere feelings.
And, as we have seen, the majority of these Christians, far from
being stuck within the limits of outmoded clichés, as one might

expect from a period which is often regarded as culturally decadent, were able to reinvigorate the concept of friendship, making it a dynamic instrument in the gradual movement of Christians towards harmony and salvation.

Notes

I INTRODUCTION

1. In his introduction to the *Penguin Book of Homosexual Verse* (Harmondsworth, 1983), p. 39, Stephen Coote expresses his belief that 'friendship' is merely a euphemism for 'gay emotion'.

2. C. S. Lewis, however, sees it as potentially dangerous to society because of the exclusivity which he considers a necessary part of it: see Lewis' chapter on friendship in *The Four Loves* (London, 1960). For a modern analysis of friendship see M. Argyle and M. Henderson, *The Anatomy of Relationships* (Harmondsworth, 1985).

3. It may seem unhelpful to make a strong distinction between 'pagan' and 'Christian' in discussing a period when the two cultures overlap in so many ways, but such a distinction is not wholly of our own making and is justifiably used of a body of ideas and literature produced by pre-Christians and non-Christians. Note the caveat expressed by J. Matthews, *The Roman Empire of Ammianus Marcellinus* (London, 1989), p. 426, in a discussion on 'pagan' religion: 'The modern historian faces a no less intractable problem of definition and should not embark on it with a vocabulary and conceptual framework that prejudge the issue.'

4. Paulinus of Nola, for instance, got into trouble with Augustine for corresponding on friendly terms with the heresiarch Pelagius – see Ep.186 among Augustine's letters addressed to Paulinus from him and Alypius.

5. R. Krautheimer in *Rome, Profile of a City, 312–1308* (Princeton, 1980), speaks of the Romanisation of Christianity, determined by the penetration of the Church hierarchy by men such as Ambrose, Jerome, Paulinus and Augustine who had been educated to a very high standard according to the traditional pagan culture of which Rome was still the focal point (see esp. pp. 33–42).

6. Cf. A. Otto, *Die Sprichwörter u. sprichwörtlichen Redensarten der Römer* (Leipzig, 1890), p. 264.

7. Cf. K. Treu, 'Freundschaft' in *RLAC* 8 (1972), p. 429, 'Vom 4.Jh. fliessen die Quellen reichlich. Durch Briefe u. autobiographische Darstellungen werden die Autoren zunehmend auch als Menschen u. Freunde fassbar. Mit der allgemeinen Übernahme klassischer Bildungstraditionen wird die Anknüpfung an die antike Freundschaft deutlicher.'

8. On the state of education in late antiquity, see the survey by H.-I. Marrou, *A History of Education in Antiquity* (trans. G. Lamb, London, 1981).

9. Basil, in Ep.91, writes to a fellow bishop of the unity of spiritual love created by letters between Christians.

10. The translation of this passage and others from Paulinus' letters is based on that of P. G. Walsh in *The Letters of St. Paulinus of Nola* (ACW vols. 35–6) (London/Westminster Md., 1967).

11. Cf. H. Koskenniemi, *Studien zur Idee und Phraseologie des griechischen Briefes bis 400 n.Chr.* (Helsinki, 1956), p. 51.

12. See e.g. Synesius Ep.88 and Ep.133.

13. Basil Ep.48. The translations of passages from Basil's letters are based on those of R. J. Deferrari in his edition of St Basil's letters for the Loeb Classical Library (London, 1926, repr. 1972).

14. Cf. Synesius Ep.53 (55 G.) and Ep.85, Augustine Ep.31 to Paulinus and Ep.186 in which he writes thus of Januarius, the bearer of this letter to Paulinus, 'At long last God has provided us with the most trustworthy of all letter-bearers, our justly cherished brother Januarius. Even if we did not write, you could learn all our news from him as from a living and intelligent letter.'

15. Basil Ep.163 and Ep.165.

16. The theorist of Greek letter-writing, Demetrius, describes a letter as an image of the soul (*De elocut.* 227 = Radermacher (1901), p. 48).

17. Cf. Koskenniemi, 'Studien', pp. 38–42, on the presence of friends through letters; Cicero, *Letters to Atticus* VIII.14.1, IX.10.1, XII.53 and XII.39.2.

18. Symmachus 4.35, 5.27, 5.29; Jerome Ep.7.2, Paulinus Ep.6.2, Basil Epp.73, 89, 100, 162.

19. See e.g. Gregory of Nazianzus Ep.30, Basil Ep.162 and Ep.165, Paulinus Ep.17.1; cf. Luther in his commentary on Gal.4:20, (trans. in J. Pelikan, ed., *Luther's Works*, St Louis, 1963, pp. 431–2).

20. E.g. Julian 288b (Ep.89b, ed.Bidez, trans. by W. C. Wright in the Loeb Classical Library edition of *The Works of the Emperor Julian*

(London, 1923, repr. 1953), vol. 2 p.297), and Eunapius, *Vitae sophistarum* VI.11.8.

21. See e.g. B. McGuire, *Friendship and Community; the Monastic Experience 350–1250* (Cistercian Publications, Kalamazoo, 1988).

22. Cf. G. Bonner, 'Augustine's attitudes to women and *amicitia*, in C. Mayer and K.-H. Chelius, eds., *Homo Spiritalis. Festgabe für Luc Verheijen* (Würzburg, 1987), pp. 259–75.

23. See Possidius, *Life of Augustine* 26 (PL 32.55); cf. St Martin as portrayed by Paulinus' friend Sulpicius Severus in *Dialogus* II.7, trans. B. Peebles in FotC, vol.7 (New York, 1949).

24. Such women were known within the Church as *subintroductae* or *agapetae*. It may be that such women are referred to by St Paul in 1 Cor.7:36, though this is denied by P. Labriolle in his article, 'Le mariage spirituel dans l'antiquité chrétienne', *Revue Historique*, 137 (1921), 204–25. For late fourth-century criticism of such relationships, see Jerome's Ep.22 and John Chrysostom's works *Contra eos qui subintroductas habent* (PG 47.495–514) and *Quod regulares feminae viris cohabitare non debeant* (PG 47.513–32). For evidence that such relationships occurred within the Syrian church and were condemned in the early fifth century, see 'The Rules of Rabbula for the Qeiama', in A. Vööbus, *Syriac and Arabic Documents regarding Legislation relative to Syrian Asceticism* (Stockholm, 1960), p. 38, no.2. Note also that in the work included among the spuria of Cyprian (CSEL 3.173–220), *De singularitate clericorum*, the text of Gal.6:2, popular among writers on friendship, is put forward in hypothetical defence of such relationships.

25. Cf. Jerome Ep.45

26. In his Ep.22 to the young Eustochium, Jerome refers to such women with the oxymoron 'meretrices univirae' (faithful whores).

27. Thomas Kelly, *A Testament of Devotion* (1941, repr. London, 1979), p. 71.

2 CLASSICAL THEORIES OF FRIENDSHIP

1. For surveys of friendship in antiquity, see especially L. Dugas, *L'amitié antique d'après les moeurs populaires et les théories des philosophes* (Paris, 1894); F. Dirlmeier, φίλος *und* φιλία *im vorhellenistischen Griechentum* (unpublished thesis, Munich, 1931); J.-C. Fraisse, *Philia, la notion de l'amitié dans la philosophie antique* (Paris, 1974); K-A. Neuhausen, ed., *M. Tullius Cicero: Laelius* (Heidelberg, 1981); E. Klein, *Studien zum Problem der 'römischen' und 'griechischen' Freundschaft* (unpublished thesis, Freiburg, 1957).

2. For some of the general differences between Greek and Roman ideas on friendship, see K. Meister, 'Die Freundschaft bei den Griechen und Römern', *Gymnasium*, 57 (1950), 5.

3. See O. Kaiser, '*Lysis* oder "Von der Freundschaft",' *ZRGG* 32 (1980), 193–4 and O. Gigon, *Kommentar zum zweiten Buch von Xenophons Memorabilien* (Basle, 1956) p. 118, on extension of the term *philia*.

4. See the article of A. W. H. Adkins, 'Friendship and self-sufficiency in Homer and Aristotle', *CQ* 13 (1963), 30–45.

5. Cf. Theognis 979–82: 'Not for me a friendship based only on words – I want actions, too. May my friend hurry to help me with his hands and money alike; rather than holding me spellbound with his words over drink, let him show me the benefits of his deeds, if he can.'

6. See the discussions of H. J. Kakridis, *La notion de l'amitié et l'hospitalité chez Homère* (Thessalonica, 1963) and D. Robinson, 'Homeric φίλος; love of life and limbs and friendship with one's θύμος', in E. M. Craik, ed., *Owls to Athens: essays presented to Sir K. Dover* (Oxford, 1990).

7. This friendship is referred to as an ideal by Seneca in Ep.88.6, Lucian (*Toxaris* 10), Plutarch in his essay *On having many friends* (*Mor*.93E), Themistius (p.330D) and Libanius (Or.1.56).

8. See e.g. Plato, *Symposium* 179E: '(Achilles) bravely chose to go and rescue his lover Patroclus.'

9. Cf. the relationship between the future king Arthur and Sir Kay where it is the younger man, Arthur, who attains prominence although he begins as the subordinate.

10. See e.g. the references by Plato (*Lysis* 214A), Aristotle (*Rhet*.1371b 16, *Eud.Eth*.1235a 7 and *Nic.Eth*.1155a 34), and in Latin, Cicero (*De senectute* 3.7), Quintilian (v.11.41), Ammianus Marcellinus (28.1.53) and Erasmus (*Adages* 1.2.22 = LB II.80B–C).

11. For a discussion of the importance of the law of revenge in Greek ethics with special reference to its use in tragedy, see M. W. Blundell, *Helping Friends and Harming Enemies: a Study in Sophocles and Greek Ethics* (Cambridge, 1989).

12. Lines 25–6 of Hesiod's *Works and Days* are cited by Plato (*Lysis* 215D) and Aristotle (*Rhet*.1381b 16, *Nic.Eth*.1155a 35–1155b 1) in discussing the nature of friendship. Cf. Gregory of Nazianzus Ep.195.

13. Theognis' line 35 is mentioned by Aristotle in his discussion at *Nic.Eth*.1170a 11–12.

14. See Theognis 125–6; cf. 457–60, 959–62.

15. For the cosmic element in *philia*, compare Empedocles' theory of

the cosmic balance between *philotes* (friendship) and *neikos* (strife) and Heraclitus' theory of the harmony of opposites (Fr.8 D–K) referred to by Aristotle at *Nic.Eth.*1155b 4–6. Also important in early Greek philosophy were the related concepts of equality and justice – see G. Vlastos, 'Equality and justice in early Greek cosmologies', *CPh* 42 (1947), 156–78.

16. On this problem, see C. J. de Vogel, *Pythagoras and early Pythagoreanism* (Assen, 1966), esp. pp. 153–5 and Fraisse, 'Philia', p. 57.

17. See Diog. Laert.8.10.23; Iamblichus, *De vita Pythagorica* 229–30; Porphyry, *De vita Pythagoreae*; Diodorus x.8.

18. Iambl., *Vit. Pyth.* 33. 237.

19. Diodorus writes (x.8) that the Pythagoreans 'laid the greatest store upon constancy towards one's friends, believing as they did that the loyalty of friends is the greatest good to be found in life'.

20. The story of Lysis and Euryphamos was recorded by Iamblichus (*Vit. Pyth.*30.185) and that of Damon and Phintias by Iamblichus (*ibid.*33.234–7) and Porphyry (*Vit.Pyth.*59–61).

21. Cicero: *De fin.*II.24.79, *De off.*III.10.45, *Tusculan Disputations* v.22,63; Diodorus x.4.3–6; Valerius Maximus IV.7; Plutarch, *On having many friends* (*Mor.*93E); Hyginus 257 (under the names Selinuntius and Moerus); Ambrose, *De off.min.*III.12.80, *De virginibus* II.5.34; Jerome, *Comm.in Matt.*18.19–20.

22. See F. Hauck's article on *Koinonia* in the *Theologisches Wörterbuch zum NT*, vol.3 (1935–8), pp. 789–810.

23. This attribution is made by Porphyry in his *Life of Pythagoras* (33), though Diogenes Laertius (7.23) states that Zeno the Stoic was the originator of the phrase.

24. Cicero, *De off.*I.17.56.

25. See Fraisse, 'Philia', p.11.

26. Blundell, 'Helping friends', esp. p. 260–73. See also N. A. Greenberg's article, 'Euripides' Orestes, an interpretation', in *HSPh* 66 (1962), 157–92.

27. For Socrates' rejection of the idea expressed by Euripides at *Medea* 809, *Ion* 1046–7 and *Heracles* 585–6, see esp. Plato, *Rep.*332E, *Gorgias* 474B and *Crito* 49A.

28. Euripides, *Hecuba* 879, *The Daughters of Heracles* 681, *Heracles* 55–6, 1425–6.

29. Fraisse, 'Philia', p. 12.

30. E.g. Alan of Lille, *Anticlaudianus* II.195–6, *Roman de la Rose* 8148–54, Erasmus' letter to James Tudor (Allen 1.366–8).

31. E.g. Aristippus, quoted by Diogenes Laertius (2.91) as talking of 'a friend for the sake of usefulness'.

32. See W. K. C. Guthrie, *The Sophists* (Cambridge, 1971), pp. 148–52.
33. E.g. Aristotle, *Rhet.*1381a; Thucydides 1.44.1, 3.70.6, 3.75.1, 7.33.6; Xenophon *Anabasis* 2.5.39; Isocrates 19.10; Democritus Fr.107 D–K.
34. Guthrie, 'Sophists', pp. 41–4.
35. This translation is that of E. C. Marchant in his Loeb edition of Xenophon's *Memorabilia and Oeconomicus* (London, 1923). Aristotle alludes to this idea at *Nic.Eth.*1170a 13 where he speaks of virtuous friendship being naturally desirable for virtuous men. Cf. *Politics* 1253a 1–2.
36. For a summary of the argument of Plato's *Lysis*, see W. K. C. Guthrie, *History of Greek Philosophy*, vol. 4, pp. 143–54; and, in the context of a discussion of its meaning, A. W. Price, *Love and Friendship in Plato and Aristotle* (Oxford, 1989), pp. 2–8.
37. On these works of Plato, see Price, 'Love and Friendship', pp. 15–102.
38. Plato, *Lysis* 216c.
39. *Ibid.*210E.
40. *Ibid.*219c–D.
41. See Price, 'Love and Friendship', pp. 3–4.
42. On p.8 of 'Love and Friendship', Price discusses the confusion created by Socrates' use of the two related meanings of *oikeios*.
43. In the words of W. Ziebis, *Der Begriff der φιλία* bei Plato (unpublished thesis, Breslau, 1927), pp. 26–7, 'Das *proton philon*, die Idee des Guten und Schönen, ist das Prinzip das alle die eint, die nach ihm streben. Dieses gemeinsame Streben macht die *oikeiotes* . . . unter Freunden aus.'
44. This more practical side to friendship is highlighted in Plato's sixth and seventh letters in which he encourages his friends to base their friendships on a shared devotion to philosophy; this will enable them to be of great benefit to one another. In the seventh letter he also indicates that he believes self-control to be essential to loyal friendship.
45. For some of the differences between Plato and Aristotle in their theories of friendship, see Fraisse, 'Philia', p. 190.
46. Cf. Aristotle, *Eud.Eth.*1234b 18.
47. At *Nic.Eth.*1156b 26–8 Aristotle refers to the popular saying, 'Men cannot know each other before they have eaten salt together.'
48. Hesiod, *Works and Days* 715; Aristotle, *Nic.Eth.*1170b 21.
49. One characteristic they share is *koinonia* which is applicable both

to the living together of friends and social relations on a wider
scale: see *Nic.Eth.*1161b 11–15.

50. Aristotle, *Nic.Eth.*1162b 16–19.

51. This agreement between proverbial statements and the Aristotelian view of the relation between self-love and friendship is also evident at *Nic.Eth.*1166a 31–2 where he refers to the popular saying that a friend is a second self.

52. Aristotle, *Nic.Eth.*1169a 19–20.

53. Kaiser, '*Lysis*', p.206, states however that Plato believed that 'Es gibt keinen Menschen, der nicht der Ergänzung durch den anderen bedarf'.

54. For the evidence for such works, see Cicero in *De finibus* IV.3.6, Diog.Laert.4.4 and 4.12; also Neuhausen, 'Laelius', p.29 and Treu, 'Freundschaft', p. 420.

55. I.e. Cicero, *Lael.*22.85; Seneca Ep.3.2; Plutarch, *On brotherly love* 8 (*Mor.*482B); Ammianus Marcellinus, 26.2.9; Rutilius Lupus 1.6 – as an example of the rhetorical device known as antimetabole.

56. Diog.Laert.7.108.

57. I.e.*poietika agatha* rather than *telika agatha*. Cf. Cicero on Zeno the Stoic in *De fin.*III.16.55.

58. Diogenes Laertius (7.124) says that Posidonius and Hecato declared that a friend should be chosen for himself, with which we may compare what Cicero writes in the *De finibus* (III.21.70).

59. The Stoic application of the term *oikeiosis* to their view of friendship may have been influenced by one of the earliest and most fundamental Greek theories on the subject, namely that friendships are best founded on the principle of like to like.

60. Cicero, *Lael.*5.18; Seneca Ep.81.12.

61. According to Clement of Alexandria (*Stromateis* v.14.95 (GCS 52.388 = *SVF* I 223), Zeno had posited that all good men are one another's friends.

62. It was an idea discussed by Zeno in his work the *Politeia* and by Chrysippus in his *On Paradoxes*; cf. F. H. Sandbach, *The Stoics* (London, 1975), pp. 25 and 43.

63. Seneca Ep.48.3; cf. Cicero, *Lael.*5.20.

64. In sorting out this problem Seneca makes use of typically Stoic paradoxes such as (Ep.9.14–15) the distinction drawn by Cleanthes who said that the wise man is not in need of anything and yet many things are necessary to him and therefore friends are necessary. Cf. Ep.9.13, 'The wise man is self-sufficient, not for living but for living happily.'

65. F.-A. Steinmetz, *Die Freundschaftslehre des Panaitios nach einer Analyse von Ciceros Laelius 'De Amicitia'* (Wiesbaden, 1967), believes

that Cicero followed Panaetius in depicting a moderate brand of Stoicism which tempered the orthodox Stoic ideal of the wise man but which continued to put forward virtue as the basis of true friendship and to stress the importance of *oikeiosis*: see Cic. *Lael*.5.19–20.

66. This seems to have been a revision of an earlier definition of friendship as 'a benevolent attitude towards someone for the sake of the one who is loved, with a similar attitude on his part', thus formulated by Cicero in his *De inventione* (II.55.166).

67. The popularity of Cicero's dialogue did however mean that Scipio and Laelius were added to the list of legendary pairs of friends, cf. *Lael*.4.15. It is likely that their friendship was particularly attractive to Cicero because it was a philosophical friendship between statesmen and Cicero saw himself as a second Laelius to Pompey's Scipio (cf. Cic.*Ep.ad Fam*.5.7). This pair of friends is referred to by the emperor Julian (*Or*.8.244C) and by Ausonius (Ep.24.37, in *The Works of Ausonius*, ed. R. P. H. Green, Oxford, 1991).

68. See e.g. the works of P. A. Brunt, '*Amicitia* in the late Roman Republic', *PCPhS* 11 (1965); 1–20, P. White, '*Amicitia* and the profession of poetry in early imperial Rome', *JRS* 68 (1978), 74–92; E. Rawson, *The Politics of Friendship: Pompey and Cicero* (Sydney, 1978); M. Gelzer, *The Roman Nobility* (trans. R. Seager, Oxford, 1969); J. Hellegouarc'h, *Le vocabulaire latin des relations et des partis politiques sous la république* (Paris, 1972); and R. P. Saller, *Personal Patronage under the Early Empire* (Cambridge, 1982); see also the bibliographies in Neuhausen, '*Laelius*' and R. O. A. M. Lyne, *The Latin Love Poets* (Oxford, 1980), pp. 291–2 n.4.

69. See Cicero, *Lael*.17.64.

70. On the stability of nature, see *Lael*.9.32 where Cicero writes that 'because nature cannot be changed, true friendship (based on nature) is eternal'. Here he follows the view of Panaetius and the Stoics generally who believed that friendship developed from nature rather than need because love and benevolence are natural to man, as is proved by the feelings of parents towards their children.

71. See Steinmetz, 'Panaitios', pp. 62–172, for his detailed analysis of the threefold division of the *Laelius*, i.e. sections 16–24, 26–32 and 33–100.

72. Like his predecessors Cicero believed that potential friends ought to be tested before one commits oneself to friendship. At *Lael*.17.64 Cicero quotes Ennius' memorable phrase 'amicus

certus in reincerta cernitur' with approval. On the question of frankness in friendship, see G. Bohnenblust, *Beiträge zum Topos περὶ φιλίας* (unpublished thesis, Bern, 1905), pp. 35–6 and Plutarch's work on flattery and friendship (*Moralia* 59B–62B). On one's duty to a friend, compare *Lael.*11.37 and Aulus Gellius, *Attic Nights* 1.3.9–10.

73. For the proverb about friendship being more valuable than the basic necessities of fire and water, see Paroem.Gr.II.766.49, Otto, 'Sprichwörter', p. 19, and Plutarch on flattery and friendship (*Mor.*51B).

74. Eating salt together could also be regarded as a symbol of friendship as in *PUniv.Giss.*25.19 (iii A.D.)

75. Sallust's phrase is referred to by Seneca Epp.20.5 and 109.16; Silius Italicus 9.406, Jerome *Adv.Rufinum* 3.9, Ep.130.12, Sidonius Apollinaris Ep.v.3.2; cf. K.–A. Neuhausen, 'Zu Cassians Traktat *De Amicitia*', in C. Gnilka and W. Schetter, eds., *Studien zur Literatur der Spätantike* (Bonn, 1975), p. 195 and Otto, 'Sprichwörter', p. 19.

76. Lactantius, *Instit.*5.9.6, Rufinus (6.559 Keil), Augustine *Ep.*82, Sulpicius Severus 1.9.3, Priscian (3.433 Keil) and Isidore *Etymologiae* 2.9.11. Cf. Ausonius *On the seven sages* 191, ed. Green, 'veritas odium parit'.

77. Cicero, *Lael.*25.92 and *De off.*1.17.56.

78. In a letter to Atticus (12.53) Cicero writes, 'Even if I have nothing to write to you, I write because I seem to talk to you.' Cf. *Ep.ad Fam.*7.5 to Caesar and 16.16.2 from Quintus.

79. See Lucretius, *De rerum natura* v.1019ff. on the role of *amicitia* in the development of society and the end of Book IV on the problems caused by sexual desire.

80. At *De fin.*II.26.82 Cicero refers to a saying of Epicurus which seems to sum up this view: 'Friendship cannot be divorced from pleasure and ... it deserves to be cultivated for the reason that without it we cannot live secure and free from alarm and therefore we cannot live agreeably.'

81. See A. Festugière, *Epicure et ses dieux* (Paris, 1968), p. 56; cf. J. Rist, *Epicurus, an Introduction* (Cambridge, 1972), p. 132.

82. In *Gnom.Vat.*23 (ed. Arrighetti p.145) it is written, 'All friendship is chosen for itself but it takes its beginning from usefulness', while Diogenes Laertius writes (10.120) that Epicurus proposed that 'friendship is prompted by our needs ... and maintained by a partnership in the enjoyment of life's pleasure', trans. R. D. Hicks (Loeb, 1950).

83. Plutarch's *Reply to Colotes* (*Mor.*111B).

84. W. Schmid, ed., *Studia Herculanensia* Fasc.1, Ethica Epicurea, Pap.Herc. 1251 (1939), col.xxii, lines 15–21.

85. It is interesting to note that according to Diogenes Laertius (10.11), Epicurus did not approve of friends holding everything in common 'for such a practice implied mistrust and without confidence there could be no friendship'.

86. Fraisse, 'Philia', p. 313, writes, 'Pour Epicure comme pour Aristote enfin, il s'agit, par l'amitié, non de découvrir un plaisir nouveau, mais de rendre tout plaisir plus vrai qu'il ne l'est dans la solitude: de même que chez Aristote, la partage d'une activité la rend plus agréable et en facilite l'exercice, de même, chez Epicure, la présence d'un ami contribue à rendre notre jouissance plus pure et plus intemporelle.'

87. One of Publilius Syrus' *sententiae* is also referred to by Jerome (Ep.107.8, cf.128.4) when he writes, 'Once when I was a boy at school I read this line, "You can hardly blame a habit which you yourself have allowed."'

88. This work of Valerius Maximus is referred to by Pliny the Elder, Plutarch, etc. Epitomes of it were also made in the fourth and fifth centuries by Julius Paris and Januarius Nepotianus.

89. Blossius was a Stoic and a close friend of Ti. Gracchus: see Cic. *Lael.*11.37 and Plutarch's life of Ti. Gracchus. Pomponius and Laetorius are mentioned as two friends of C. Gracchus who accompanied him in flight after his last battle on the Aventine; they prevented him from committing suicide and then held the bridge over the Tiber in the manner of Horatius Cocles until Gracchus had swum to the other side; see e.g. Plutarch's life of C. Gracchus and Orosius 5.12.7.

90. Plut. *On having many friends* (*Mor.*93E).

91. Plutarch also mentions Chilo (regarded, like Cleoboulos of Lindos, as one of the seven sages), whom Aulus Gellius highlights in his discussion of friendship in the *Attic Nights*, where Chilo is portrayed as doubting whether he should support his friend or the law in cases where they conflict. In connection with this problem Aulus Gellius mentions the earlier discussions of Theophrastus and Cicero, criticising them for giving too general an answer to the problem. He also refers to a saying of Chilo quoted by Plutarch in the first book of his work on the soul, to the effect that enmities and friendships are closely interdependent.

92. Prodicus' story of Heracles' choice is told by Xenophon in the *Memorabilia* (II.1.21) and in a speech on the subject of friendship by the late fourth-century orator and imperial tutor, Themistius.

93. In support of this theory Maximus quotes *Iliad* 22.262 when

Achilles, on the point of refusing mercy and killing Hector, says, 'Lions do not come to terms with men nor does the wolf see eye to eye with the lamb.'

94. J. Rist, *Eros and Psyche* (Toronto, 1964), p. 82.

3 SOME PROBLEMS OF CHRISTIAN FRIENDSHIP

1. S. Kierkegaard, *The Works of Love* (trans. D. F. and L. M. Swenson, Princeton, 1946), p. 37; cf. James Boswell's account in his life of Samuel Johnson, of Johnson's argument that Christianity and friendship are incompatible, with Mrs. Knowles' persuasive counter-argument. See also K. Treu, 'φιλία und ἀγάπη: zur Terminologie der Freundschaft bei Basilius und Gregorius Nazianzenus', *StudClas* 3 (1961), 421, 'Der Begriff der *agape* ersetzt die *philia*'; H. Hagendahl, *The Latin Fathers and the Classics* (Gothenburg, 1958), p. 358, 'In antiquity, friendship was cultivated, not only among the Pythagoreans, as a cornerstone of human society and a blessing of life; from the rise of Christianity it had to yield to charity'. Cf. L. Vischer, 'Das Problem der Freundschaft bei den Kirchenvätern', *ThZ* 9 (1953), 176.

2. J. H. Newman, *Parochial and Plain Sermons* (London, 1868), vol.2, no.5, p. 55; cf. Bishop Jeremy Taylor in 'A discourse of the nature, measure and offices of friendship' (London, 1657), who wrote, 'So that to your question, how far a dear and perfect friendship is authorized by the principles of Christianity? The answer is ready and easy. It is warranted to extend to all mankind; and the more we love, the better we are and the greater our friendships are, and the nearer we are to God; let them be as dear and let them be as perfect, and let them be as many as you can; there is no danger in it; only where the restraint begins, there begins our imperfection ... it were well if you could love and if you could benefit all mankind; for I conceive that is the sum of all friendships.'

3. P. Hinnebusch, *Friendship in the Lord* (Indiana, 1974), p. 9, writes, '... friendship in the Lord is never two people closed in on themselves. Each of the friends is fully open to the Lord and open to other friends in such a way that the friendship is always part of a larger community'. Cf. A. Sage, 'La contemplation dans les communautés de vie fraternelle', *RecAug* 7 (1971), 285–6.

4. A. Nygren opened the discussion by presenting this dichotomy forcefully in his book *Agape and Eros: a Study of the Christian Idea of Love* (trans. P. S. Watson, London, 1953); others, such as J. Burnaby, have had to accept his dichotomy in order to discuss it,

in his book *Amor Dei: a Study of the Religion of St Augustine* (London, 1938).

5. For a discussion of the meanings of these words, see Paeslack's article, 'Zur Bedeutungsgeschichte der Wörter φιλεῖν lieben, φιλία Liebe, φίλος Freund, in der LXX u.im N.T.', *Theologia Viatorum*, 5 (1953–5), 51–142, and Treu, 'Freundschaft', p. 424.

6. Peter Abelard, *Planctus David super Saul et Jonathan*, G. Vecchi, ed. (Modena, 1951), no.6, e.g. lines 45–6:

> Plus fratre mihi, Jonatha,
> In una mecum anima...

7. See e.g. Theognis 643–4, 'Drinking companions often become friends, but they desert when harder times come.' Cf. G. Stählin in the *Theologisches Wörterbuch zum N.T.*, vol.9 (1973), p. 154, 'Sir.6:5–17 bietet sogar eine kleine zusammenhängende Abhandlung, vergleichbar mit den entsprechenden Stücken in griech. u. hellen. Literatur.' In connection with his comments on Sir.6:6 the seventeenth-century exegete Cornelius a Lapide compares thoughts on *polyphilia* expressed by Theognis, Hesiod, Aristotle, Cicero and Lucian. On Sir.6:10, cf. Horace *Carm.*i.35.26–8 and R. Nisbet and M. Hubbard, *A Commentary on Horace Odes* i (Oxford, 1970).

8. Philo, *De plantatione* 104–6, *SVF* iii.432.

9. Philo, *Special laws* i.70, *On the virtues* 35.

10. The idea of friendship between man and God is an important one in Philo which can be found in later Christian writers, too, though it is not made much of in the ethical, non-mystical discussions about friendship which prevail among those writers of late antiquity who are the subject of this study. See Stählin, 'φίλος', p. 156 and the article by E. Peterson, 'Der Gottesfreund', *ZKG* 42 (1923), 161–202.

11. For the essential agreement between pagans and Christians about the important place of *unanimitas* in friendship, see Cornelius a Lapide's *Commentary on Ecclesiasticus*, p. 162, where he refers to Cicero, Cassian and Ambrose on the subject.

12. For references to Ps.54:7 in the context of friendship (usually in personal letters), see e.g. Basil Epp.47 and 140, Greg.Naz.Ep.42 and Paulinus of Nola Epp.18.8 and 38.9.

13. Aug.*En.in* Ps.103.13.

14. See the commentaries of Augustine and Jerome on this psalm. Augustine appropriately also refers to Acts 4:32–5 in commenting on this passage.

15. Aug.*Tract*.17.9 on the Gospel of John, *De diversis quaestionibus* 71.1.
16. Basil Epp.91, 114, 172, 191, 203, 258; Augustine Ep.73.3.6; cf. *En.in Ps*.147.9, *Tract*.25.6 on the Gospel of John, in which Augustine uses the same text to point to the perfection of love which will exist at the end of time.
17. Basil Ep.65; cf. Aug.Ep.211.12.
18. See H. D. Betz, *Plutarch's Ethical Writings and Early Christian Literature* (Leiden, 1978), p. 237, nn.33 and 34.
19. John Chrysostom, Hom.1 in Coloss.(Field, ed., vol.5, pp. 176–8).
20. For recent linguistic studies of *philia* and *amicitia*, see e.g. those by Treu, 'Terminologie', and H. Petré, *Etudes sur le vocabulaire latin de la charité chrétienne* (Louvain, 1948).
21. John Chrysostom Hom.7 in 2 Tim.(Field, ed., vol.6, p. 227) Aug.*De Trin*.6.5.7; cf. Aelred of Rievaulx who allows himself to take the step narrowly avoided by Augustine: in quoting 1 John 4.16 he writes (*De spiritali amicitia* 1. 69–70), 'Deus amicitia est'.
22. In his commentary on the sixth chapter of Ecclesiasticus (pp. 60–1), Cornelius a Lapide quotes side by side Chrysostom's Hom.61 in Matt.(PG 58.588) which speaks of the indissolubility of *agape* founded on Christ, Jerome's letter to Rufinus (Ep.3) in which he writes, echoing Cicero, 'A friendship which can cease to exist was never genuine', and the mention in Cassian's sixteenth *Conference* (16.3) of 'the faithful and indissoluble bond of friendship which can only be created on the basis of equality of virtues'.
23. This is not to deny that Christians recognise that there were still many social inequalities in Christian society and that equality in this sense was an ideal towards which men must strive in love: see Aug.*Tract*.8.5 on the Epistle of St John. On attitudes to the idea of the equality of all human beings in antiquity and its relation to Christian values, see J. Rist, *Human Value* (Leiden, 1982), pp. 153–4.
24. Burnaby, 'Amor Dei', pp. 307–8.
25. In Ep.272 Basil again set friendship and love of neighbour side by side when he writes to Sophronius, 'For I consider that I am just as good as any of those renowned for friendship, both because I have never been caught offending against friendship and because I have received from God the commandment to love...'
26. O. M. T. O'Donovan, *The Problem of Self-love in Augustine* (New Haven, 1980); cf. Burnaby, 'Amor Dei', pp. 116–26; Nygren, 'Agape', pp. 216–17; G. Outka, *Agape, in Ethical Analysis* (New Haven, 1972), esp. ch.2; and Betz, 'Plutarch', pp. 367–94 on Plutarch's *De laude ipsius*.

27. For such allegations, see *The Penguin Book of Homosexual Verse*, S. Coote, ed. (Harmondsworth, 1983), G. Vidal, *Julian* (New York, 1977) and J. Boswell, *Christianity, social tolerance and homosexuality* (Chicago, 1980). Coote includes poems of Ausonius and Paulinus in his anthology; cf. Boswell, 'Christianity', pp. 133–4 on Ausonius and Paulinus; Vidal, 'Julian', p. 129, writes, 'If Gregory ever made such a prophecy, it must have been whispered in Basil's ear when they were in bed together.'

28. Erasmus in his Prolegomena to the 1508 edition of the *Adages* writes eloquently of the value accorded to friendship by both pagans and Christians (LB II.6E–7A):

> If anyone were to consider more carefully and thoroughly that Pythagorean dictum about friends holding everything in common, he would never find such an important point of human happiness summed up so succinctly. For what else was it that Plato tried to put forward in so many volumes, if not the benefits of the community and of friendship which is the basis of community life? What else was it that Christ, the head of our religion, was getting at? It is true that he gave only one commandment to love to the world, telling us that on this one commandment hang all the law and the prophets. But what does love urge, if not that everyone should share everything?

4 FRIENDSHIP IN THE LIVES AND THOUGHT OF BASIL AND OF GREGORY OF NAZIANZUS

1. Gregory's autobiographical poem *De vita sua* is printed in PG 37.1029–166, while the funeral oration (*Or.*43) is in PG 36.493–605.
2. *Or.*43.17 (PG 36.520).
3. *De vita sua* 225ff. (trans. D. M. Meehan, FotC vol.75, Washington DC, 1987); cf. *ibid.* 476–81, *Or.*43.20 (PG 36.521). For the idea that 'There is no such solid bond of union as thinking the same thoughts', cf. Cicero, *Pro Plancio* 2.5.
4. *Or.*43.19 (PG 36.521).
5. Field, ed., vol.5, p. 335.
6. *Or.*43.80 (PG 36.601); cf. Abelard, *Planctus David super Saul et Jonathan*,

> Et me post te vivere
> Mori sit assidue
> Nec ad vitam anima
> Satis sit dimidia.'

7. For the idea of complete unity and harmony behind the use of this image, we may compare *Or.*43.22 where Gregory compares

his relationship with Basil to that of the sons of Actor (cf. *Iliad* 11.749 and 23.638; Plutarch *On brotherly love* (*Mor*.478c)). For the image of the yoke in friendship, see Ausonius Ep.24, ed. Green, to Paulinus.

8. L. Vischer, 'Das Problem der Freundschaft bei den Kirchenvätern', *ThZ* 9 (1953), 197, writes, 'Es war ihm nicht möglich, das Menschliche und Persönliche vor Gott auszulöschen und die Freundschaft gleichsam jenseits des Menschlichen und Persönlichen zu finden.'

9. On the dispute between Basil and Gregory in the years after 370, see R. Ruether, *Gregory of Nazianzus: Rhetor and Philosopher* (Oxford, 1969), pp. 34–41.

10. An account of the whole episode as it affected their friendship is found in Gregory's poem *De vita sua*, lines 386–491 and in chapters 58–9 of *Or*.43.

11. See Ruether, 'Gregory of Nazianzus', p. 40, 'On this basis the son was reconciled to his father, although he remained at enmity with Basil', *New Catholic Encyclopaedia* (1967), vol.6, p. 791, 'The result of the affair was a rift in the friendship of Gregory and Basil, and the old intimacy was never restored'; Vischer, 'Problem der Freundschaft', p. 177, 'Sie (i.e. their friendship) ... brach auseinander'.

12. *Or*.43.80 (PG 36.601–4).

13. E.g. Ep.131.3 and Ep.133.2.

14. *Or*.43.22 and Ep.156.

15. In Gregory's Ep.11 he quotes Euripides' *Phoenician Women*, line 1446.

16. Gregory, Ep.162.

17. Ep.165; cf. Plotinus *Ennead* 3.6.1, 3.8.8; 4.4.44; Iamblichus, *Vit.Pyth*.24.106.

18. Basil Ep.83; Aristotle, *Nic.Eth*.1155a.

19. Basil Ep.133 and Ep.154.

20. For the mildew/grain image cf. Basil, *Hom.de invidia* 5 (PG 31.380A) and Plato, *Rep*.609A.

21. Nauck *TGF* Fr. 902.

22. E.g. at Basil Epp.114 and 172.

23. Ep.70 and 243.

24. See e.g. Basil Ep.5.

25. Plato, *Alcib*.126c 4–5.

26. See also Basil Epp.65 and 92.

27. Basil Epp.28 and 266; cf. use of *homognomon*, e.g. at Ep.68.

28. Cf. Basil Epp.65,70,92,122,129,191,210,243,265,266 for additional uses of *homopsychos* in connection with Christian unity.

29. E.g. Basil Ep.20.

30. E.g. Basil Ep.359.

31. For Basil's ideas on contemplation, see his homily 'Attende tibi ipsi' (Rudberg, ed., pp. 35–7), Ep.8 and Ep.233.

32. For Platonic influences on Basil's thought, see E. Fialon, *Etude littéraire sur saint Basile* (Paris, 1861), pp. 137–45.

33. In a letter (Ep.159) in which Basil goes on to discuss certain aspects of the Nicene creed, he starts by saying, 'What could be sweeter to a man who prays that he may always associate with God-fearing men and derive some of the profit such association yields than such letters as help us in our search of the knowledge of God?'

34. Basil, *Moralia* (PG 31.700A–869C), *RFT* (*ibid.*889A–1052C), *RBT* (*ibid.*1080A–1305B), *Introd. to ascetic life* (*ibid.*620A–625C), *On the renunciation of the world* (*ibid.*625C–648C), *On ascetic discipline* (*ibid.*648C–652D).

35. *RFT* 3; it is interesting to note that the emperor Julian in his Ep.89b (ed. Bidez) bases his criticism of the Christian monks on the same view of man's nature: the monks are perverse because they deny a way of life natural to man when they choose the solitary life.

36. See F. Hauck, 'κοινός κοινωνία', in *Theologisches Wörterbuch zum N.T.*, vol.3 (1935–8), pp. 804–10.

37. W. F. Adeney, *The Greek and Eastern Churches* (Edinburgh, 1908), p. 158.

38. See Basil, *RFT* 34–5.

39. On the importance of fraternal correction, see *Moralia* 50–4 (PG 31.776–81).

40. Cf. *RBT* 175, *RBT* 227, *RFT* 7 and Ep.295 to a group of monks under his supervision. In *RFT* 7 Basil uses the term συζῆν of the monastic community, reminding one of an Aristotelian characteristic of friendship.

41. *Moralia* 60, *RFT* 7 and *RFT* 24.

42. The authenticity of the two sermons has been doubted: E. Amand de Mendieta speaks of these two works as of very doubtful authenticity, in *L'ascèse monastique de saint Basile* (Maredsous, 1949), p. xxvi, and D. Chitty, in *The Desert a City* (Oxford, 1966), pp. 66–7 and p. 78 n.29, argues against their authenticity. The view expressed in the first sermon is echoed in the second (PG 31.885A) and in the *Monastic Constitutions* 29 (PG 31.1417D–1420C).

5 JOHN CHRYSOSTOM AND OLYMPIAS

1. It is true, as Elizabeth Clark writes in *Jerome, Chrysostom and Friends* (Lewiston, NY, 1979), p. 43, that, 'Nowhere in his letters to women does Chrysostom theorize about the possibility of

friendship between the sexes', though he does theorise about the possibility of equality between the sexes: see Ep.170.

2. These letters to Olympias are edited by A. Malingrey in Sources Chrétiennes, vol.13 (Paris, 1947).

3. In fact all 242 extant letters from John Chrysostom were written during the period of exile.

4. On these aspects, see A. Malingrey in the introduction of her edition of the letters to Olympias (n.2 above).

5. Sources for details of Olympias' life include the Life of St Olympias in *Analecta Bollandiana* 15 (1896), 409–23, probably a work of the later fifth century; Palladius' *Dialogus*, written about 408 and his *Lausiac History*, both of which are particularly valuable because Palladius appears to have known both Chrysostom and Olympias personally; also the ecclesiastical histories by Sozomen and Socrates, both works of the fifth century.

6. The text of this poem is found in PG 37.1542–50.

7. It is interesting to note that in his letter Ep.66 (67 in Garzya's edition) Synesius urges the implacable Theophilus to bury the hatchet with regard to Chrysostom who has by now been dead for about five years!

8. For an account of the Origenist controversy, see e.g. B. J. Kidd, *A History of the Church to A.D.461* (Oxford, 1922), vol.II, pp. 429–48, with reference to Chrysostom's involvement and the events leading to his downfall. Cf. O. Chadwick, *John Cassian, a Study in Primitive Monasticism*, first edition (Cambridge, 1950), pp. 33–6 and W. S. Crawford, *Synesius the Hellene* (London, 1901), pp. 411–14.

9. Cardinal Newman wrote of Chrysostom in his *Historical Sketches* (London, 1872–3), vol.II, p. 137, that 'he was indeed a man to make both friends and enemies, to inspire affection and kindle resentment; but his friends loved him with a love stronger than death and his enemies hated him with a hatred more burning than hell, and it was well to be so hated, if he was so beloved'.

10. Nicephoras Callistes, *Hist.Eccl.*13.24 (PG 146.1012B). The apocryphal work, the Acts of St Paul and St Thecla can be found in an English translation in *The Apocryphal New Testament*, M. R. James, ed. (repr. Oxford, 1955), pp. 272–81; on Paul and Thecla, see also P. Brown, *The Body and Society* (London, 1989), pp. 156–9.

11. As Clark, 'Jerome', p. 56, writes, 'The equality so necessary for true friendship has been achieved by perceiving women as men.' Cf. Jerome, Ep.71.3.

12. Ep.170 to Italica, written in 406 (PG 52.709–10).

13. On the kind of education shared by Christians such as Chrysos-

tom, Basil and Gregory of Nazianzus, as well as by the future emperor Julian, see J. Bregman, *Synesius of Cyrene* (California, 1982), p. 44 and pp. 139–40; on Chrysostom's early life and education, see J. C. Baur, *John Chrysostom and His Time*, 2 vols. (London, 1959), vol.I, chapters 1–3.

14. Chrysostom *De sacerdotio* I.I (trans. G. Neville, SPCK, London, 1964).
15. Chrysostom Hom.7 in 2 Tim.(Field, ed., vol.6, p.227); Hom.40.3 in Act.Apost.(PG 60.285).
16. Cf. Chrysostom Hom.2 in 1 Thess.2.7–8 (Field, ed., vol.5, pp. 331–6).
17. Chrysostom Hom.7 in 2 Tim.(Field, ed., vol.6, pp. 221–31).
18. Chrysostom Hom.40.4 in Act. Apost.(PG 60.286).
19. Cf. Basil's use of the term *homopsychoi*.
20. Chrysostom Hom.2 in 1 Thess.(Field, ed., vol.5, p. 336).
21. In Ep.8 to Olympias Chrysostom emphasises how much Paul loved his followers and friends by using the example of 2 Cor.2:12–18 where Paul, who has borne so much with perfect patience, admits that he is devastated at not finding Titus at Troas; cf. what Paul writes at 1 Thess. 2:17–18 and 3:1–2:22.
22. Field, ed., vol.5, pp. 334–5.
23. PG 57.587–8.
24. There were of course other women at Constantinople supporting Chrysostom, while at Rome we know of Italica and Anicia Faltonia Proba and her daughter-in-law Juliana (all later correspondents of Augustine) who worked on his behalf. See Epp.168–70.
25. Cf. Chrysostom Ep.14.1(b).
26. Cf. Chrysostom Ep.7.5(e).
27. See Chrysostom's Epp.2 and 4.
28. As for instance in his Ep.8.11(b).
29. See e.g. Chrysostom's Ep.12.1(b).
30. See Chrysostom's Ep.9; Cucusus was a village in the mountains of eastern Turkey, from where Chrysostom was to be taken to Pityus, a fortified port on the N.E. coast of the Black Sea, though he died at Comana, between Caesarea and Cucusus.
31. On Chrysostom's appreciation of the value of rebuke, see further his work *De mutat.nomin.*III (PG 51.131–6), Hom.9 in 2 Tim. (Field, ed., vol.6, pp. 243–52) and the homily on David and Saul 3.4 (PG 54.699–701).
32. Cf. Chrysostom's Hom.7 in 2 Tim.(Field, ed., vol.6, pp. 221–31).
33. Chrysostom was well aware of the dangers of sin, as is clear from

his correspondence with Olympias whom he reminds in Ep.7.1(c) that sin alone is to be feared and he frequently shows that he considers her *athumia* (despondency) sinful and destructive (e.g. in Ep.8.3(d) where he describes it as inspired by the devil and spiritually destructive).

34. Cf. Chrysostom Hom.3.4 in Gen.(PG 53.36–7) and his homily on Rom.12:20 (Field, ed., vol.1, pp. 376–80).
35. Cf. Chrysostom's Hom.60.3 in Matt.(PG 58.588) and Hom.9 in Eph.4:2 (Field, ed., vol.4, pp. 198–206).
36. Chrysostom Ep.8.12(d).
37. Cf. Chrysostom Ep.42 to Candidianus or Ep.56 to Romulus and Byzus.

6 SYNESIUS OF CYRENE

1. For a discussion of the different suggestions as to the date of Synesius' birth, see D. Roques, *Synésios de Cyrène et la Cyrénaique du Bas-Empire* (Paris, 1987), ch.2.
2. A. D. Nock, *Early Gentile Christianity and its Hellenistic Background* (London, 1928), p. 158, points to a similarity between the experience of the emperor Julian and Augustine 'in that each ends in a return to something which has all the time been in the background'; G. Bonner, *St Augustine of Hippo, Life and Controversies* (Norwich, 1986), pp. 45–6 says of Augustine at the time of his conversion that he 'thought he could have a synthesis of the philosophy and the religion, as did many other Christians of his age, always with the proviso that, in the last resort, when the two systems conflicted, Neoplatonism would have to give way to Christianity'. The opposite was of course true for Synesius in a similar position.
3. For a near-contemporary reference to Hypatia see the history of Socrates, the mid-fifth century historian (7.15).
4. See e.g. Synes.Epp.137–46 to Herculian.
5. These were the works *On kingship* and possibly *On providence*; for the political situation at Constantinople and Synesius' position there, see J. Bregman, *Synesius of Cyrene* (California, 1982), pp. 49–59 and G. Dagron, *Naissance d'une capitale, Constantinople et ses institutions de 330 à 451* (Paris, 1974), p. 73.
6. Aurelian is said to have built a church in which he buried Isaac, one of the monks of Constantinople who was a sworn enemy of John Chrysostom. Three of Synesius' letters to Aurelian survive (Epp.31, 38(35 G.), 34(47 G.)).

7. On contemporary military activity in the Pentapolis in the years 395–405, see Roques, 'Synésios', ch. 5.

8. For a survey of different answers to this question, see the introduction to Bregman, 'Synesius'.

9. T. Kobusch, 'Studien zur Philosophie des Hierokles von Alexandria', *Epimeleia*, 27 (1976), p. 21; additional support is given by Kobusch's suggestion that the Neoplatonist Hierocles of Alexandria was influenced by certain Christian doctrines e.g. creation *ex nihilo*, though this view is strongly rejected by I. Hadot in 'Ist die Lehre des Hierokles vom Demiurgen christlich beeinflusst?', in A. M. Ritter, ed., *Kerygma und Logos, Festschrift für Carl Andresen* (Göttingen, 1979), pp. 259–71.

10. See the description of this violent scene by Charles Kingsley in his novel *Hypatia* (London, 1889).

11. As F. Lapatz writes in the introduction to his book, *Lettres de Synésios* (Paris, 1870), p. vii, of people like Synesius, 'Ils n'ont point d'autre fanatisme que celui de l'antiquité: leur grand divinité, c'est le génie grec, et leur coreligionnaire, celui qui fait ses délices de Platon. Ils prolongent dans la société nouvelle, je ne dirai pas l'ésprit, mais la phraséologie et comme le cérémonial littéraire de l'ancienne.'

12. *Synesii Cyrenensis Epistolae*, A. Garzya, ed. (Rome, 1979). The popularity of Synesius' letters is shown by the large number of MSS. of them as indicated in the Prolegomena to Garzya's edition, as well as in the laudatory references to them in many later, particularly Byzantine, writers.

13. In fact W. H. C. Frend, in his review of Roques' book, 'Synésios', in *JbAC* 32 (1989), p. 206, likens Synesius to Basil of Caesarea in his concern for others and in his efficiency in his work as bishop.

14. Crawford, 'Synesius', ch. 11, 'The friends of Synesius' and G. Grützmacher, *Synesios von Cyrene: ein Charakterbild aus dem Untergang des Hellenentums* (Leipzig, 1913), ch. 4, 'Die Freunde des Synesios aus seiner alexandrinischen Studienzeit' and ch. 8, 'Der Freundeskreis des Synesios in Konstantinopel'.

15. See Bregman, 'Synesius', pp. 30–1; On the tetractys as 'the epitome of Pythagorean wisdom', see W. F. M. Burkert, *Lore and Science in Ancient Pythagoreanism* (Cambridge, MA, 1972), p. 72. On the concept of the trias in Neoplatonic thought, see W. Theiler, *Die chaldäischen Orakel und die Hymnen des Synesios* (Halle, 1942). It was a term occasionally used in Christian theology to apply to the Trinity, from the time of Theophilus of Antioch in the second century A.D.

16. Synes.Epp.48(50 G.),61,71,74,88,100–3,129,131,134,150–3, written during the period 402–10.
17. Cf. Lapatz, 'Lettres', p. 382, Photius *Bibl.*26 (PG 103.61).
18. For a discussion of Synesius' style, see P. X. Simeon, *Untersuchungen zu den Briefen des Bischofs Synesios von Kyrene* (Paderborn, 1933), pp. 40–53; C. Martha, *Etudes morales sur l'antiquité* (Paris, 1905), pp. 319 and 330, offers a less positive view of the profundity of his style.
19. For the attractions of 'deificari in otio', see Aug.Ep.10.2 to his close friend Nebridius, written in 389 or 390.
20. Cf. Synes.Ep.124 in which he applies the same line of Homer to his friendship with Hypatia.
21. E.g. in Ep.138 to Herculian Synesius alludes to Plato's *Lysis* 216c which itself alludes to Theognis, line 17.
22. Cf. Synes.Ep.152, Plato, *Symp.*192E, Arist.*Nic.Eth.*1168b 11.
23. Synes.Epp.137,139 and 140 to Herculian and Epp.101,103 and 151 to Pylaemenes.

7 AMBROSE OF MILAN – CICERONIAN OR CHRISTIAN FRIENDSHIP?

1. On Ambrose's education, see F. Homes Dudden, *The Life and Times of St Ambrose*, 2 vols. (Oxford, 1935), vol.i.
2. In this respect he had the edge over Augustine who was prevented by his lack of familiarity with Greek from steeping himself in the works of the Greek Fathers and philosophers.
3. Cf. Augustine's use of Cicero's *De oratore* in Book IV of his *De doctrina Christiana*.
4. G. Madec, *Saint Ambroise et la philosophie* (Paris, 1974), p. 84, writes, 'L'intention affichée de saint Ambroise est donc celle de l'opposition de la sagesse biblique et chrétienne à la philosophie, bien plutôt que le souci de réaliser et de justifier une 'synthèse' des deux morales', while A. F. Coyle, 'Cicero's *De Officiis* and the *De Officiis Ministrorum* of St Ambrose', *Franciscan Studies*, 15 (1955), p. 224, puts forward the opposite view when he writes, 'In his treatise *De Officiis Ministrorum*, modelled after the work of Cicero, St Ambrose produced the first synthesis of Christian morality in the West ... Ambrose was the first to treat the whole matter systematically, wherein he combines what was best in Stoicism with the new conceptions of Christianity.'
5. Ambr. *De off.min.*II.11.36–7.
6. See e.g. H. Chadwick, *Early Christian Thought and the Classical Tradition* (Oxford, 1966), pp. 13–14, showing that both Jews (e.g.

Josephus and Philo) and some early Christian apologists (e.g. Justin, Origen and Clement) had used this argument to prove the dependence of Greek civilisation on Jewish culture. Ambrose uses a similar argument in Ep.28.1 (81 B.), Ep.37.28 (54 B.), *De excessu fratris Satyri* 1.42 and the *De bono mortis* 10.45. Augustine (*De doctr.Chr.*II.28.43) expressed his admiration for Ambrose's attitude but it was an argument which he rejected in later life (see *De civit.Dei* 8.11; *Retr.*2.4).

7. R. Thamin, *S. Ambroise et la morale chrétienne au IVème siècle* (Paris, 1895), p. 230, Homes Dudden, 'Life and Times', vol.II, pp. 532–3, H. Hagendahl, *The Latin Fathers and the Classics* (Gothenburg, 1958), p. 358.

8. Cf. Arist. *Nic.Eth.*1162b 12 and 1169b 10.

9. Cic.*De off.*III.10.46, *Lael.*13.44.

10. That Ambrose does indeed have these passages in mind is clear from the fact that he continues, 'We ought not, like children, to change our friends at a whim' which is similar to the context of *Lael.*19.67.

11. Hagendahl, 'Latin Fathers', p. 371.

12. Cic.*De off.*III.10.44.

13. Cf. Cic.*Lael.*20.74

14. Ambr.*De off.min.*III.22.133; cf. Cic.*Lael.*21.81–2.

15. Ambr.*De off.min.*III.22.135.

16. Ibid.I.7.24.

17. Sabinus was the bishop of Placentia to whom Ambrose addressed Epp.45–9, 58 (=25,27,24,23,26,28 B.).

18. Cf. Jerome Ep.115 in which he urges his addressee, Augustine, to sport with him in their letters on the field of Scripture, though this suggestion does not find favour with Augustine (Ep.82) who thinks Jerome is trying to trivialise the seriousness of their exegetical enterprises.

19. Ambr.Ep.48.7 (23 B.); cf. Cic. *Lael.*17.62–18.66.

20. J. Matthews, *Western Aristocracies and Imperial Court 364–425* (Oxford, 1975), p. 191.

21. Ambr.Ep.4 (19 B.).

22. Ambr.Epp.29 and 57 (79 and 11 B.).

23. In this connection it is interesting to note the difference indicated by P. Brown, *Augustine of Hippo; a biography* (London, 1967), p. 95, between Augustine and Ambrose in their use of pagan, particularly Platonic material: 'Ambrose, who also read Plotinus, patently ransacked his author: it is possible to trace literal borrowings from Plotinus in the bishop's sermons. For Augustine,

however, Plotinus and Porphyry are grafted almost imperceptibly into his writings as the ever present basis of his thought.'
24. Ambr.*De viduis* 14 (PL 16.235).

8 ST JEROME

1. Jer.Ep.3.5 and 3.6. The second of these two extracts is quoted by
   Alcuin in a letter written to his friend Paulinus of Aquileia at the
   end of the eighth century (Ep.28, MGH Epist.IV p.70).
2. Cf. Phaedrus, *Fab.Lib*.III.9.1, 'The name of friend is a common
   one but loyalty is rare.'
3. For a description of these friends, see e.g. J. N. D. Kelly, *Jerome,
   His Life, Writings and Controversies* (London, 1975), pp. 18–19.
4. Cf. the account given by Ponticianus in Augustine's *Confessions*
   (VIII.6.15) of a dramatic renunciation of worldly life which took
   place at Trier a few years after Jerome spent some time there.
5. Chromatius later became bishop of Aquileia and maintained
   friendly relations with Jerome at a distance for many years. For
   more information on this friend of Jerome, see the collection of
   essays in *Chromatius Episcopus 388–1988*, Y.-M. Duval, ed. (Udine,
   1989).
6. Cf. Horace *Carm*.II.17.5.
7. Cf. Basil Ep.156.3.
8. See Kelly, 'Jerome', pp. 121 and 128.
9. For examples of Jerome's abuse against Rufinus, see Kelly,
   'Jerome', p. 256 and D. S. Wiesen, *St Jerome as a Satirist* (Ithaca,
   NY, 1964).
10. Jerome's hypocrisy or inability to see his own malice is perhaps
    best illustrated by his warning, in Ep.125, against indulging in
    malicious gossip which is immediately followed by a devastat-
    ingly spiteful picture of a backbiter – clearly meant to represent
    Rufinus!
11. I.e.Epp.48,49, 57, 66, 84 (with Oceanus) and 97 (with Marcella).
12. See Jerome's preface to his commentary on Hosea in which he
    addresses Pammachius, defending his attitude to Origen (CCL
    76.5).
13. Jer.Ep.166 written in 397.
14. Jer.*Adv.Jovin*.I.41–9; see Wiesen, 'Jerome', Ch. 4, for other uses
    by Jerome of satire against women and marriage, notably in
    those letters he addressed to widows trying to persuade them not
    to undertake second marriages.
15. Jer.Ep.45.3.

16. See Jerome's Ep.127.2,4,6 on Marcella's chastity and Ep.108.5,6,19 on Paula's rejection of second marriages and renunciation of family ties.
17. See Jerome's Ep.108.5,10,16 on Paula's generosity.
18. Cf. Jer.Ep.108.
19. Jer.Ep.45.2.2; E. Clark, 'Theory and practice in late ancient asceticism', *Journal of Feminist Studies in Religion*, 3 (1987), p. 35.
20. Cf. Paulinus Ep.29.9 in which, in a lengthy eulogy of Rufinus' friend Melania, he describes how she 'tore her only son from her breast' in order to devote herself whole-heartedly to the ascetic life.
21. For an allusion to Marcella's death, cf. Jerome's preface to his commentary on Ezechiel (CCL 75.3).
22. As well as the letters addressed to Marcella and Paula, few of which survive, Jerome dedicated his commentaries on Ecclesiastes, Micah, Nahum, Zephaniah, Haggai, Galatians and Ephesians to Paula and Eustochium, and the commentary on Daniel to Marcella and Pammachius jointly.
23. The discussion of Scriptural problems played a large part also in the correspondence between Abelard and Heloise after their dedication to separate religious establishments and the change in their intimate relationship from a physical to a spiritual one. See B. Radice in *Medieval Women Writers*, K. M. Wilson, ed. (Manchester, 1984), p. 98.
24. Cf. Jer.Ep.127.5 for the friendship uniting these three women.
25. Jer.*Adv.Jovin.*I.47.
26. See Jer.Ep.22.
27. Jer.*Comm.in Ep.Gal.*4.16 (PL 26.382).
28. Jer.*Adv.Ruf.*I.1.
29. Another possible reference to Theophrastus' work on friendship is to be found in the preface to the third book of Jerome's commentary on Hosea (CCL 76).
30. See the commentary of R. Nisbet and M. Hubbard on Horace's first book of Odes (Oxford, 1970) for the literary lineage of this phrase from Horace *Carm.*I.3.8.
31. Notably in many of his letters, in the short commentaries on the Psalms (CCL 72), in the fifty-nine tractates on the Psalms (CCL 78), the three biographies of the early hermits Paul, Malchus and Hilarion (PL 23), as well as Jerome's translation into Latin of several Pachomian writings.
32. For a similar view of the relation between the eremitic and the coenobitic life, see Cassian, *Conference* 18.5–6.

9 PAULINUS OF NOLA

1. Ambrose Ep.58 (28 B.); Aug.*De civit.Dei* 1.10 and Ep.27; Jerome Ep.118.5.
2. Gregory of Tours, *Liber de gloria confessorum* 110(107); Gregory the Great, *Dialogues* Bk.3.
3. Paulinus, however, plays down the 'achievement' of his renunciation in a letter to Severus (Ep.5.4), arguing that his withdrawal happened gradually and was therefore less painful than that of his friend; but C. E. Stancliffe, *St Martin and His Hagiographer: History and Miracle in Sulpicius Severus* (Oxford, 1983), p. 30 n.2, reverses the perspective when comparing their conversions for she points out that Severus 'did not make as clean a break with his past life as Paulinus'.
4. See J. Szöwerffy, *Weltliche Dichtungen des lateinischen Mittelalters* (Berlin, 1970), pp. 97 and 155, for the importance of friendship to Paulinus and his place in the development of the *Freundschaftskulte* of the Middle Ages.
5. There are seven letters extant from Ausonius to Paulinus, of which nos.17–20 were written before Paulinus' move to Nola, followed by Nos.21, 22 and 24. There is some confusion as to the correct numbering of Ausonius' letters in different editions; I have used the numbering of R. P. H. Green in his edition and commentary, *The Works of Ausonius* (Oxford, 1991).
6. Paulinus *Carm.*10.83.
7. See e.g. Ep.4.3 to Augustine where Paulinus writes, 'If one thinks of the office we share, you are my brother. But if one considers your maturity of mind and thought, you are my father though you may be younger in years.' Cf. Jerome Ep.58 to Paulinus where Jerome reprimands Paulinus for showering praise on him: 'You measure me by your own virtues and you who are great extol me who am little . . . Do not, my dear brother, judge me by the number of my years . . . and do not think me better than you because I began to fight in God's army before you.'
8. See Auson.Ep.24.96 and 110.
9. Cf. Paulinus Ep.32.1 to Severus, and Augustine Ep.28 to Jerome where he writes of his relationship with Alypius.
10. P. Fabre, *S. Paulin de Nole et l'amitié chrétienne* (Paris, 1949), pp. 164–7.
11. Cf. Paulinus Ep.16 to the pagan Jovius, urging him to seek Christ.
12. Stancliffe, 'St Martin', p.16 but cf. Fabre, 'Amitié chrétienne', p. 277.

13. It seems that Paulinus himself had met Martin at Vienne, as is evident from Ep.18.9.
14. Stancliffe, 'St Martin', p. 19.
15. The extant letters to Severus were written over the period 395–404; see further P. Fabre, *Essai sur la chronologie de l'oeuvre de S. Paulin de Nole* (Paris, 1948).
16. See Paulinus Ep.17.1 for one expression of his disappointment.
17. A. Buse, *Paulin, Bischof von Nola und seine Zeit*, 2 vols. (Regensburg, 1856), vol.1, p. 98, describes the closeness of their relationship in the following fulsome terms, 'Das innigste Band jedoch unter allen verknüpfte ihn mit Sulpicius Severus. Ihre Herzen waren gleichsam miteinander verschmolzen; bei der unverbruchlichsten Treue, der ruckhaltlosesten Vertraulichkeit, war ihre gegenseitige Liebe eine so grosse, so heilige, dass nur eins noch hinzutreten konnte, nämlich die Liebe Christi.'
18. In Ep.7.3 after alluding to Terence, Paulinus writes, 'But why should I speak in the language of foreigners, since our own store is adequate for all things?' And in Ep.22.3 he mentions his resolution not to read the works of Classical poets – a decision comparable to that of Jerome, notably described in Jerome's Ep.22. See Walsh in ACW, vol.40 (NY, 1975), pp. 4–6 for Paulinus' use of Classical forms in poetry even after his conversion, and W. Erdt, *Christentum und heidnisch-antike Bildung bei Paulin von Nola* (Meisenheim-am-Glam, 1974), pp. 288–309.
19. The idea that Paulinus' love for his friends will continue after death is movingly expressed at the end of poem 11 to Ausonius in lines 49ff., probably the most famous lines of Paulinus' poetry.
20. Paulinus Ep.42 where he is quoting Sir.9:15, a text which understandably recurs quite frequently in Christian writings about friendship.
21. Paulinus Ep.6.2 to Augustine.
22. Fabre, 'Amitié chrétienne', p. 294.
23. See e.g. Ep.12 to Amandus and Ep.39 to Aper and Amanda.
24. Paulinus Ep.18.1 to Victricius.
25. Paulinus Ep.5.1 and Ep.23 to Severus.
26. In Ep.6, for instance, Paulinus writes to Augustine, 'Nor is it surprising that we are together though apart and acquainted though unknown to each other for we are members of the one body.'
27. Paulinus Ep.5.10; cf. Ep.13.3 and Ep.18.3.
28. See esp. Paulinus Ep.4.5 to Augustine.
29. Paulinus Ep.3.4.

30. Cf. Paulinus Ep.11.3, Ep.32.1 and for a similar idea expressed some twenty-five years later, Ep.51.3.
31. Jerome, for instance, interprets Matt.24:40 as applying to the different fates awaiting Christians and Jews or orthodox and heretic for their handling of the same material of Scripture; John Chrysostom, in his commentary on Matthew, takes this verse to signify that some rich people will be saved, some not.
32. Cf. Paulinus Ep.11.12 where he refers to himself as Severus' 'amicus' and Ep.13 where he writes of his spiritual 'amicitia' with Pammachius.
33. Paulinus Ep.32.1 in which he writes, 'You, I say, are the greater and better part of me. You are my rest and joy. You are a pillow for my head and a dwelling for my mind which I hope and trust in the Lord will remain accessible to me not merely in this life but also forever, through his gift and in his body and spirit.'
34. Peter Brown, *The Body and Society* (London, 1989), p. 15, notes that the popular ideal of frankness and honesty in friendship was sometimes found existing between husband and wife in pagan and Christian marriages.
35. Ausonius Ep.22.31 where he uses the language of Juv.6.566, to which Paulinus replies (*Carm.*10.192) that she is no Tanaquil but a Lucretia. Ambrose (Ep. 58 = 28 B.) describes Therasia as rivalling her husband in virtue and dedication and Augustine writes of her (Ep.27.2) that she 'is also made visible to your readers, not as one leading her husband into luxury, but rather as leading him back to strength in his innermost being. We salute her also with the greetings owed to you alone because she is joined in close union with you and is attached to you by spiritual bonds which are as strong as they are chaste.'
36. Gregory of Tours, *Liber de gloria confessorum* 110(107).
37. For the widespread belief among Christians that the ascetic life could make women equal to men, see the introduction and the chapter on John Chrysostom and Olympias. Gregory of Tours also speaks of Therasia as her husband's equal.
38. See Paulinus Ep.18.5 to Victricius where he speaks of 'the conduct of married couples subject to God who secretly live as brother and sister'.
39. Augustine Ep.31; cf. Jerome's letter to Marcellinus and Anapsychia (Ep.126) in which he addresses them jointly as 'domini' and 'filii'.
40. E.g. Horace *Carm.*11.5.1 and retained in the word 'conjugal'.
41. Our sole source for the details of Felix's life are the two biographical poems dedicated to him i.e. Paulinus' poems 15 and 16.

42. Each year from 395–407 Paulinus composed a long poem dedicated to Felix to celebrate the day of his death which Paulinus regarded as his true birthday for then he was born into heaven. These poems can therefore be seen as variations on the ancient theme of the *genethliakon* or birthday poem. Among Paulinus' poems these so-called Natalicia are numbered thus in the order of their composition: 12–16, 18, 23, 26–8, 19–21, 29.

43. Peter Brown, *The Cult of the Saints* (London, 1981), p. 56, implies that the term *amicus* is used when he writes, 'Felix was not a timeless idealized figure: he was very much a *patronus* and an *amicus* as Paulinus and his readers recognized such beings, only too well, in the tight-knit world of the Roman aristocracy and its dependents.'

44. Paulinus' use of the metaphor of spiritual estate which will bring forth spiritual produce in his letter to Aper and Amanda (Ep.39.1) could be applied to his relations with Felix as well as to his friendships with the living – and this gives added support to an interpretation which regards his relationship with Felix as a friendship. 'In matters of the world', he writes, 'a farm is more valuable when it responds with abundant produce to the greedy prayers of its farmer or when it charms with its beauty the eyes of its self-indulgent owner. It is the same with our spiritual estate, with, that is to say, our holy brothers whom Christ's love has joined to and bestowed on us as a permanent possession. He is accounted the richer soil who shows greater concern for us and brings us a larger harvest by provision of the blessings which bring salvation.'

45. Fabre, 'Amitié chrétienne', p. 345.

46. Paulinus Ep.5.15 and Ep.17.3.

47. For a study of the different terms used in the language of Roman patronage, see R. P. Saller, *Personal Patronage under the Early Empire* (Cambridge, 1982).

10 MONASTICISM AND FRIENDSHIP

1. See F. R. Hoare, *The Western Fathers* (London, 1954), pp. xix–xx; cf. W. H. C. Frend, *The Early Church*, 3rd edition (London, 1971), p. 200.

2. For anti-monastic feelings within the Church at this period, compare the ideas expressed by Helvidius, Jovinian and Vigilantius as they can be gleaned from the polemical works of Jerome. See also the article by L. Gougaud, 'Les critiques formulées

contre les premiers moines d'Occident' in *Revue Mabillon*, 24 (1934), 145–63.

3. See L. Vischer, 'Das Problem der Freundschaft bei den Kirchenvätern', *ThZ* 9 (1953), 199.

4. On the Syrian origins of monasticism, see A. Vööbus, *A History of Asceticism in the Syrian Orient* (Louvain, 1958, = CSCO, vol.184), vol.1.

5. See e.g. Jerome Ep.22.34–6 where he describes three different kinds of ascetic life.

6. The letters of Antony are printed in PG 40.972–1000 and an English translation of them has been made by D. Chitty (Fairacres Publications, vol.50, Oxford, 1975). Athanasius' *Life of Antony* is found in PG 26. A Latin translation was made by Jerome's friend Evagrius of Antioch before 379, in which form it had an immediate and powerful influence in the West.

7. In his *Confessions* (VIII.12.29) Augustine relates how he was influenced by Antony's example in using the *Sortes Vergilianae* method to make a decision about his future at the crisis of his conversion.

8. Plato, *Rep.*VII.514–21.

9. Antony Ep.3.4.

10. Antony Ep.4.3.

11. Athanasius' *Life of Antony*, ch. 3 (PG 26.844); cf. the story told in the Sahidic *Life of Pachomius* (in the edition of Th. Lefort, Louvain, 1943) and quoted by H. Bacht in *Studia Anselmiana* 38 (1956), 104, which confirms Antony's approval of a harmonious community life for Christians.

12. Athanasius' *Life of Antony*, ch. 44 (PG 26.908).

13. PL 73.880, no.27.

14. PL 73.974, no. 7.

15. E.g. PL 73.1014, no. 18 and 1039.

16. *Verba Seniorum* III.96 (PL 73.777–8, no. 96).

17. *Ibid.* v.10.23 (PL 73.916, no.23).

18. *Ibid.* VII.28.4 (PL 73.1050, no.4), with allusion to Matt.24:12.

19. Palladius, *Historia Lausiaca* 32 (C. Butler, ed. (Cambridge, 1904), vol.II, p. 88). The nature of Pachomius' conversion was also significant: in 312 he was conscripted to fight in the war between Licinius and Maximius; while a soldier, he and others were incarcerated one night and were brought food by a group of Christians; brought up as a pagan, Pachomius was struck by the Christians' practical compassion and was fired with enthusiasm

to become one of them so that he, too, could love and serve others in a spirit of obedience.

20. On the Pachomian sources, see D. Chitty, 'Pachomian sources reconsidered', *JEH* 5 (1954), 38–77; also Th. Lefort in CSCO, vol.159, pp. vi–ix. For an English translation of the Rule of Pachomius, see *Pachomian Koinonia* (Cistercian Studies, vol.46, Kalamazoo, 1981), vol.II, pp. 141–95.

21. This work is printed in CSCO, vol.159, pp. 1–24 and CSCO vol.160 (French trans.), pp. 1–25; for an English translation, see vol.III of 'Pachomian Koinonia', pp. 13–46, (Cistercian Studies, vol.47, Kalamazoo, 1982).

22. CSCO, vol. 160, p. 21.

23. This short work is found in CSCO, vols.159 and 160, pp. 75–80; for an English translation, see vol.III of 'Pachomian Koinonia', pp. 145–51.

24. For a more detailed description of the characteristic behaviour of such a friend, see Lefort (CSCO, vol.160) pp. 77–8 (Engl.trans. by A. Veilleux in Cistercian Studies, vol.47, p. 149): 'Some from your circle go out with a made-up face; they wear a bandeau around their face; they put this black thing over their eyes under pretext of illness; they have numberless rings attached to their handkerchief and on their belt, fringes that flap behind them like calves frisking about in an enclosure. Often they bathe quite naked without necessity; they wear soft shoes on their feet ... they mince along in the assembly; they accost their friends with a boisterous laugh, like the noise of thorny twigs crackling under a cooking pot ...'

25. CSCO, vol.160, pp. 47–8.

26. On the connection between the coenobitic ideal and the early Christian community, see A. Levis, 'Koinonia e comunidade no monacato pacomiano', *Claretianum* 15 (1975), 269–327. Note that Pachomius says that each monk should form one single heart with his fellow monks, which is reminiscent of the words of Acts 4:32 (CSCO, vol.160, p. 2).

27. K. Heussi, *Der Ursprung des Mönchtums* (Tübingen, 1936), p. 124, denies that Pachomius mentions this text; for the opposite view, see H. Bacht, 'Antonius u. Pachomius. Von der Anachorese zum Cönobitentum', *Studia Anselmiana*, 38 (1956), 92–3.

28. See A. de Vogüé, 'Monachisme et Église dans la pensée de Cassien', *Théologie de la vie monastique* (Paris, 1961), pp. 218–19.

29. Horsiesius, *Liber*, ch.9 (A. Boon, ed., *Pachomiana Latina*, Louvain, 1932, pp. 113–14).

30. Cassian, *De incarn.*7.30–1.
31. The text of the sixteenth *Conference* can be found in CSEL, vol.13 and, with a French translation, in Sources Chrétiennes, vol.54 (Paris, 1958).
32. Cf. *Conference* 1.1 (CSEL 13, p. 7) for Cassian's description of their friendship and the fact that it was said of them that they had one mind and one soul in two bodies; cf. K.–A. Neuhausen, 'Zu Cassians Traktat "De Amicitia"', in C. Gnilka and W. Schetter, eds., *Studien zur Literatur der Spätantike* (Bonn, 1975), pp. 200–2.
33. Cf. Cic.*Lael.*20.74.
34. Cf. Neuhausen, 'Cassians Traktat', p. 195 and Sallust, *Catil.*20.
35. On the Evagrian ideal of spiritual perfection or *apatheia*, see E. Pichery in the introduction to vol. 1 of Cassian's *Conferences* (Sources Chrétiennes, vol. 42, Paris, 1955), pp. 45–9; Cassian does not himself use this Greek term, taken over by such theologians as Clement of Alexandria from the Stoics, but the ideal of purity and calmness put forward by Cassian is recognisably influenced by the ascetic theories of Evagrius of Pontus. On Cassian's relation to Evagrius, see e.g. O. Chadwick, *John Cassian, a Study in Primitive Monasticism*, 2nd edition (Cambridge, 1968), pp. 92–3 and P. Courcelle, *Late Latin Writers and their Greek Sources* (Cambridge, MA, 1969), pp. 229–30.
36. Chadwick, 'John Cassian', 1st edition (Cambridge, 1950), p. 107.
37. See A. Fiske, 'Cassian and monastic friendship', *American Benedictine Review*, 12 (1961), 193.
38. Cf. Neuhausen, 'Cassians Traktat', pp. 196–7 and the *Historia Monachorum* 21 (PL 21.443), where the author describes the semi-eremitic monks at Nitria as living separately but joined inseparably in spirit and faith and love.
39. Cf. Paulinus of Nola Ep.6.2 to Augustine.
40. Cf. Cicero *Lael.*11.36–12.43 and Aulus Gellius 1.3. Fiske, 'Cassian', p. 201, writes, 'This is again Cicero's teaching transposed to the inner life.'
41. Cf. Cassian, *Conference* 15.7 on humility.
42. Cf. Cassian *Conference* 16.7 and 16.13 where he cites 1 John 4:16 and Rom.5:5.
43. Gen.37:3–4.
44. The commentary of Alardus of Gaza on the works of Cassian was first published in 1616 and reprinted in PL 49–50.
45. Fiske, 'Cassian', p. 200.

11 ST AUGUSTINE

1. See M.A. Macnamara, *Friendship in St Augustine* (Fribourg, 1958); P. Brown, *Augustine of Hippo; a biography* (London, 1967), pp. 61ff., 155–6, 160–1, 180 and 201; K. Treu, 'Freundschaft', *RLAC* 8 (1972), cols. 418–34; R. J. O'Connell, *Art and the Christian Intelligence in St Augustine* (Oxford, 1978), p. 62, 'And yet, however awkward one may deem his efforts to integrate the love of neighbour into his scheme, the evidence is clear that it strongly affects his values, his thinking and eventually his aesthetic.'

2. 'Luminosus limes amicitiae' (*Conf.*II.2.2).

3. See J. Boswell, *Christianity, social tolerance and homosexuality* (Chicago, 1980), p. 135: he erroneously implies that this was a homosexual relationship, for which there is no evidence despite the tender terms in which Augustine speaks of this friend.

4. Aug.*Solil.*I.12.20.

5. Cic.*Lael.*6.22; on Augustine's failure to develop a satisfactory friendship with Proba and other women in her family, see the discussion of E. Clark, 'Theory and Practice in late ancient asceticism', *Journal of feminist studies in religion*, 3 (1987), 25–46.

6. Brown, 'Augustine', p. 180; J. McEvoy, 'Anima una et cor unum: friendship and spiritual unity in Augustine', *Rec.Theol.* 53 (1986), 42.

7. The work entitled *Liber de amicitia* (printed among Augustine's works in PL 40.831–44) is not by Augustine but is a plagiarism and summary of the twelfth-century work *De spiritali amicitia* by Aelred of Rievaulx. The work of Peter of Blois, *De amicitia Christiana*, which used to be attributed to Cassiodorus, contains much from Augustine.

8. Aug.*Conf.*IV.6.

9. G. de Nerval, *Aurélia* I.389.

10. Aug.*Ep.*82.31 to Jerome; cf. E. Osborn, *Ethical patterns in early Christian thought* (Cambridge, 1976), p. 166, 'In his account of glory, as in that of virtue, justice and commonwealth, Augustine draws on and transforms the values of Roman culture . . . To this list could be added friendship.' Osborn here points out the frequency with which Augustine used *vera* in connection with such traditional Roman concepts as *pietas, religio* and *veritas*, and this is true also of *amicitia*.

11. Aug.*Solil.*I.3.8.

12. Aug.*De div.quaest.83* (31.3).

13. Aug.*De serm.Dom.in monte* I.11.31; cf. *Conf.*VI.7.11 where Augustine uses the phrase 'amicitiae benevolentia'.

14. Aug.*De Gen.liber imperf.*59.
15. CSEL, vol.60, p. 43.
16. In connection with the association of *amor* and *amicitia* in Cicero, cf. M. Fronto's letter to the emperor Marcus Aurelius (1.3.4f.) in which he distinguishes between *amor*, based on affection, and *amicitia* which is dependent on mutual services.
17. Aug.Ep.155.3.11; for this formulation of the idea expressed at Prov.27:6, see Ralph Waldo Emerson's essay on friendship, in *The Selected Writings of Ralph Waldo Emerson* (New York, 1940).
18. Aug.Ep.82.5.36.
19. Ep.22.5; Aurelius is mentioned along with Alypius as a close friend of Augustine by Paulinus in his Ep.6.
20. Aug.Ep.28.1 written in 394–5.
21. Aug.*De civit.Dei* 12.21.
22. Cic.*Lael.*16.59.
23. Aug.*De fide rerum invisib.* 11.4 where he writes, 'All friendship will then be destroyed for it cannot exist without mutual love.'
24. O'Connell, 'Art', p. 171.
25. See e.g. Augustine's *Sermo* 385, *En.in Ps.*140, *Tract.*10 on the Epistle of John and *Tract.*65 on the Gospel of John.
26. Aug.*De mor.Eccl.Cath.*26.49.
27. O. M. T. O'Donovan, *The Problem of Self-love in Augustine* (New Haven, 1980), p. 4 and p. 112.
28. Aug.*De doctr.Chr.*1.3.3–4.
29. Cic.*Lael.*21.80.
30. Aug.*Conf.*IV.9.14.
31. It is significant that in quoting the second part of the twofold commandment in the *Speculum*, composed in the last years of his life, Augustine can quote it as 'diliges amicum tuum sicut teipsum'.
32. Cf. Aug.*De disciplina Christiana* III.3, *De catechizandis rudibus* 26.50, *En.in Ps.*14.3, *En.*8.2 in *Ps.*118, *Sermo* 90.7, *Sermo* 359.9. *De doctr.Chr.*1.30.32, *Quaest.in Levit.*73 and *Sermo* XVI (ed. Denis).
33. O'Connell, 'Art', p. 139, writes of this change, 'Augustine's sensitivity to the phenomenon of human friendship, a sensitivity undoubtedly enhanced by his concern with the Christian law of love, has led him to make a momentary adjustment of his categories touching the order of goods – an adjustment that tends precisely to accord the created human scene a greater value than a rigorous application of that order of goods would logically warrant.'
34. On the impossibility of a broad extension of love in this life, cf.

Aug. *De doctr.Chr.*1.28.29, *Tract.*8.4 on the Epistle of John and *De civit.Dei* 19.14.

35. Aug.Ep.130.13.
36. Aug. *De civit.Dei* 19.13.
37. Aug.*De div.quaest.83* (71.5); cf. *De Gen.cont.Manichaeos* 1.2.4 where Augustine, in the context of a discussion about knowing the will of God, ridicules the idea that one can know the will of another human being unless he is your friend.
38. Aug. *Enchiridion* 32.121.
39. See L. Verheijen, 'Spiritualité et vie monastique chez S.Augustin: L'utilisation monastique des Actes des Apotres 4:31, 32–5, dans son oeuvre', in *Jean Chrysostome et Augustin: Actes du colloque de Chantilly* (Paris, 1974), pp. 118–20.
40. It is remarkable that a similar exhortation to transform enemies into friends is found expressed by an early Greek philosopher: according to Diogenes Laertius (1.91) Cleoboulos of Lindos (c.600 B.C.), the author of many moral precepts, said that one must benefit one's friend so that he becomes more of a friend and one must benefit one's enemy so as to make him a friend.
41. That Augustine regarded *frater* and *amicus* in a Christian context as synonymous is indicated by a passage from *En.in Ps.*122.5 in which he quotes as parallel John 15:15 and Gal.4:7.
42. Aug.*Tract.*65.1 on the Gospel of John.
43. Aug.*De ordine* 11.18.48.
44. Cf. H. Petré, *Etudes sur le vocabulaire latin de la charité chrétienne* (Louvain, 1948), p. 322, who observes that unity is a new concept, essential to Christianity but not highly valued among Classical writers except in discussions about friendship e.g. at Cic.*Lael.*21.81 and 25.92.
45. P. Brown, *The Body and Society* (London, 1989), p. 398.
46. Aug.Ep.142.1.
47. See e.g. Aug.Ep.9 to Nebridius and Ep.267 to Fabiola.
48. Cf. Aug.*De Trin.*9.4.6.
49. A. Sage, 'La contemplation dans les communautés de vie fraternelle' *RecAug* 7 (1971), 263.
50. Aug.*Tract.*5.7 on the Epistle of John and *Tract.*17.8 on the Gospel of John; cf. *De Trin.*8.8.12.
51. Aug.*De Trin.*6.5.7.
52. Cf. P. Courcelle, *Les Confessions de saint Augustin dans la tradition littéraire: antécédents et postérité* (Paris, 1963), p. 26; L. Verheijen, *Nouvelle approche de la règle de saint Augustin* (Begrolles-en-Mauges,

1980), p. 238; A. Sage, *La vie religieuse selon saint Augustin* (Paris, 1972), p. 181.

53. A. Zumkeller, *Das Mönchtum des hl. Augustinus*, 2nd edition (Würzburg, 1968), p. 37.

54. On Augustine's attitudes to women, marriage and friendship between the sexes, see Clark, 'Theory', and G. Bonner, 'Augustine's attitudes to women and *amicitia*', in C. Mayer and K.-H. Chelius, eds., *Homo Spiritalis. Festgabe für Luc Verheijen* (Würzburg, 1987).

55. Aug.*Conf*.viii.6.14–15; cf. *Conf*.x.43.70 where Augustine admits he had at one time been attracted by the solitary life.

56. Verheijen, 'Nouvelle approche', p. 211, draws particular parallels between Augustine's early work *De ordine* and the *Regula* as e.g. between *De ordine* ii.18.48, 'What else do friends strive for but to become one? And the more they are one, the more they are friends' and the precept, expressing a similar idea but in more Biblical language (with allusions to Ps. 67:7 (68:6) and Acts 4:32), in the *Regula*, 'Firstly because you are gathered together so that you may live in complete harmony and share one soul and one heart.'

57. Aug.*Epp*.3–12, 14 to Nebridius; G. Bonner, *St Augustine of Hippo; life and controversies* (Norwich, 1986), p. 107.

58. Aug.*Sermo* 355.

59. Zumkeller, 'Mönchtum', p. 71.

60. Augustine's ideas on the monastic life come out most clearly in such works as the *De moribus Ecclesiae Catholicae*, the *De opera monachorum*, the *De sancta virginitate*, Epp.210–11, *En.in Ps*.131 and 132, *Sermones* 355 and 356 and the *Regula ad servos Dei*.

61. Aug.*Conf*.iv.6.11; cf. *Conf*.ii.5.10 where Augustine speaks of friendship as a delightful bond uniting many into one. It should be noted that he also uses Acts 4:32 to apply to the ideal spiritual unity within Christian marriage – see *De bono coniugali* 18.21.

62. Sage, 'Contemplation', pp. 248–50.

63. Cf. Aug.*En.in Ps*.104(105).3, 'Love has both found him (God) through faith and seeks to have him by sight where he will then be found so as to satisfy us and no longer need to be sought.'

64. E.g. Arist. *Eud.Eth*.1245b 5.

CONCLUSION

1. See W. V. Harris, *Ancient Literacy* (Harvard, 1989), who reckons that the overall literacy of the western provinces under the Empire never even reached 5–10 per cent of the population. I

would not agree with Harris' argument that the system of schools declined in late antiquity 'under the influence of the anti-educational priorities of the Christians' (p. 312). The Christians who are the subject of this study, though neither educated by the Church nor for the Church, show that a very high standard of education could still be reached, and valued, among Christians during the fourth and early fifth centuries.

2. K. Hopkins, 'Conquest by book', in *Literacy in the Roman World*, Journal of Roman Archaeology, supplementary series no.3 (Ann Arbor, Mi., 1991), pp. 146–7.

3. S. Collins, 'Monasticism, utopias and comparative social theory', *Religion* 18 (1988), 114–15, has pointed to the way in which a similar attitude to friendship developed among Buddhist monks as in Christian monasticism. The monk Anuruddha, for example, says to the Buddha of his friend, 'We have different bodies but assuredly only one mind.' For the value put on friendship in Buddhist monasticism, see also *The Book of Kindred Sayings*, 5 vols., C. A. F. Rhys Davids and F. L. Woodward, trans., Pali Text Society, 1917–30, I.112f. and v.2, 27, 29f.

4. John of Salisbury, Ep.147, in *The Letters of John of Salisbury*, W. J. Millor and C. N. L. Brooke, eds., vol.II (Oxford, 1979).

5. P. Brown, *The Body and Society* (London, 1989), pp. 13, 15, 113, on friendship within pagan marriage.

Editions and translations of primary sources

Editions of principal primary Classical and Patristic sources, with English translations where available.

Ambrose, *De officiis ministrorum*, PL 16
  Letters, PL 16; trans. in FotC vol.26, Sister M. M. Beyenka (Washington, 1954)
Antony, *Letters*, PG 40; *The Letters of Saint Antony the Great*, trans. Derwas Chitty (SLG Press, Oxford, 1975)
Apophthegmata Patrum [Sayings of the Fathers], Latin Collection: PL 73; Alphabetical collection, trans. Benedicta Ward (London, 1975)
Aristotle, *Nicomachean Ethics*, I. Bywater, ed. (Oxford, 1894); trans. in *The Complete Works of Aristotle*, J. Barnes, ed. (Princeton, 1984), vol. 2, pp. 1825ff.
Augustine, *Confessions*, CCL vol. 27; trans. R. S. Pine-Coffin (Penguin Classics, Harmondsworth, 1961)
  Epistles, CSEL vols. 34,44,57; trans. in FotC vols. 12, 18, 20, 30, 32, Sister W. Parsons (Washington DC, 1951–6)
  Tractates on the Gospel of St John and on the Epistle of St John, trans.in vol.7 of *The Nicene and Post-Nicene Fathers*, P.Schaff, ed. (Michigan, repr. 1974)
  Rule of St Augustine, with intr. and comm. by T. J. van Bavel, trans. R. Canning (London, 1984)
Basil of Caesarea, *The Letters*, with trans. by R. Deferrari (Loeb, London, 1972), 4 vols.
  RFT (The Long Rules), PG 31; *Moralia, Ascetical treatises*, trans.in FotC vol. 9, Sister M. Wagner (Washington DC, 1962).
Cassian, John, *Conférence 16*, E. Pichery, ed., Sources Chrétiennes 42 (Paris, 1955); trans.C. Luibheid (New York, 1985).
Cicero, *Laelius (De amicitia)*, with trans.by W. A. Falconer (Loeb, London, 1923)

Gregory of Nazianzus, *Letters*, P. Gallay, ed. (Budé, Paris, 1964, 1967), 2 vols.
De Vita Sua, PG 37.1029–166; trans.in FotC vol.75, D. M. Meehan OSB (Washington DC, 1987), pp.77ff.
Funeral Oration on Basil the Great, PG 36.493–605; trans.in FotC vol.22, L.P. McCauley etc. (repr.Washington DC, 1968).
Jerome, *Letters*, J. Labourt, ed.with French trans. (Budé, Paris, 1949–63), 8 vols; *Select Letters*, with trans.by F. A. Wright (Loeb, London, repr. 1980); *Letters 1–22*, trans.in ACW vol. 33, C. C. Mierow (London and Westminster, MD, 1963); *The Correspondence (394–419) between Jerome and Augustine of Hippo*, trans.C. White (Lewiston, NY, 1990)
John Chrysostom, *Letters*, PG 52; *Letters to Olympias*, A.-M. Malingrey, ed. with French trans., Sources Chrétiennes 13 (Paris, 1947)
On the Priesthood, A.-M. Malingrey, ed.with French trans., Sources Chrétiennes 272 (Paris, 1980); trans.by G. Neville (SPCK, London, 1964)
Homilies on Galatians, Ephesians, etc., F. Field, ed. (Oxford, 1849–62); trans. in vol.13 of *The Nicene and Post-Nicene Fathers*, P. Schaff, ed. (Michigan, repr.1976)
Pachomius, *Rules*, trans.by A. Veilleux in *Pachomian Koinonia 2*, pp.145–85 (Cistercian Studies no.46, Kalamazoo, 1981)
Paulinus of Nola, *Letters*, CSEL vol.29; trans. in ACW vols.35–6, P. G. Walsh (London and Westminster, MD, 1967), 2 vols.
The Poems of St Paulinus of Nola, CSEL vol.30; trans.in ACW vol.40, P. G. Walsh (New York, 1975)
Plato, *Lysis*, with trans.by W. R. M. Lamb (Loeb, London, repr.1975)
Synesius, *Letters*, A. Garzya, ed. (Rome 1979); trans.A. Fitzgerald (Oxford, 1926)

Select bibliography

Adkins, A. W. H., 'Friendship and self-sufficiency in Homer and Aristotle', *CQ* 13 (1963), 30–45

Amand de Mendieta, E., *L'Ascèse Monastique de saint Basile* (Maredsous, 1949)

Bacht, H., 'Antonius u. Pachomius. Von der Anachorese zum Cönobitentum', *Studia Anselmiana* 38 (1956), 66–107

Baur J. C., *John Chrysostom and his Time*, 2 vols. (London, 1959)

Betz, H. D., *Plutarch's Ethical Writings and Early Christian Literature* (Leiden, 1978)

Blundell, M. W., *Helping Friends and Harming Enemies: a Study in Sophocles and Greek Ethics* (Cambridge, 1989)

Bohnenblust, G., 'Beiträge zum Topos περὶ φιλίας' (unpublished thesis, Bern, 1905)

Bonner, G., *St Augustine of Hippo: Life and Controversies* (Norwich, 1986)
'Augustine's attitude to women and *amicitia*', in *Homo Spiritalis. Festgabe für Luc Verheijen*, C. Mayer and K.-H. Chelius, eds. (Würzburg, 1987), pp.259–75

Boswell, J., *Christianity, social tolerance and homosexuality* (Chicago, 1980)

Boularand, E., 'L'amitié d'après saint Ambroise dans le *De Officiis ministrorum*', *Bulletin de litt.éccl és*, 73 (1972), 103–23

Bregman, J., *Synesius of Cyrene* (California, 1982)

Brown P., *Augustine of Hippo: a biography* (London, 1967)
The Cult of the Saints (London, 1981)
The Body and Society (London, 1989)

Brunt, P. A., '*Amicitia* in the late Roman Republic', *PCPhS* 11 (1965), 1–20

Burnaby, J., *Amor Dei; a study of the religion of St Augustine* (London, 1938)

Buse, A., *Paulin, Bischof von Nola u.seine Zeit*, 2 vols. (Regensburg, 1856)

Chadwick, H., *Early Christian Thought and the Classical Tradition* (Oxford, 1966)

Chadwick, O., *John Cassian, a study in primitive monasticism* (1st edn. Cambridge, 1950, 2nd edn. 1968)

Chitty, D., *The Desert a City* (Oxford, 1966)

Clark, E. A., *Jerome, Chrysostom and friends* (Lewiston, NY, 1979)
'Theory and practice in late ancient asceticism', *Journal of Feminist Studies in Religion*, 3 (1987), 25–46

Coote, S., ed., *The Penguin Book of Homosexual Verse* (Harmondsworth, 1983)

Courcelle, P., *Les Confessions de saint Augustin dans la tradition littéraire: antécédents et postérité* (Cambridge, MA 1963)
Late Latin Writers and their Greek Sources (trans. H. E. Wedeck, Cambridge, MA, 1969)

Coyle, A. F., 'Cicero's *De Officiis* and the *De Officiis Ministrorum* of St Ambrose', *Franciscan Studies*, 15 (1955), 224–56

Crawford, W. S., *Synesius the Hellene* (London, 1901)

Dagron, G., *Naissance d'une capitale, Constantinople et ses institutions de 330 à 451* (Paris, 1974)

Dirlmeier, F., *'φίλος u. φιλία im vorhellenistischen Griechentum'* (unpublished thesis, Munich, 1931)

Dugas, L., *L'amitié antique d'après les moeurs populaires et les théories des philosophes* (Paris, 1894)

Eisenstadt S. N. and Roniger L., *Patrons, Clients and Friends* (Cambridge, 1984)

Erdt, W., *Christentum u. heidnisch–antike Bildung bei Paulin von Nola* (Meisenheim-am-Glam, 1974)

Fabre, P., *Essai sur la chronologie de l'oeuvre de S.Paulin de Nole* (Paris, 1948)
S.Paulin de Nole et l'amitié chrétienne (Paris, 1949)

Festugière, A., *Epicure et ses dieux* (Paris, 1968)

Fialon, E., *Etude littéraire sur saint Basile* (Paris, 1861)

Fiske, A., 'Cassian and monastic friendship' *American Benedictine Review*, 12 (1961), 190–205
Friends and Friendship in the Monastic Tradition (Mexico, 1970)

Fraisse, J.-C., *Philia, la notion de l'amitié dans la philosophie antique* (Paris, 1974)

Frend, W. H. C., *The Early Church* (3rd edn, London, 1971)
Review of Roques' book on Synesius, *JbAC* 32 (1989) 203–6

Gelzer, M., *The Roman Nobility* (trans. R. Seager, Oxford, 1969)

Grützmacher G., *Synesios von Cyrene: ein Charakterbild aus dem Untergang des Hellenentums* (Leipzig, 1913)

Hagendahl H., *The Latin Fathers and the Classics* (Gothenburg, 1958)

Hauck, F., 'Die Freundschaft bei den Griechen und im Neuen Testament' in *Festgabe für Th.Zahn* (Leipzig, 1928), pp.211–28 *Theologisches Wörterbuch zum N.T.*, Vol. 3 (1935–8), pp. 789–810

Hellegouarc'h J., *Le vocabulaire latin des relations et des partis politiques sous la république* (2nd edn, Paris, 1972)

Heussi, K., *Der Ursprung des Mönchtums* (Tübingen, 1936)

Hinnebusch, P., *Friendship in the Lord* (Indiana, 1974)

Hoare, F. R., *The Western Fathers* (London, 1954)

Homes Dudden, F., *The Life and Times of St Ambrose*, 2 vols. (Oxford, 1935)

Kaiser, O., '*Lysis* oder 'Von der Freundschaft'', *ZRGG* 32 (1980), 193–218

Kakridis, H. J., *La notion de l'amitié et l'hospitalité chez Homère* (Thessalonica, 1963)

Kelly, J. N. D., *Jerome, his Life, Writings and Controversies* (London, 1975)

Kierkegaard, S., *The Works of Love* (trans. D. F. and L. M. Swenson, Princeton, 1946)

Klein, E., *Studien zum Problem der 'römischen' und 'griechischen' Freundschaft* (unpublished thesis, Freiburg, 1957)

Koskenniemi, H., *Studien zur Idee und Phraseologie des griechischen Briefes bis 400 n.Chr.* (Helsinki, 1956)

La Bonnardière, A.-M., 'Portez les fardeaux les uns des autres: éxègese augustinienne de Gal.6:2', *Didaskalia* I (1971), 201–15

Lapatz F., *Lettres de Synésius* (Paris, 1870)

Lapide Cornelius A, *Commentaria in Acta Apostolorum* (Antwerp, 1627) *Commentaria in Ecclesiasticum* (Antwerp, 1643) *Commentaria in prophetas minores* (Antwerp, 1646)

Lewis, C. S., *The Four Loves* (London, 1960)

Lienhard, J. T. H., *Paulinus of Nola and Early Western Monasticism* (Bonn, 1977)

McEvoy, J., 'Anima una et cor unum; friendship and spiritual unity in Augustine', *Rec.Theol.* 53 (1986), 40–92

McGuire, B., *Friendship and Community: the Monastic Experience 350–1250* (Cistercian Publications, Kalamazoo, 1988)

MacKendrick, P., *The Philosophical Books of Cicero* (London, 1989)

McNamara, M. A., *Friendship in St Augustine* (Fribourg, 1958)

Marrou, H.-I., *A History of Education in Antiquity* (trans. G. Lamb, London, 1981)

Martha, C., *Etudes morales sur l'antiquité* (Paris, 1905)

Matthews, J., *Western Aristocracies and Imperial Court 364–425* (Oxford, 1975)

The Roman Empire of Ammianus Marcellinus (London, 1989)

Meilander, G., *Friendship, a Study in Theological Ethics* (Notre Dame, Indiana, 1981)

Meister, K., 'Die Freundschaft bei den Griechen und Römern', *Gymnasium* 57 (1950), 3–38

Morison, E., *St Basil and His Rule: a Study in Early Monasticism* (Oxford, 1912)

Neuhausen K.-A., 'Zu Cassians Traktat *De Amicitia*', in *Studien zur Literatur der Spätantike*, C. Gnilka and W. Schetter, eds. (Bonn, 1975), pp. 181–218

Ed., M. *Tullius Cicero: Laelius* (Heidelberg, 1981)

Nygren, A., *Agape and Eros: a Study of the Christian Idea of Love* (trans. P. S. Watson, London, 1953)

O'Connell, R. J., *Art and the Christian Intelligence in St Augustine* (Oxford, 1978)

O'Donovan, O. M. T., *The Problem of Self-love in Augustine* (New Haven, 1980)

Osborn, E., *Ethical Patterns in Early Christian Thought* (Cambridge, 1976)

Otto, A., *Die Sprichwörter u. sprichwörtlichen Redensarten der Römer* (Leipzig, 1890)

Outka, G., *Agape, an Ethical Analysis* (New Haven, 1972)

Petré, H., *Etudes sur le vocabulaire latin de la charité chrétienne* (Louvain, 1948)

Pizzolato, L. F., *L'amicizia cristiana*, Antologia dalle opere di Agostino di Ippona e altri testi di Ambrogio, Gerolamo e Paolino di Nola (Turin, 1973)

'L'amicizia nel *De Officiis* di S. Ambrogio e il *Laelius* di Cicero', *Richerche storiche sulla chiesa ambrosiana nel XVI centenario* IV (Milan, 1974), pp. 53–67

Porter R. and Tomaselli S., eds., *The Dialectics of Friendship* (London, 1989)

Price, A. W., *Love and Friendship in Plato and Aristotle* (Oxford, 1989)

Rawson, E., *The Politics of Friendship: Pompey and Cicero* (Sydney, 1978)

Rist, J., *Epicurus, an Introduction* (Cambridge, 1972)

Human Value (Leiden, 1982)

Robinson, D., 'Homeric φίλος; love of life and limbs and friendship with one's θύμος', E. M. Craik, ed., *Owls to Athens, essays presented to Sir K. Dover* (Oxford, 1990)

Roques, D., *Synésios de Cyrène et la Cyrénaïque du Bas-Empire* (Paris, 1987)

Ruether, R., *Gregory of Nazianzus: Rhetor and Philosopher* (Oxford, 1969)

Sage, A., 'La contemplation dans les communautés de vie fraternelle', *RecAug* 7 (1971), 245–302
La vie religieuse selon saint Augustin (Paris, 1972)
Saller, R. P., *Personal Patronage under the Early Empire* (Cambridge, 1982)
Sandbach, F. H., *The Stoics* (London, 1975)
Simeon, P. X., *Untersuchungen zu den Briefen des Bischofs Synesios von Kyrene* (Paderborn, 1933)
Stählin, G., '*φίλος, φίλη, φιλία*', *Theologisches Wörterbuch zum N. T.*, vol. 9 (1973), pp. 144–69.
Stancliffe, C. E., *St. Martin and his Hagiographer: History and Miracle in Sulpicius Severus* (Oxford, 1983)
Steinmetz, F.-A., *Die Freundschaftslehre des Panaitios nach einer Analyse von Ciceros Laelius 'De Amicitia'* (Wiesbaden, 1967)
Stower, S. K., *Letter Writing in Greco–Roman Antiquity* (Philadelphia, 1989)
Thamin, R., *S. Ambroise et la morale chrétienne au IVème siècle* (Paris, 1895)
Treu, K., '*φιλία* und *ἀγάπη* : zur Terminologie der Freundschaft bei Basilius und Gregorius Nazianzenus', *StudClas* 3 (1961), 421–27
'Freundschaft', *RLAC* 8 (1972), cols.418–34
Verheijen, L., 'Spiritualité et vie monastique chez S. Augustin: L'utilisation monastique des Actes des Apôtres 4:31, 32–5 dans son oeuvre', *Jean Chrysostome et Augustin: Actes du colloque de Chantilly* (Paris, 1974), pp. 93–123
Nouvelle approche de la règle de S. Augustin (Begrolles-en-Mauges, 1980)
Vischer, L., 'Das Problem der Freundschaft bei den Kirchenvätern', *ThZ* 9 (1953), 173–200
Vogel, C. J. de, *Pythagoras and Early Pythagoreanism* (Assen, 1966)
Vööbus, A., *A History of Asceticism in the Syrian Orient* (Louvain, 1958)
Wallace Hadrill, A., *Patronage in Ancient Society* (London, 1989)
White, P., '*Amicitia* and the profession of poetry in early imperial Rome', *JRS* 68 (1978), 74–92
Wiesen D. S., *St Jerome as a Satirist* (Ithaca, NY, 1964)
Ziebis, W., 'Der Begriff der *φιλία* bei Plato' (unpublished thesis, Breslau, 1927).

Index

INDEX OF THE MOST COMMON CLASSICAL STATEMENTS CONCERNING FRIENDSHIP

INDEX OF BIBLICAL CITATIONS